THE MONEY DIET

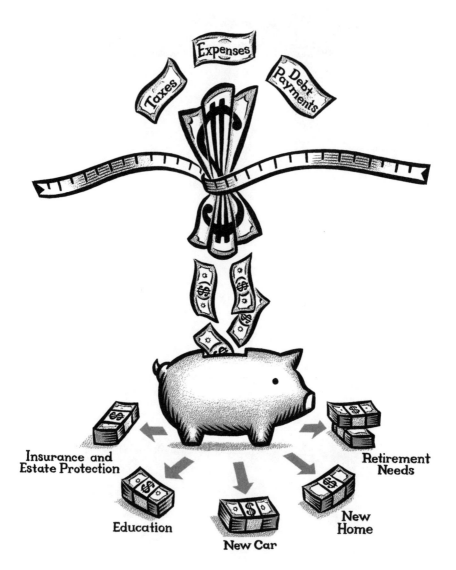

The Money Diet Method

THE MONEY DIET

Reaping the Rewards
of Financial Fitness

GINGER APPLEGARTH
CFP, CLU, ChFC

VIKING

VIKING
Published by the Penguin Group
Penguin Books USA Inc., 375 Hudson Street, New York, New York 10014, U.S.A.
Penguin Books Ltd, 27 Wrights Lane, London W8 5TZ, England
Penguin Books Australia Ltd, Ringwood, Victoria, Australia
Penguin Books Canada Ltd, 10 Alcorn Avenue,
Toronto, Ontario, Canada M4V 3B2
Penguin Books (N.Z.) Ltd, 182–190 Wairau Road,
Auckland 10, New Zealand

Penguin Books Ltd, Registered Offices: Harmondsworth, Middlesex, England

First published in 1995 by Viking Penguin, a division of Penguin Books USA Inc.

1   3   5   7   9   10   8   6   4   2

PUBLISHER'S NOTE
This publication is designed to provide accurate and authoritative
information in regard to the subject matter covered. It is sold with the understanding
that the publisher is not engaged in rendering accounting or other professional service.
If financial advice or other expert assistance is required, the service of a competent
professional person should be sought.

LIBRARY OF CONGRESS CATALOGING IN PUBLICATION DATA
Applegarth, Ginger.
The money diet: reaping the rewards of financial fitness/Ginger Applegarth.
p.   cm.
Includes index.
ISBN 0–670–85680–0
1. Finance, Personal—Planning.   2. Financial planners.   I. Title.
HG179.A66   1995
332.024—dc20   94–31389
CIP

This book is printed on acid-free paper.
∞
Printed in the United States of America
Set in Sabon
Illustrations © 1994 by Tim Grajek
Charts design by Desktop Publishing & Design Company, Boston, MA

For my children, Alden Keene Bevington
and Elizabeth Rickey Bevington

Preface:
Why the Money Diet?

IF 54,000 LETTERS to the *Today* show is any indication, Americans need—and want—a money diet.

In 1993, the *Today* show featured my five-part series called "The Money Diet," based on my experience over the years as a financial adviser to the rich and not-so-rich alike. To help viewers of the series get started on their own money diets, NBC agreed to distribute my six-page guide to the series, called "Applegarth Advice," which contained practical tips and simple worksheets to help people start to take control of their financial lives. Steve Friedman, executive producer of *Today* at the time, felt we would know the series had been a success if we received 15,000 letters. But then the mail started pouring in and did not let up for a month. All told, over 54,000 viewers took the time to write NBC and request a guide. What had been said that caused such a powerful reaction?

The letters and comments we received provided compelling evidence of what was on viewers' minds. In letter after letter people spoke of anxiety about the future—anxiety about retiring, educating children, paying for a parent's nursing home, or buying a house as a single person. A few older viewers wrote letters explaining exactly how they had worked to achieve their goals—and then asked, "Was this the right thing to do?" And the stationery bearing requests for the

"Money Diet" information came from viewers from every walk of life; we received both engraved personal letterhead and pages ripped out of a child's notebook. Even banks, insurance companies, stock brokerage firms, colleges, and government agencies responded.

What is obvious from the mail we received is that many Americans are worried about their finances, and they ought to be. The month after "The Money Diet" aired, the annual Consumer Confidence Index, which measures Americans' view of future economic conditions, was at a ten-year low. For those of us who entered the workforce before the mid-1970s or who as children watched our parents' standard of living rise until that time, the feeling was that things generally got better and that we could plan our own finances around that expectation. In fact, when I first started writing financial plans in the 1970s, it was considered routine to estimate an 8+ percent annual pay increase, with hefty employer pension contributions to boot. Most of us were raised to believe that our standard of living would be higher than our parents' and that our children's would be better yet. But somewhere along the way the country's budget deficit mushroomed, and we as a nation started saving less for the future and borrowing more to finance today's lifestyle. The result is that for the first time family economic progress is in real danger.

Americans' standard of living doubled between 1947 and 1973, a period of twenty-seven years. Before that, our standard of living took thirty-six years to double. But at the rate our standard of living has "improved" during the period of 1973 to 1991, some experts estimate it will take as long as *268 years* to double. That rate reflects an average increase of less than one-half of 1 percent a year; with that kind of "improvement," no wonder it doesn't feel as if things are getting better (and the fact is, in a number of those years they've actually gotten worse).

If as a nation we are already having trouble with our finances, the worst is yet to come. The Deficit Reduction Bill (passed in 1993) was designed to remove $500 billion from the U.S. economy over the next several years to reduce the deficit. If the measure works, it means that less credit is going to be available to consumers. The results of deficit reduction (higher taxes for some and cuts in government programs for others), combined with potential increases in medical-related costs (our premiums and our taxes) due to insurance reform, may mean that Americans are simply going to have to make do with less.

Problem 1: It's not just that our financial lives have changed, but that our jobs and our lifestyles have changed dramatically as well. We will have more years and more things to pay for than our parents did. Our life expectancy has increased twenty years since 1920 and Social Security is not going to be able to pay for all those extra retirement years. And, as elderly parents remain in their own households rather than moving in with their children, and as single-person households continue to grow, the cost as a group for extended families is higher than when family members pooled their resources and lived together under one roof. Through it all, the national debt continues to mushroom: Three-fourths of our total national debt was accumulated in the twelve years ending in 1992.

Problem 2: At the same time most of us were taught that our financial circumstances would improve as we moved through adulthood, we were not taught how to live within our means today. (And if we were taught how, the teaching was probably predicated on those familiar increased expectations.) Just look at the way we manage our financial lives. Almost 50 percent of us have no personal budgets, and financial disaster (as measured by the tripling of the personal bankruptcy rate since 1980) now hits all income and net worth levels. In fact, many people are simply financially ignorant, are averse to dealing with their money problems, and lack motivation to change regardless of how many zeros are at the end of their salaries or net worths. A number of my clients have six-figure incomes and seven-figure net worths, but money has served only to complicate their lives. They just have more income, more expenses, and more taxes to worry about and must handle the pressure of meeting larger goals while maintaining a much higher standard of living. It is not at all clear that more money means more happiness. At the same time that one of my middle-income clients was agonizing over $20,000 of credit card debt, an affluent client was agonizing over how to pay back almost $100,000 of credit card debt and bank account overdrafts. Just because some people grew up with lots of money doesn't mean they learned any more about money than their poor cousins did. In fact, in my experience they probably learned much less because no one was telling them, "No, we can't afford it right now"; as a result, their adult money habits are geared to a very high, seemingly inflexible standard of living.

Most of us were never taught what to do when the rate of growth starts to decline, much less what to do when it starts getting worse. One thing we do know is that we can no longer measure our financial success by the old standards. We worry constantly about meeting our financial goals. Many of us don't even know what those goals should be. We might have some idea of what our present situations are by seeing whether our bank statement balances are going up or down, but it is hard to know where we will stand in a few years. We never expected that just getting by would be so difficult. Since almost everyone else we know *appears* to be doing fine, we tend to think something is wrong with us. Financial pressures also put a strain on our personal relationships; in fact, money is the number one cause of marital arguments.

Problem 3: Our culture and our advertising media just make it harder to see reality. All those advertising dollars are spent for one purpose: to persuade us to part with our hard-earned dollars. And that power of persuasion is very strong! Not only does the media tell us we *need* more things, it also tells us we need to be *seen* with more things, teaching us every day that our net worth is a measure of our true worth. In a recent *Worth* magazine survey, more than half the respondents said the one feature they would most like to change about themselves is the amount of money they have. You may disagree, but wouldn't you rather have people think you are wealthy than poor? So we work to keep up pretenses, and it is embarrassing to ask for help.

The next time you sit down to watch the news on television, observe the kind of mixed messages you receive. Here is what often happens: The nightly network news comes on, reporting grim economic statistics—inflation is up, people are having trouble staying even, or they are over their heads in debt. Cut to the commercial. What do the carefully scripted images show? The happy family vacation or romantic couples' cruise, or the car, or the candlelit restaurant, or even the credit card itself—all spelling an escape from reality! We are only human, so which message do we remember? The more inviting one (spending brings happiness), not the one that keeps us up at night worrying about our financial futures.

WHERE WE ARE

■ We can't figure it out.

Our confidence in our own financial abilities is at an all-time low. Almost all the clients I have worked with in recent years have admitted to me that they are embarrassed about some aspect of the way they have handled their money, even if those decisions made perfect sense. Some examples? "I know I should have saved more when I was younger"—from an accountant who had never planned to retire but was forced out at age fifty-five by his firm. "I know I should not have spent so much on the house"—from the woman who spent twice her budget in renovations. "I know we should have bought more insurance on my wife"—from the widower with small children. "I know I should not have given a relative that money to invest"—from more than one client who never saw it again. "I know I should have been more organized"—from almost everybody!

■ Instead of saving, we're spending.

If you are still buying into the idea that things will be the way you expected them to be (or the way your parents think they *should* be), it is easy to be tempted to overspend; not only is it hard to save money, you may even end up using debt to finance your lifestyle today at the expense of saving for the future.

The rate at which we as a nation save our money—compared with the rates of other industrialized countries—is appalling. We save about *4 percent* of our income, while in these other countries people save 12 to 18 percent of their incomes. And, to make matters worse, this slow savings rate is coupled with our reliance on credit card debt as a way of life, a reliance that may have been fostered by past tax laws that encouraged us to go into debt by making credit card interest fully tax-deductible until 1986! For example, as a nation we put off paying for over half of what we charge, and in one recent year alone Americans paid more than $38 billion in credit card interest. We get ourselves in debt and are so busy paying off the past that we cannot adequately save for the future. It makes us wonder, Have we lost our money minds?

■ Changing habits is hard.

How we spend and save our money often has as much (or more) to do with habit than actual need or how much we have in the bank. We are used to doing things a certain way, and change is very difficult. And who has the time, the knowledge, and the willpower to make painful changes in his or her lifestyle? Habits rule the day. I certainly know this from my own experience. I recently realized that when I go to the grocery store I always buy the same cut-rate items. When I go to a restaurant, I can never bring myself to order the most expensive thing on the menu, even if it is the only thing that looks appealing. But I am satisfied with only the most expensive computer and stereo equipment. Why? *I have no idea,* but the consequences obviously have a major impact on my spending. These actions are purely a matter of habit. Some clients tell me, "No matter how much my monthly paycheck is, I always spend *exactly* that amount—without even realizing it!" (The solution? Have your savings withheld from your paycheck before it gets into your hands.) As one prospective client said to me, "We live hand to mouth—on half a million dollars a year."

Our spending and saving behavior is not limited to (or even based on) actual economic need, either. I see this time after time when I work with clients to pare their budgets. Two different clients may have approximately the same incomes, number of children, amount of income taxes due, and mortgage payments, but the amount of money they say they absolutely "must" have for expenses can vary by tens of thousands of dollars. And while one such client considers saving $1,000 a year a real hardship, another cannot sleep at night unless $10,000 is squirreled away by July 1 each year.

How we spend and save our money doesn't seem to have a lot to do with our economic station in life. In my experience, the wealthy often become overwhelmed because their finances are constantly in flux due to changes in stock, bond, and real estate prices as well as tax law revisions. The middle class is so busy trying to make it from month to month that they don't ever have a chance to look at the "big picture," either. Clients always seem relieved to know that others behave the same way they do about money because somehow they imagine their friends all manage their finances better. *It is not true.*

The bottom line is that times have changed, but our expectations, knowledge, and patterns of spending and saving have not. One result? If Americans keep spending, saving, and investing the way they have been, three-fourths of us over the age of twenty will have *less than half* the money we need in order to retire at the same standard of living we currently enjoy. Indeed, many Americans are already waking up to this reality and are part of the "new frugality" of the nineties, which is the exact opposite of the excessive consumer consumption of the eighties that helped get us into this money mess! An example of this new frugality? According to a 1993 *Brand Week* poll, 61 percent of Americans said that if they had extra money, they would put it into savings.

GETTING TO WHERE WE WANT TO BE

I have asked my clients and friends why financial advice has not helped them make decisions on their own. The consensus has been clear. They have pointed out that financial advice is usually focused at the "micro level": "Buy this stock," "sell this mutual fund," "don't buy gold," "pay off your car loan," "avoid variable life insurance." Moreover, on this "micro level" the advice is often confusing. Let's say you decide you want to buy some mutual funds, so you buy three financial magazines. You examine their top picks, and most of the choices are different! Financial advice is often conflicting, and it is impossible to see how your decision affects your overall financial situation. In general, the focus is on *implementation* (usually product purchase), not on *developing an overall plan of action*.

The first step in developing a plan is figuring out which type of money person you are. Financial planning is always a trade-off of the short term versus the long term; the key is to keep short-term *wants* from taking priority over long-term *needs*. Usually you can recognize yourself in one of these three categories:

- You spend less than your take-home pay and are saving every year. You are probably OK for the short term and may be OK for the long term.
- You spend *exactly* what you bring home and are not saving at all. In the short term you may be fine unless unexpected expenses come up, but your long-term goals are in jeopardy.
- You spend more than your take-home pay. Chances are you have got major short-term *and* long-term problems. Even if you have only recently started this bad habit and have savings from the past, you will end up using your savings just to meet your current spending and to service the debt you've accumulated.

It is all too easy to get so focused on the short term that you forget the long term altogether. And, for short-term decisions, emotions usually rule the day. Who hasn't bought something totally superfluous because they were depressed ("I deserve this") or elated ("I deserve this")?

Once we recognize our spending patterns, we need to address our financial phobias. The reality is, we may enjoy thinking about certain aspects of our finances (such as investing, the perennial favorite) because they are pleasurable—they involve winning! But we may hate thinking about disability insurance or dying or losing our jobs, or we may be filled with anxiety when we think about retirement or how we are going to pay for college. If we know, deep down, that our financial reality may not be a pretty picture, it is hard to plow through personal financial guides that read like textbooks or are so thick with worksheets that it would take months of weekends just to complete them. My clients have told me that two things were missing in most of these books: *help in overcoming their aversion* to dealing with money and *motivation to do something* about their finances. From these wise clients, the Money Diet was born.

THE MONEY DIET

At first glance, something called the Money Diet may simply sound like a gimmick. In reality, however, I chose to base my checkbook advice on well-known waistline advice because dieting is the one thing virtually all Americans are familiar with. After all, 50 million Americans are dieting at any given point in time! Wouldn't it be terrific (and good for the country as well) if 50 million Americans were working on their personal financial plans at the same time! Most Americans know roughly how much they weigh (although they will not always admit it) but may not know their total assets. Most Americans know how to diet, but if their personal finances are in total disarray, with the bill collector knocking at the door or the college tuition due, they don't have a clue about how to address the situation. Americans keep trying to lose those extra pounds—just like they vow to spend less this month, cut up those credit cards, buy some insurance, save more for retirement, or call the lawyer about a will. Believe it or not, the processes of financial planning and dieting are almost identical.

Think about how you diet. First you look at your current weight; you get on the scale or look in the mirror and realize what you see may not be what you want. In financial planning terms, this means figuring out what you own and owe as well as how you are spending and saving your money. So, Step 1 of the Money Diet is **Getting on the Financial Scales.** Second, you set a goal—how much you want to weigh. The financial analogy? The goals of how much you want for retirement, how much to pay for a new house, how much it will cost to send the kids to college or to do whatever else is important to you. In the Money Diet, Step 2 is **Setting Financial Goals.** The third dieting step is to design a plan to help you get from your current weight to your ideal weight. With money, this means developing an overall strategy—a financial plan—to try to reach your goals. But at the same time you are losing weight, you need to protect your health by eating right and exercising, which is analogous to protecting against financial disasters such as illness, death, and disability. All of these needs are covered in Step 3 of the Money Diet, **Developing Your Money Diet Plan.** The last step in a diet is getting on the scales periodically to see how well you are maintaining your ideal weight. In financial planning terms, this is the periodic financial review or "checkup." That's why Step 4 of the Money Diet is **Sticking to Your Money Diet.**

It is easier to ignore your finances than your weight. With your finances, you may get statements once a month, but you can always run up your credit cards and lines of credit if you have to, and you can go your entire life without opening a savings account. There is nothing staring you in the face reminding you that unless you change something about the way you manage your money, you will not be able to meet your financial goals in five, ten, or twenty years. But you have to deal with your weight every day when you look in the mirror, put on your clothing, or get on the scale. It is equally important to periodically assess your financial situation even if no red flags have popped up to tell you there is trouble in financial paradise. It may well be that you're doing fine day-to-day but are in for a rude awakening a few years down the road if you don't start making changes *now.*

Thus far, I have painted a grim picture of financial realities in the 1990s and beyond. But it doesn't have to be this way, and the future is grim only if we postpone making changes. There are opportunities every day, every time you pull out your wallet, checkbook, or credit card, to change your financial destiny. We Americans can work miracles under pressure; all we need is to recognize a problem and learn some ways we can change, and we are off and running toward a solution. As an adviser, I know each of us can make powerful changes to take back control of our finances.

You have just as many chances to change when you go on a money diet as you do when you go on a food diet—in the way you think about, plan for, and use money. Think of how many times a day the thoughts of money come into your head. In fact, as an exercise for today and tomorrow, keep track of how many times you directly or indirectly think of money. You will probably be amazed at the results. If you are like most people, you will find that—in addition to thinking about money every time you open your wallet or checkbook or pull out your credit card—many of your thoughts about other things and people revolve around money: "I can't afford that." "It's too expensive." "That looks cheap." "How much did it cost?" "How could they afford that?" "I wish I could buy that." "I'm lousy with money." "I got a good deal." "I can't afford to take a vacation." And so on.

Just as thinking about food provides an opportunity to change your eating habits, thinking about money provides the opportunity to change your money habits. There is an old saying that "every action serves to maintain or change a habit." Any change in the way you deal with money is a start. It may be as little as the video you have decided not to rent or as large as the decision to call the lawyer for a will after all these years of meaning to, but *any change is a start.*

The Money Diet is not a psychological treatise on why people overspend, are incapable of balancing their checkbooks, run up credit card debt, buy investments that always lose money, don't buy a shred of life insurance, or don't have a clue about their finances even if they have $400,000 sitting in a money market account. I am not a therapist, and I have seen people headed toward financial disaster for lots of different reasons, many of which are totally out of their control, whether it's a major illness, a job termination, or an unwanted divorce.

First and foremost, *The Money Diet* is a practical guide to improving your chances of reaching your financial goals in the face of an uncertain economic future that is *not all your fault.* It deliberately focuses on the big picture. Indeed, you have to focus on the big picture to avoid getting blindsided; a carefully designed stock portfolio can disappear overnight if you get sued in a car accident and have inadequate liability insurance. And, without knowing the big picture, you may feel there's no reason to change. The big picture will give you the knowledge and the motivation to spend less, pay less in taxes, and get out of debt so you can save more, as well as protect yourself from personal or financial catastrophe.

The Money Diet is filled with real-life examples of how people are coping with their money. I have found that the best teacher is someone who has encountered and solved the same problem. Every client I have ever worked with or person who has spoken with me about his or her finances in connection with the *Today* show has taught me something that I can pass on to you, which may make it easier for you to manage your money. I am grateful for those who gave permission to share their stories here. Americans are truly ingenious when it comes to money—like the young woman we featured on *Today* who controlled her credit card spending by freezing the cards in an ice block in the freezer! There's more in the chapters to follow.

The Money Diet approach is as simple as I could make it. I have tried to limit the number and size of the worksheets included. But keep in mind that the shorter the worksheets the easier they are to understand and be motivated by—that's why I call them Willpower Worksheets. Each worksheet you complete will strengthen your willpower to make changes because you can see the future in black and white. If you consider yourself a novice at financial planning, and find the Willpower Worksheets overwhelming at first glance, skip one (or all of them!) for now and just read the text. The book contains hundreds of tips, facts, and client stories that will give you the confidence and motivation to go back and complete the worksheets you really need. Money is complex enough these days; my guess is that an easy-to-read, sometimes humorous book will be the best way to meet *my* goal of having you read *The Money Diet* from start to finish—and then make some changes in your personal finances.

Like other financial planning guides, *The Money Diet* is filled with advice and tips, but that knowledge is worthless unless you use it, and to use it you need motivation. In a nutshell, the goal of this book is to help you *overcome any aversion* you have to dealing with money, give you the *knowledge* you need to plan, and then give you the *motivation* to act. But *The Money Diet* it not saying that all life decisions should be made "by the numbers." If we did that, no one would ever have any fun! We would never take vacations, we would never buy new cars or new clothes, we would live in one-room apartments, we would never have children, our kids would never move out until they were married, no one would ever choose such important but low-paying careers as teaching or being an artist, and no one would *ever* marry a nonworking spouse or someone making a lower income! Keep in mind that financial planning is always a balance between reality and dreams.

Unlike some other financial authors, I make no claims of being a millionaire myself; however, I do have one qualification that makes me uniquely suited to write a book of this nature—my own experience. In fact, my life would make terrific soap-opera material if it were not true.

My personal finances unraveled during a seven-year disability I suffered starting in the late 1970s. By the time I was twenty-five, I had graduated from college, married, produced a son, earned two financial planning designations, and somehow managed to finagle a challenging part-time job as a financial planner that left ample time for my family. Physical exercise was a big part of my life: I played basketball through elementary and high school, biked through France in college, and even played two sets of tennis the day before my son was born. In short, sitting still and depending on others for everything was the last thing in life I ever imagined could happen to me. But it did, and I found myself bedridden for most of the years between 1979 and 1985 due to a congenital back problem that manifested itself during my second pregnancy. After being told that I might never walk unassisted again, and spending as much as six months at a time without getting out of bed, I agreed to take a chance on experimental surgery and a body cast for almost a year. A bedpan in Boston was a far cry from my debutante years growing up in Atlanta! I was one of the lucky ones—the surgery was a success. Even more important than surgery, however, was the ongoing emotional (and sometimes financial) support provided by family and friends. This singular experience taught me personal and financial coping skills, but more important, it taught me empathy, which I now try to share with others every day of my life. Whenever I find myself starting to judge someone's past financial decisions, I remind myself that had I not agreed to that operation, I would probably be on Medicaid today—and would have been unable to care for my two children.

Before I got sick, I took money for granted; there was enough to live well on and save for the future at the same time. I assumed my income, spending, and saving would just keep increasing. I was wrong on all counts. There are advantages, however, to learning this lesson earlier rather than later in life. Although I am not better off financially, the psychological benefits are enormous. I have discovered how exhilarating it is to realize the true value of money (mainly, what it *can't* buy you), learned to downsize my spending habits and expectations for the future, and taken control of my finances for the first time in my life. In my practice I have seen what works—and doesn't work—with clients of all income and net-worth levels. I know that even if getting your finances under control seems impossible, it is *very* possible; but it is a process of thousands of little steps along the way. You never know when your money survival skills will be tested; no one is immune from job loss or cutbacks, death, disability, huge medical expenses, divorce, lawsuits, fires, or car accidents. For example, four months before I started writing this book, I was accidentally hit by a car. Because I already had experienced the financial impact of a disability, I was immediately able to cut back our household spending and start planning for any needed lifestyle changes in the event I could never regain the full use of my right leg. The medical jury is still out, but because I have already "planned for the worst," I have improved my chances that "the worst" will be manageable. Accidents can happen to anyone; if you get your finances in shape *now*, you too will be prepared no matter what surprises the future may bring.

As you read, keep in mind a few rules, all designed to make it as easy as possible to follow the Money Diet. **First**, details come last! We are looking at the big picture here. It is much more important to get an overall look at your finances than to spend all your time figuring out whether to prepay your second mortgage (which may, in fact, *not* be a good idea, depending on your overall financial situation). **Second**, estimates are fine. My rule: Once you have your papers organized, any number that takes over ten minutes to locate should be estimated for now. **Third**, proceed through *The Money Diet* from beginning to end—don't jump around. The first part (chapters 2 and 3) is designed to help you figure out where you stand; the second part (chapter 4) helps you set financial goals, the third part (chapters 5 through 16) explains how to develop your own financial plan; and the fourth part (chapters 17 and 18) makes sure the plan will work for you year after year as your situation changes. **Fourth**, keep in mind that if you "come up short" in your current planning, *you are not alone*. These changes may not be easy, but the longer you wait to make them the more difficult they will be. Still, I guarantee that you will feel so much better once you have taken a realistic look at your financial situation that these changes will seem worthwhile. You can console yourself with the thought that you are taking steps that most of your friends and family should be taking as well but aren't. **Fifth,** remember that we are working from today on. Do not fault yourself for past money mistakes. You are now taking positive steps to change your financial future! **Sixth,** *The Money Diet* is meant to be an introduction to, not a substitute for, professional individual financial planning. Nothing would make me happier than if you were to read through to the last page, close the book, and make a beeline to the nearest phone to call a professional financial adviser. In fact, an entire chapter is devoted to helping you find just such a person. Just as you should consult a doctor before starting a food diet, be sure to consult a professional adviser before taking any of the major steps in this book.

Finally, as you read the book and put the Money Diet into action, make notes of what works—and doesn't work—for you. I am eager to learn of your own money management tricks and tips, your successes and failures to date, and what advice you have for others. Of course I want to know if *The Money Diet* has changed your life for the better, but I also want to know what part or parts you have not found useful. Please be specific! At the back of the book, you will find an address where you can send me your comments. Remember, you may have just the bit of advice that others in your situation can use to make a better life for themselves, their families, and their futures too. That's what *The Money Diet* is all about!

Acknowledgments

THE MONEY DIET is the result of a collaborative effort of many colleagues, clients, family and friends. Unfortunately, space only allows me to mention some of these fine people.

First and foremost, Steve Friedman, former Executive Producer of *Today*, agreed to an entire week's worth of segments to present "The Money Diet" series to viewers; he then honored his promise to send my "Applegarth Advice" guide to everyone who wrote in, even when "everyone" turned out to be 54,000 people. Bryant Gumbel and Katie Couric understood the subject matter's importance to viewers. Producer Stephanie Becker turned my ideas into segments that viewers could easily understand, and Mary Alice O'Rourke and Tammy Haddad provided key support for "The Money Diet" series from concept to reality.

Colleen Mohyde of the Doe Coover Agency saw the potential for a Money Diet book before anyone else did and took on the task of shopping it to publishers, negotiating contracts, and providing invaluable professional and moral support at every step of the process. Pam Dorman, Executive Editor of Viking, put her credibility on the line by first purchasing the rights to the book and then taking pains not to pressure me when medical issues postponed delivery of the manuscript. Others at Viking who have been particularly helpful and involved are Cathy Hemming, Carolyn Carlson, Michael Geoghegan,

Giulia Melucci, David Nelson, Katy Riegel, Laurie Rippon, Teddy Rosenbaum, Paul Slovak, and Neil Stuart.

Financial planning is a complex subject because it touches on so many specific areas—legal, tax, investment, insurance, etc.—and a number of experts provided important assistance. They include Oliver Fowlkes, JD; Shari Levitan, JD; James Margolis, CLU; David Mohning, Director of Financial Aid for Vanderbilt University; Warren J. Roy, CPA; Lee Simmons and Charlotte Rush of MasterCard International. My assistant, Kathy Chianca, assumed substantial additional client responsibilities at the same time she was studying to earn her own financial planning designation. Warner Henderson, my partner at Applegarth Henderson Advisors, Inc., served as sounding board for much of the book, especially the investment chapter. He also took on overall management of our firm so that I could concentrate on writing *The Money Diet*. Erin Lehman of Harvard University served as my research assistant and should be credited for uncovering many of the most interesting statistics included in *The Money Diet*.

Marc Kaufman at Desktop Publishing and Design in Boston transformed my complicated handwritten charts into easy-to-follow Willpower Worksheets. Gloria Papile transcribed the manuscript and cheerfully made revisions to every draft from first to last, with assistance from Randy English at two key points in the process. Judy Campbell patiently created fictitious people, using a variety of financial and personal factors, and then filled out sets of the worksheets as these "alter egos" to test the worksheets' logic and accuracy. Any errors remaining in text or worksheets are my responsibility alone.

I started writing *The Money Diet* four months after a serious automobile accident, making sustained concentration difficult. Wendell Pierce, M.D., and Stanley Sagov, M.D., should be credited with providing medical and moral support far beyond what the Hippocratic Oath mandates. On a personal note, I would like to thank Anne Hogeland and Rickey Bevington for helping to foster that concentration at several key points in time. Finally, I am grateful for my entire family, who took this book project on as a family endeavor and encouraged me to keep on writing no matter what the latest medical prognosis was. This includes my parents, Bill and Alice Applegarth; my siblings, Anne McGugin, Susan Murphy, and Paul Applegarth; and my children, Alden and Rickey Bevington.

My thanks to all of you.

Contents

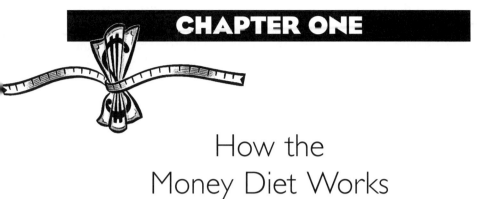

CHAPTER ONE

How the
Money Diet Works

I WILL NEVER forget the couple who were my first real clients when I was just starting out in the 1970s. After passing all the exams for the Certified Financial Planner and Chartered Life Underwriter designations, I finally persuaded a financial planning firm in Atlanta to take me on as a junior planner. My first assignment was to prepare a financial plan for a couple I will call the Petersons (all the names in this book have been changed). The Petersons were in their forties (exactly twenty years older than I was at the time; in hindsight, a bad match from the start!). I carefully gathered all the information I needed about their current situation, helped them think about their goals and dreams, and spent time getting to know them so I could understand how they each handled money. Back then, personal computers were not available, so it took me weeks with a calculator to check and recheck all their financial projections and my recommendations.

I will also never forget my anticipation in presenting my first detailed plan to the Petersons. My anticipation soon turned to humiliation, though, when they opened the report and read my first recommendation. To meet their goals, I had calculated that this couple needed to save $26,000 a year—on a $50,000-a-year income! Needless to say, I lost them as clients. I still think of them every time I am writing a plan; I wonder whether they were able to survive the shock I gave them and not swear off financial planners for life.

What did I do right? Just as my textbooks instructed me to do, I told the Petersons how much they needed to save to reach their goals, after making a host of assumptions about inflation, their income, taxes, etc. What is more important, however, is what I did wrong. I fell squarely into the trap that a financial planner is supposed to avoid at all costs: giving clients totally unrealistic advice that is impossible to fulfill, thereby making them feel like total failures. I learned a valuable lesson that day because these clients never bothered to listen to all my other recommendations that would have made the $26,000-a-year annual savings target a little more possible. Too much reality, too fast, can scare clients into inaction, perhaps permanently.

So if I were to spend the rest of this book proving to you that to meet your goals you need to save so much money and invest so aggressively that you can't sleep at night, you no doubt would be too depressed to take my advice. It is true that most of us will need to make changes if we want to meet our goals. But all of us have opportunities, *every day*, to make decisions that will improve our financial futures.

Let us start out with the first positive thing about your financial future: how much money you are likely to make for the rest of your life, probably the largest number in your financial future. The table entitled **How Much Will You Make the Rest of Your Life? (With 5 Percent Annual Increases)** on page 3 shows how much you will likely earn from now until you reach age sixty-five if your income increases 5 percent a year until retirement at that age. For example, if you are thirty-five now and earning $40,000 a year, your total projected salary to age sixty-five is well over $2.6 million. In fact, the next table, **How Much Will You Make the Rest of Your Life? (If Your Income Remains the Same)** on page 4, shows that you will still earn $1.2 million even if you never get another raise. If you are married and both employed, you can calculate the future income for each of you and then add them together for a family total. If you are married and one of you is not currently working, you can use the chart to figure out what the "added value" would be to your family if the unemployed spouse returned to work. Those lifetime-earnings numbers look

How Much Will You Make the Rest of Your Life?
(With 5 Percent Annual Increases)

Age	Earnings	$10,000	$20,000	$30,000	$40,000	$50,000	$60,000	$70,000	$80,000	$90,000	$100,000
20		$1,597,002	3,194,003	4,791,005	6,388,006	7,985,008	9,582,009	11,179,011	12,776,012	14,373,014	15,970,016
25		$1,207,998	2,415,995	3,623,993	4,831,991	6,039,989	7,247,986	8,455,984	9,663,982	10,871,980	12,079,977
30		$903,203	1,806,406	2,709,609	3,612,812	4,516,015	5,419,218	6,322,422	7,225,625	8,128,828	9,032,031
35		$664,388	1,328,777	1,993,165	2,657,554	3,321,942	3,986,331	4,650,719	5,315,108	5,979,496	6,643,885
40		$477,271	954,542	1,431,813	1,909,084	2,386,355	2,863,626	3,340,897	3,818,168	4,295,439	4,772,710
45		$330,660	661,319	991,979	1,322,638	1,653,298	1,983,957	2,314,617	2,645,276	2,975,936	3,306,595
50		$215,786	431,571	647,357	863,143	1,078,928	1,294,714	1,510,499	1,726,285	1,942,071	2,157,856
55		$125,779	251,558	377,337	503,116	628,895	754,674	880,452	1,006,231	1,132,010	1,257,789
60		$55,256	110,513	165,769	221,025	276,282	331,538	386,794	442,051	497,307	552,563

Find the age nearest yours in the left-hand column, then move to the right until you reach the column for the annual income nearest yours. This shows your total lifetime income henceforth, assuming your income goes up 5 percent a year and you retire at 65.

How Much Will You Make the Rest of Your Life?
(If Your Income Remains the Same)

Age	Earnings	$10,000	$20,000	$30,000	$40,000	$50,000	$60,000	$70,000	$80,000	$90,000	$100,000
20		$450,000	900,000	1,350,000	1,800,000	2,250,000	2,700,000	3,150,000	3,600,000	4,050,000	4,500,000
25		$400,000	800,000	1,200,000	1,600,000	2,000,000	2,400,000	2,800,000	3,200,000	3,600,000	4,000,000
30		$350,000	700,000	1,050,000	1,400,000	1,750,000	2,100,000	2,450,000	2,800,000	3,150,000	3,500,000
35		$300,000	600,000	900,000	1,200,000	1,500,000	1,800,000	2,100,000	2,400,000	2,700,000	3,000,000
40		$250,000	500,000	750,000	1,000,000	1,250,000	1,500,000	1,750,000	2,000,000	2,250,000	2,500,000
45		$200,000	400,000	600,000	800,000	1,000,000	1,200,000	1,400,000	1,600,000	1,800,000	2,000,000
50		$150,000	300,000	450,000	600,000	750,000	900,000	1,050,000	1,200,000	1,350,000	1,500,000
55		$100,000	200,000	300,000	400,000	500,000	600,000	700,000	800,000	900,000	1,000,000
60		$50,000	100,000	150,000	200,000	250,000	300,000	350,000	400,000	450,000	500,000

Find the age nearest yours in the left-hand column, then move to the right until you reach the column for the annual income nearest yours. This shows your total lifetime income henceforth, assuming your income remains the same and you retire at 65.

From The Money Diet, by Ginger Applegarth.

pretty high, don't they? That is the good news because *what you do with the dollars you earn over your lifetime determines how you will live.* Of course, if you have already retired, you may no longer have earned income, but you can add up your future Social Security and pension income.

Unfortunately, reality means that you cannot keep everything that you earn. You will have to pay taxes, you will have living expenses, and you may have debt payments. This means that you will have to achieve all your future goals with the money that is left over, as well as with your existing assets and their earnings.

How can anyone possibly plan for the future with so many factors to think about? This is a problem I have pondered for years as I have tried to come up with a way that would easily allow clients to keep their overall financial picture in mind so that short-term temptations do not get in their way. In order for financial planning to be most useful for you, it's smart to keep the big picture in mind so that every time you make a financial decision (when you pull out your wallet, checkbook, or credit card; sign a form with changes to your retirement plans; or fill out an insurance application), you will instantly get an overall idea of how that decision might affect your financial future. Otherwise, you get overwhelmed by the details and may be unable to see the forest for the trees. I call this the "bog-down" factor; I am reminded of it every time I am too cheap to pay for covered parking in the winter and then pay $30 in dry-cleaning bills because I have ended up drenched by snow and spattered by mud. Keeping this "big picture" in your mind's eye will motivate you to think of your finances in future terms instead of in present terms. Otherwise the short-term temptation to overspend, skimp on insurance, settle for the guaranteed low-rate certificate of deposit (CD), etc., will win every time.

You may have noticed the chart called **The Money Diet Method** at the beginning of this book. This chart illustrates better than I can explain in words exactly how the Money Diet works. Now is a good time to look at how **The Money Diet Method** would function in a perfect world.

At the top of the picture, your income dollar is being squeezed. We all know that feeling. The first squeeze comes from taxes. Your dollar shrinks. The second squeeze comes from expenses. Your dollar shrinks again. The third squeeze is debt payments. Whatever you have left over is savings, or the dollar bills you see floating down to the piles of money. These dollars are put into investments such as bank accounts, stocks, mutual funds, a home; each goal is represented by a pile of money at the bottom of the chart. You save and invest your money now so that you can meet your goals in the future. This is the real key to the Money Diet process because *what you do with the dollars you earn over your lifetime determines how well you will be able to live.*

In **The Money Diet Method** the piles of money at the bottom of the picture represent what you have been able to save in life thus far to meet your goals. If you have accumulated savings over the years, you may have mentally stacked up different piles—one for each goal. You may have even actually segregated your savings into different accounts, such as an individual retirement account (IRA), a special investment account for education, etc. Of course, whatever savings dollars you have been able to put in these piles may not be enough by themselves to meet your goals. But through the magic of investing, the piles of money can grow larger each year, even if you do not add another penny of savings.

For starters, let's assume you have been able to set aside sufficient annual savings and have invested it well enough to end up with all the money you need to meet each of your goals. When the time comes to pay for one of your goals, you will hand over the stack of money you have saved for just that purpose, leaving the other stacks in place to grow until another stack must be traded for your next goal. Then you come to your last and largest goal: retirement. (You may say that retirement is not a goal, but at some point you *will* retire—if you don't die first.) At that point, there may be no more annual savings to add to the pile. But in this perfect scenario, there is enough money in the pile so that, coupled with pension and Social Security income, it is more than enough for your retirement needs. Finally, at the end of your life, there is even money left in the pile to bequeath to your heirs when you die. In this scenario you are able to achieve the lifestyle you want, saving what is left over for the future, with enough money to meet your goals. This is the Money Diet in a perfect world.

Alas, the world is not perfect. Most of us need to make changes in our money-management ways if we want to meet our goals. Often, these changes seem overwhelming. But just by looking at **The Money Diet Method** you can see where these changes can be made. This is where the *diet* comes in. The first thing you can do is make sure that money is left over after what I call the "TED" squeeze. TED = *Taxes, Expenses,* and *Debt payments.* To reduce the TED squeeze you must do everything you can to reduce your taxes, cut your expenses, and start to pay down your debts now so that you are not paying high debt interest charges. This increases those savings dollars floating down to the piles. Then, to make your piles of money grow even more rapidly, you can modify your investment strategy for greater overall investment return. Strategies for achieving these goals will be covered in more detail in later chapters.

Fortunately, the TED squeeze and investment strategy you choose are not the only determinants of your financial future. Other circumstances and events will affect the size of those piles of money over your lifetime. If you work for an employer who is setting aside retirement money for you, that goes straight to your nest egg at retirement (or perhaps even if you leave your job before then). If you are fortunate enough to inherit money, at some point that too will increase your investment dollars. If your child receives a scholarship to attend college, the amount required to meet your education goal for your family will be smaller so that more money can go to the retirement pile. The goal is to accumulate as much money in the various piles as possible and reduce the amount you will need to withdraw for one or more of your goals.

Most people can make big changes in some of these areas and none at all in others. Every person's financial situation is unique. What is right for someone else may not be right for you, but the Money Diet *process* and the *habits* it teaches are right for just about everyone. With this book, you can construct your own unique Money Diet. After all, the most effective food diets are those that are realistic, contain foods you like, and do not require major changes in your lifestyle.

The Money Diet will not work without some measure of protection for both your income and your assets. What needs protecting? If your income is lost through disability, then regular living expenses and unexpected expenses such as medical bills will have to come out of your assets. Your family may even have to use up the education, house, or retirement piles just to pay the bills. And you have to be protected against the loss of your automobile, home, or other assets, as well as protected against lawsuits. The invisible circle around the Money Diet is insurance, which is the only way to provide all the protection you need to be certain that the Money Diet can work when you start and maintain it.

You may note I have not mentioned increasing your income as a way to help your Money Diet, but I "neglected" to do so for two reasons. First of all, your income is often the one thing over which you have the least control. If you think about it, the size of your income may result from factors such as your parents' economic status; whether they were able to send you to college or specialized schools; what talents, skills, and gifts you were born with; who you know; where you live; what you like to do; and just plain luck. For instance, I can trace my connection with the *Today* show back to a single phone call on a Friday evening several years ago. I was on my way out the door when the phone rang, but I paused to pick it up. The *Today* producer who was calling me, Stephanie Becker, later told me that after a couple more unanswered rings she would have hung up and called the next person on her list. Now *that* is an example of supreme good fortune.

This example just goes to show that some small thing you do today might have far-reaching implications for the future. And even if your money situation does not look terrific, anything can happen. Still, good fortune remains a factor we cannot control or count on.

The second reason the Money Diet does not rely on increasing your income is that doing so does not always result in higher savings. All too often we make ourselves miserable by thinking that if only we could earn more we would be able to save all that extra income. Unfortunately, it ain't necessarily so. You may imagine that your neighbor, your boss, or your brother who has a much higher income than you do can save much more each year than you can. I have found that this just is not true. Why? People with higher incomes pay higher income taxes and generally have much higher standards of living and expenses, so their savings rate may in fact be less than yours. And whereas you may be happy to live in a modest but comfortable house, their higher expectations may trap them in a lifestyle where only an expensive house in the nicest neighborhood will satisfy them. The assumption that someone who makes more than you do is in better financial shape than you are is often incorrect.

Let me use two hypothetical families as an example. The Smiths have a $35,000 annual income and save $7,000 a year. The Joneses are fortunate enough to make $200,000 a year, and they are saving $15,000 through retirement plans. The Jones family is in better financial shape, right? *Wrong.* First of all, the Joneses are saving 7½ percent of their income, versus 20 percent for the Smiths. Second, the Joneses' standard of living is so high that even though they are making retirement plan contributions, they have to turn right around and cash in at least that much in investments to pay their bills. Their actual annual savings is a negative number because their expenses, taxes, and debt payments total more than their income. They feel compelled to live above their means because all their friends and family are wealthy and they do not want their financial problems to become known. Who has a worse financial situation? The Joneses. Whose financial future looks brighter? I would bet on the Smiths in a minute.

Now that you know it's not how much you make but how much you save and how you invest those savings, you may feel motivated to start making changes sometime soon. But instead of waiting until you get your next raise, until Christmas is over, until the house is redecorated, or until the car loan is paid off, make a commitment to start the Money Diet now. The sooner you get started, the better the chances are that you can meet your goals. Why? The beauty of compound interest, or investment return. Let's take two examples. John, aged forty-five, decides to start saving for retirement and contributes $2,000 a year for twenty-one years (including age sixty-five) into an IRA plan in which contributions are tax-deductible and no taxes on earnings are taken out until he retires. Let's say he invests well and gets a 10 percent return every year. His total payments are $40,000. The total value of his IRA at age sixty-five is $128,000.

John Sr. tells his twenty-five-year-old son, John Jr., about his plan and tells him to do the same. John Jr. does not always follow his father's advice, but he realizes that this bit of advice makes good sense. So John Jr. contributes $2,000 a year for the same twenty-one years, then stops after age forty-five, leaving his money untouched in his IRA for another twenty years until he is sixty-five. Like John Sr., he pays $40,000 into the plan, but his total value at sixty-five is over *$860,000,* or over *seven times as much.* Why? The difference is compound interest; John Jr.'s account had twenty more years to grow. This is why it is important to set goals as early as possible in life and start to save for them: You'll end up *paying less* for those same goals!

The whole point of financial planning (and the Money Diet) is to give you more control over your financial life. And it can work. By the end of this book, you will feel empowered to increase your income, reduce your taxes, reduce your expenses, properly insure yourself against disasters, increase your savings, and improve your investment strategies so you have a better chance of transforming your dreams into reality.

STEP ONE

GETTING ON
THE FINANCIAL SCALES

CHAPTER TWO

Your Current Weight: What You Own and Owe

ONE OF THE MOST important things to remember when you start the Money Diet is that numbers *do lie*. Of course, they don't lie when you add them up and get a "report card" of your financial life to date. But they *do* lie when it comes to measuring how skilled you are at managing money as well as forecasting your future financial success. Before you start trying to diet, it's smart to get on the scales so you can figure out your weight-reduction goal and then design a diet to meet that goal. Chapters 2 and 3 form Step 1 of the Money Diet— **Getting on the Financial Scales**.

We've mentioned two ways to measure your financial success: determining your net worth and figuring out how much you are currently spending and saving. This chapter deals with the first of those measurements—net worth, or what you own minus what you owe.

YOU ARE NOT WHAT YOU OWN

At first glance, of course, a $100,000 net worth would indicate better money skills than a $10,000 net worth. That $100,000 should go a lot further than $10,000 in meeting someone's financial goals, but keep in mind that the person with the $100,000 net worth is likely to have much higher goals than the person with the $10,000 net worth. The more affluent family is used to a higher standard of living and probably does not want to reduce that standard. And if your neighbor's goals are much larger than yours, you both may be in the same financial position relative to your goals. It may have taken much more self-discipline and skill with money for you to accumulate $10,000 than for your neighbor to have accumulated $100,000. This is especially true when it comes to inherited money. Some of the least deserving people I know in the "self-disciplined" and "skilled with money" categories are those who have inherited the most money.

In the last chapter, we looked at some of the factors that might have an impact on your income. Let's look now at the factors affecting your net worth. The amount you have been able to save on an annual basis and your investment performance are the most direct determinants of your net worth because dollars are actually added to your bottom line, but what about these other, less obvious factors that help determine how much you can save and how well you invest?

Age How many years have you been able to save? People in their fifties are likely to have a lot more assets than people in their twenties because this older generation has had many more years to save and more years during which to invest those savings.

Parents Have you received any inheritances, or are you in fact exhausting both your parents' assets and your own to support them in their old age?

Health Have you been hit with high medical bills and/or the inability to work due to illness or a restrictive disability? I have painful first-hand experience with this dilemma; the effects of my seven-year disability still show up in my own net worth statement.

Marital Status Are you married? Does your spouse work, or are you supporting two people? Does your spouse work at a good job that allows you to save large amounts of money each year? Did you "marry money"? Have you undergone a costly divorce? All these factors can have a monumental impact on your bottom line.

Children Do you have any children? It has been estimated that it costs up to $500,000 to raise a child from infancy to adulthood, including college expenses. This is not an argument to dissuade you from having children, but to reassure you that there may be several good reasons—all with your last name!—why your net worth is not as high as that of someone else your age. For example, I recently counseled a couple who do not have children and who want to retire early. Looking at just their income, I originally thought their goal was unattainable. Then I tallied up what they owned and owed, or the size of their current net worth. Compared to other couples with the same income, my clients are substantially better off. Their annual savings is higher because they are not supporting children, and they don't have to use up assets to pay college tuition.

Career Choice Did you choose a low-paying career, or have you chosen not to work so that you can devote your time to your family? Teaching is a perfect example of a low-paying career choice; teachers play a vital role in our children's future, but the profession pays much less than many others. Part-time versus full-time work is also an issue. I recently calculated the cost of "cutting back" for a client who contemplated reducing her hours: Her net worth would be $30,000 lower after four years of reduced hours than it would be if she continued to work full-time and saved the extra money.

Geographic Area Do you live in Manhattan or Montana? Dallas or Dubuque? Everyone knows that it is more expensive to live in certain parts of the country. For example, one of the people we featured on the *Today* show was able to purchase a house in South Bend, Indiana, for just over $50,000. In some areas of the country, you cannot even buy a parking space for that!

Economic Status of the Country Were you hit very hard by the recession of the late 1980s through no fault of your own? You may not have changed the way you saved or invested your money, but you may have lost your job or your business or experienced a reduction in income because no one had money to purchase your company's goods or services. I cannot even count the number of people I know who were adversely affected by the last recession.

Behavior of the Stock Market Have you ever opened a retirement plan or investment statement and panicked because the value dropped a lot in just one month? The exact same portfolio of investments may be worth 20 percent less this year than it was last year, even though you have not changed one investment in the portfolio. Everyone is affected by the behavior of the stock and bond markets if they own any stocks, bonds, or mutual funds.

Now that you know some of the uncontrollable factors affecting net worth, you probably feel better about your own net worth, but you also may feel tempted to throw up your hands and say, "Why bother reading the rest of this book? It's all out of my control anyway." But just as with losing weight, you have to look at all the factors affecting your net worth, then focus on those over which you have some control. You can then exercise your control by choosing the combination of money management steps that you know you can actually accomplish and that will produce positive results.

GETTING ORGANIZED

So how do you determine your net worth? On the surface, this exercise appears simple. Even the most disorganized person can write out a list of his assets (what he owns) and liabilities (what he owes). This is exactly what we do regularly when we apply for a mortgage or car loan or update a credit card application. If it's so simple, why haven't more of us done it? It is always much easier to deal with our finances when someone else is analyzing the numbers and when there is a deadline; we have an immediate incentive to pull the information together. Or we may avoid doing this exercise because we do not want to start thinking in materialistic terms; sitting down and listing our assets may seem a little greedy.

Sometimes it is painful for us to look at the numbers on a balance sheet because they may not jibe with the numbers it would take to maintain the image the world holds of us. In the late 1980s, it was not uncommon for people who had heavily invested in commercial real estate to have *negative* net worths (what they owed was more than what they owned), accompanied by little or no cash flow. They were being hurt on all sides: Their tenants were going out of business, so rents were not coming in; mortgage payments still needed to be made; and there were very few commercial real estate buyers to take property off their hands at any price. To the outside world, these people may have seemed as wealthy as ever, but in reality they may have had virtually no income and were headed toward financial disaster. By filling out a net worth statement for a personal line of credit, a person in this situation might realize for the first time the necessity of making financial changes.

So if, despite hesitations, you know your financial net worth is key, what is the first step? *Getting organized,* or improving the system you already have if need be. Some people think I am organized by nature, but nothing could be further from the truth. Early in my adult life, after looking for a bank statement for an entire day and still not finding it, I realized that I hated looking for something more than I disliked getting my records organized, so I vowed I would never have to mount such an APB search again!

If you are like most people, you are probably more organized in your work life than in your personal life. Why? In your work, you are usually answering to somebody else! The Money Diet test of adequate organization in your personal finances is to ask yourself this question: "Can I get my hands on any major piece of paper referring to my financial situation in ten minutes (except for the contents of the safe-deposit box)?" If the answer is yes, congratulations. If not, you need to improve your organization system. First ask yourself what one major reason is keeping you from being organized. More often than not, the culprit is a poor (or nonexistent!) filing system or the habit of letting papers pile up with the idea that you will file them on the weekend (or at the end of the month, the end of the year, tax time, and so on) instead of "filing as you go."

If you are not satisfied with your current system, here is a simple one that takes only about an hour to set up. You will find it in **The Money Diet Quick Filing System** (page 18). First, you need a small filing cabinet, or a large filing box if you don't have too many files. You also need folders (I prefer hanging ones) for the categories you

The Money Diet Quick Filing System

Taxes

Current Year

Next Year

Household Files

Kitchen

Major Appliances

Small Appliances

Audio/Video/TV

Lawn & Garden

Home Furnishings

Miscellaneous

Financial Files—One for Each Individual Item

Credit Cards

Bank Accounts

Investment Accounts

Retirement Plans

Real Estate Property

Automobile

Employee Benefits

Insurance

One Annual File for Each Person in Your Household

Current Year

Next Year

One File with Lined Paper to Keep Ongoing Records

House Capital Improvements

House Repairs

continued on next page

From *The Money Diet*, by Ginger Applegarth.

The Money Diet Quick Filing System (cont.)

Current

Bills to Be Paid
_____

12 Monthly Files for Miscellaneous Paid Bills
_____

Pending
_____

To Do
_____

see listed in the worksheet: one file for each of your bank or investment accounts; one for each of your retirement plans; and one for
each piece of real estate, each automobile, and each credit card you
have. For taxes, it is also smart to set up a current-year income tax file
with envelopes for different types of income, deductions, and taxes
(and make a file for the coming year at the same time so you are ready
to go next January 1). Keep this year's income tax file handy so that
you can just throw receipts and papers pertaining to your taxes *as
you collect them* in the appropriate envelopes and worry about them
at the end of the year. I also have one file for current bills to be paid,
twelve monthly files for miscellaneous bills that were paid during the
last year, a general "to-do" file, and a "pending" file (for things that
require action on somebody else's part). To keep track of warranty
cards, instructions, purchase receipts, etc., I have one file for each category of household items: kitchen items, major appliances, audio/
video/TV equipment, sports gear, lawn and garden stuff, pets, and so
on. A file that contains notebook paper for recording all household
capital improvements and the corresponding receipts is a very useful
way to keep track of all of the expenditures you make that might be
used to offset any capital gain you incur when you sell your house. Finally, I keep one file for insurance policies and another for employee
benefits.

You may wonder why I am not including monthly files here for
statements received. Instead, I use separate files for each credit card,
bank account, etc., because credit cards and bank accounts rarely end

on the last day of the month (then I find myself spending ridiculous amounts of time figuring out in which month the statement should go). This may sound like an unusual problem, but I cannot tell you how many times clients have told me the same thing.

One of the best pieces of advice I ever received was the suggestion to create a file every year for each person in my household. These files provide an easy place to collect greeting cards, important letters, newspaper clippings, photos, artwork, report cards, mementos, etc. Even now that my children are in their teens, one of the activities they most enjoy doing from time to time is pulling out these old files and seeing the "time capsule" for each of the years of their lives.

FIGURING OUT YOUR CURRENT NET WORTH

Now that you are organized, it is time to figure out your financial weight—what you own and what you owe. (Remember to estimate for any number that will take you over ten minutes to find!) If you are not organized now or you cannot get all the information you need, go ahead and complete the exercise based on estimates; then when you have the accurate information, go back and redo it. Using estimates will at least get you started, and getting started will motivate you to keep going on your Money Diet. But do not make any major financial decisions until you replace those estimated numbers with accurate ones. If you use estimates, you may be pleasantly surprised at how on target you were when you track down the actual numbers! If not, this may be a sign that your financial "perception versus reality" is out of sync. If you are like many people, you may start to feel some resistance because you're thinking, Do I really want to know what I'm worth? But you *have* to know where you stand today so that you have a starting point from which to measure all of your future financial progress. These are the first Willpower Worksheets, so make note of how motivated you are to improve your finances when you see the bottom line.

The **Simplified Net Worth Statement** (page 22) gives you a snapshot of where you are today. The **Detailed Net Worth Statement** (page 24) is a more detailed version, which I have included so that you can list individual assets and liabilities. You will need this information in other chapters, so it is definitely worth taking the time to complete this worksheet now. As you proceed through these exercises, keep in mind that some assets may be missing here. For instance, it may be impossible to determine the value today of any company retirement plans that do not provide you with a current account balance but that instead describe your benefit as a monthly income at retirement. We will take these assets into account later.

Here are some tips to help you find out what you own and owe:

1. Shut off the critical voice in your head that says "I should have done it sooner/differently/the way Dad did." These thoughts will only make it more difficult to embark upon the Money Diet. Remember, you are starting fresh today!

2. Do not compare the results of your exercise with what you think another person's situation might be. Remember how deceiving appearances can be! And above all, do not compare your net worth to some unrealistically high ideal of success you carry around in your head. The goal of *The Money Diet* is to make you feel *better* about your financial life, not worse.

3. If you are married, you should probably complete these exercises jointly. But keep in mind that it is always a good idea for each spouse to have some assets in his or her own name.

4. When you get to the category of "house," ignore how much you paid for it and instead estimate what you could probably sell your house for today, less a realtor's fee of about 5 percent. Multiply what you believe the current market value of your house is by 0.95 (95 percent) to arrive at what you would receive if you sold it and used a realtor.

5. In examining your bank accounts, investments, and retirement plans, look at the current "account value" figures that are on these various statements. It is always useful to look at these statements and compare them with previous ones to see whether the balances have gone up or down in the last year. If so, find out why they've changed and make a note to yourself; this can give you some useful insights into your financial affairs. The reasons for the up or down activity can be legion: a change in the value of the investment; cash withdrawals; cash deposits; interest or dividends paid.

6. If you own a permanent life insurance policy that has cash

Simplified Net Worth Statement

What you OWN

A. Bank Accounts	A.
B. Investments	B. +
C. Retirement Plans	C. +
D. House (Market Value)	D. +
E. Cars	E. +
F. Personal Property	F. +
G. Other Assets	G. +
H. What you OWN (add lines A–G)	H. =

What you OWE

I. Mortgage	I.
J. Credit Cards	J. +
K. Car Loans	K. +
L. Other Debts	L. +
M. What you OWE (add lines I–L)	M. =

Your NET WORTH

H. What you OWN	H.
M. Less: What you OWE	M. –
N. Equals: Your NET WORTH	N. =

From *The Money Diet*, by Ginger Applegarth.

surrender value, include this amount with your other investments. People often confuse *cash surrender value* (what you get if you cash in the policy today) with *death benefit* or *face amount* (what your beneficiaries would receive in the event of your death).

7. When it comes to cars, I find that clients sometimes list the purchase price of their cars without taking into account the fact that these automobiles may be worth much less now due to substantial depreciation. Of course, cars and personal property are not really investment assets because—unless you are willing to sell them—their values usually are not available to meet your goals. Still, it is smart to include *some* value for them; they may be saleable in an emergency, and listing them also shows you where you have been spending some of your hard-earned savings. In fact, if more of your assets are in cars, personal property, etc., than in investment and retirement accounts, this is a danger sign that you may be spending too much on "now" and not saving enough for "later."

8. For your liabilities (what you owe), keep things simple by using your last statement balances instead of trying to add on any new purchases or subtract out any payments from the last statement. The loan amounts are for the actual amount you would need to pay off the loan now; do not include any future interest. When reviewing your loan statements, you may be shocked at how high your current mortgage balance is relative to the original amount. In the early years of most loans, most of your payment goes to pay interest.

Once you have completed either or both worksheets, you are ready to answer the question of how much you are worth. The answer is easy. On either worksheet, subtract M, your liabilities (what you owe), from H, your assets (what you own). The answer, your current net worth, is N. I hope you'll be pleasantly surprised by what you have just learned about your assets and liabilities as well as about your own abilities to organize and put your financial information down on paper. This is the first major step in financial planning, and it is one that many people simply never get around to taking. I often suggest that clients keep their net worth figures in mind whenever they are making financial decisions so that they can ask themselves, "Will this increase or decrease my net worth for the future?"

Detailed Net Worth Statement

What you OWN	ASSETS
Checking	
Savings/CDs	+
Money Market Accounts	+
A. Bank Accounts	**A. =**
Mutual Funds	
Stocks	+
Bonds	+
Life Insurance (Cash Value)	+
Annuities	+
Investment Real Estate	+
B. Investments	**B. =**
Savings — 401(k) and 403(b)	
Company Plan	+
IRA	+
Keogh	+
C. Retirement Plans	**C. =**
D. House (Market Value)	**D. =**
Car #1	
Car #2	+
E. Cars	**E. =**
F. Personal Property	**F. =**
Loans Receivable	
Collectables	+
Business Interest	+
Other	+
G. Other Assets	**G. =**
H. What you OWN (add lines A–G)	**H. =**

continued on next page

From *The Money Diet*, by Ginger Applegarth.

Detailed Net Worth Statement (cont.)

What you OWE   DEBTS

First Mortgage	
Home Equity Loan	+
I. Mortgage	**I. =**
VISA	
MasterCard	+
Other	+
Other	+
J. Credit Cards	**J. =**
Car #1	
Car #2	+
K. Car Loans	**K. =**
Education	
Life Insurance	+
Other	+
Other	+
Other	+
L. Other Debts	**L. =**
M. What you OWE (add lines I–L)	**M.=**

Your NET WORTH

H. What you OWN	**H.**
M. Less: What you OWE	**M. −**
N. Equals: Your NET WORTH	**N. =**

From *The Money Diet*, by Ginger Applegarth.

If you were *not* happily surprised by what you have just learned (even if you came up with a negative net worth), it is not necessarily time to worry. *The Money Diet* is full of advice and tips to help you increase your bottom line so that your net worth will grow ever larger. You are already halfway to knowing your current financial weight because calculating your net worth produces a dollar figure for how much you have been able to save thus far in your life. Once you have completed the next chapter, which covers calculating your expenses and savings so you can chart your *future* net worth, you will have a firm grasp of exactly where you stand today. And knowing where you stand today will make it possible to accurately identify the steps you must take to make the Money Diet help your money grow in the future.

Your Current Weight:
What You Are Spending
and Saving

IF THE THOUGHT of actually sitting down and figuring out how much you are spending and saving seems a bit overwhelming, just imagine how you would react if, right now, your phone suddenly rang with a *Today* producer on the line asking if you would like to bare your soul about your spending habits in front of millions of people! Believe it or not, this actually happened to three loyal *Today* viewers who were among the 54,000 people who wrote in to NBC for "Applegarth Advice," the guide to "The Money Diet" series.

Our financial-planning-on-wheels tour went south to North Carolina, continued west to South Bend, Indiana, and finished in upstate New York. Each home and family we visited was different—a couple with small children, a young woman just starting out in her career, and an "empty nest" couple facing retirement. They had different incomes, net worths, and concerns about money, but they all agreed on one thing: of the seven Willpower Worksheets in "Applegarth Advice," they found **Spending and Saving** (reprinted in this book on page 28) to be the most intimidating. They agreed, however, that this worksheet probably also ended up being the most enlightening. It will also probably increase your willpower to stick to your Money Diet more than any other worksheet in the book. In fact, if you only complete one Willpower Worksheet in this book, make it **Spending and Saving.**

Spending and Saving

Checking Accounts	Total Monthly Deposits ("Credits")	Total Monthly Withdrawals ("Debits")
Month 1		
Month 2		
Month 3		
Month 4		
Month 5		
Month 6		
Month 7		
Month 8		
Month 9		
Month 10		
Month 11		
Month 12 (last month)		

	Total Deposits	Total Withdrawals
	A.	F.
	B.– Social Security and income taxes paid by check	B.– Social Security and income taxes paid by check
	C.+ All other non-tax expenses withheld	C.+ All other non-tax expenses withheld
	D.+ Saving and retirement plan contributions withheld	G.+/- Increase/decrease in consumer debt in last 12 months
	E.= After-Tax Annual Income	H.= Total Annual Expenses

After-Tax Annual Income	E.
Less: Total Annual Expenses	H. –
Your Annual Savings	I. =

So, if you are thinking at this point that you would just rather skip this chapter, your sentiments are entirely normal. After all, almost half of Americans have no budget, and we can only surmise that just as many have little idea where their money goes or how much they are saving each year. So, even if you start to find this exercise a bit intimidating (and most people do), I recommend you complete it. Virtually all the clients I have ever worked with who completed this exercise have found that they were spending more than they thought and have since found painless ways to decrease their spending simply by paying more attention to where their money goes.

In chapter 1, we talked about how the Money Diet works. As with all financial planning, there are only two real ways for you to build assets to meet your future goals. The first is to increase your annual savings, and the second is to invest those savings for a higher return. Just like a food diet (where you need to assess your eating habits), with financial planning you need to know your current money consumption habits in order to make positive changes. You have already gotten on the financial scales to find out what you own and owe; now it's time to stay on those scales and see how you are spending and saving your money. And just as starting on a diet and keeping track of every bite you put in your mouth automatically makes you eat less, looking at your spending habits automatically makes you start to spend less and save more.

The **Spending and Saving** worksheet takes about an hour to do, but it will be one of the most productive hours of your financial life. And the bonus is how good you will feel after you complete it, even if the news is not what you would have hoped. (I am still touched and amused when middle-aged clients report back to me that they were so proud of themselves for doing this exercise that they even told their parents, just to prove how responsible they are!)

One problem for many people is that they use ATMs, pay by credit cards, have paychecks automatically deposited into their bank accounts, and have debt payments automatically deducted from them; not surprisingly, they feel out of touch with their money. Somehow it does not seem as if they are dealing with real dollars and cents—it almost seems like Monopoly money. An important positive side effect of this exercise is counteracting this feeling; it automatically makes you value each dollar more (and therefore makes it more difficult for you to part with it for frivolous things).

The goal of **Spending and Saving** is to help you see how much you are currently saving to help meet your goals. In later chapters we will talk about ways that you can spend less and save more if you choose to do so. You will need the following documents from the previous twelve months to get started:

- your checking account statements
- credit card statements
- investment statements

It is also important to have on hand:

- a current pay stub showing year-to-date income and withholdings for taxes, insurance, etc.
- last year's W-2 or pay summary showing income and withholdings
- a calculator

Finally, you need an hour of uninterrupted time.

Before you get started filling out this worksheet, make sure you have gathered all the documents you need so you can avoid having to stop in the middle to look for something. (If you are like me, stopping in the middle often means the task never gets finished.) Make a commitment to yourself to finish this exercise in one sitting. I recommend to clients that to avoid interruption they make an appointment with themselves for a certain date and time when their home will be quiet and other family members will be out of the house. Do not worry about cents and round to the nearest $10, $100, or even $500 if you want to. Do *whatever it takes* to make this exercise easy for you. And remember not to chastise yourself when you see how much money has been passing through your hands. Keep in mind that you are merely reviewing the past; in fact, the more waste you identify in the past twelve months, the easier it will be to cut out waste in the future.

This Willpower Worksheet is critical to the Money Diet because when you have finished it you will have many of the numbers needed to complete the rest of the exercises in the book. For example, you will have figured out your after-tax income, which will allow you to see whether you have too much debt (chapter 6) and how large a mortgage you can likely afford (chapter 11). You will know what your total annual expenses were for the year ending last month, which will tell you not only how much life and disability insurance you need (chapter 14) but also how much retirement income you should plan for (chapter 9). Finally, by figuring out your annual savings, you can develop a strong investment strategy (chapter 8) and figure out whether public or private college makes the most sense for your children (chapter 10).

If you are married, be sure to include all the checking accounts that are used to meet family goals and expenses. (Sometimes my married clients each keep small, separate checking accounts for personal expenses so they do not have to account for that money to their spouses. If you are in this situation, decide with your spouse whether to include or exclude them, but be fair! Both of you should play by the same rules.) If you are single and have more than one checking account, add them together and put the sum under total deposits. In **Spending and Saving**, spaces are provided for you to add up all the deposits in your checking accounts for the last twelve months. Month one is last month. Month twelve is one year ago this month. The steps are as follows:

FIGURING YOUR AFTER-TAX INCOME

1. Add up all your monthly checking account deposits for the year. These are usually listed as "credits" in your statements. Start with last month and go back until you have added in twelve months of statements. Write your total for the last twelve months in the box marked A, Total Deposits.

2. If you wrote any checks for income taxes or Social Security taxes out of these accounts, write that amount twice—in the boxes marked B (there are two of them). For example, if you had to write a check for $1,500 when you filed your tax returns last year, "$1,500" should be written in both boxes marked B, Social Security and in-

come taxes paid by check. Since you cannot spend that money, we want to make sure it is not included in your after-tax income or your expenses. Otherwise, it would look like you had $1,500 more after-tax income or spent $1,500 more in living expenses than you actually did.

3. Add up all the non-tax-related items you had withheld from your paychecks during the last year. These include insurance premiums, company parking-space costs, child care payments, and amounts that were withheld under an expense reimbursement plan. Write the total twice in the boxes marked C, All other non-tax expenses withheld. Otherwise, this amount is not counted in your income or expenses—it is as if it did not exist!

4. Take a look at your pay stubs and see if you have had any retirement plan contributions or other savings taken out of your paychecks before they were deposited in your checking account; figure out the total for the last twelve months and write the sum in box D.

5. To arrive at your after-tax annual income (after federal, state, local, and Social Security taxes), follow the addition and subtraction directions in boxes A through D. From your Total Deposits (A), you will be subtracting taxes paid by check (B) and adding all the amounts you had withheld (C and D). The result is your after-tax annual income (E).

FIGURING YOUR EXPENSES AND DEBT PAYMENTS

6. Add up all your checking account withdrawals for the year. These are usually listed as "debits" in your statements. Write your total in the box marked F, Total Withdrawals.

7. In Box B you already wrote the amount of taxes you paid by a check from your account. Taxes are not really living expenses and you can't just decide to cut back on your tax payments. (Actually, you can, but the IRS would quickly cure you of that notion!) You also already filled in box C with all your other withholdings besides taxes.

8. In the next part of the exercise, add up all your credit card balances and other loan balances (except for mortgages) at the end of

last month. Then add them up for the same date one year ago. Subtract the balances of one year ago from one month ago. If your new balance is higher than your old balance, that increase needs to be added to your expenses because these are new expenses you incurred in the last twelve months that you haven't paid for by check. For example, if this year's total is $4,000 and last year's was $3,000, you spent an additional $1,000 this year and it should be added to your expenses. Write this difference in your consumer (non-mortgage) debt in box G. If last month's debt balances are lower than last year's, congratulations! Technically, we shouldn't count this debt reduction as savings, because you spent this money to pay off your debts instead of putting it in a savings account or other investment. But with the Money Diet, it is important to figure out how much less you are spending than earning, and how much you can save each year until you reach your goals. It is also encouraging to see that once your debts are paid off, those loan payments can be redirected to a savings or investment account.

9. Subtract your Total Annual Expenses (line H) from your After-Tax Annual Income (line E). The number you end up with, on line I, is your Annual Savings for the period of time ending last month. If it looks suspiciously high or low, think about unusual one-time checking account deposits you might have made in the last twelve months: a bonus, gift, or investment sale. That would make your savings look artificially high. And if you paid off any debts, wrote any checks to make investments, or had any unusual expenses that were paid with money from your checking account or with your credit cards, that would make your savings look artificially low. Your annual savings will change every year, but you have already taken a big step by finding out what your savings was for last year. And if you find that your savings number is negative, do not panic; Step 3: **Developing Your Money Diet Plan** will show you lots of ways to turn that negative savings number into a positive one. In fact, this worksheet alone should give you the willpower to spend less.

I wish I could guarantee that you will be pleased with the results of this exercise. I am, however, 100 percent sure that you will be glad that you took the time to do it. As one young woman told me after completing this Money Diet exercise, "It was the hardest thing I have ever done, but the best thing I have ever done. I have never learned so much about myself in such a short period of time."

In the last chapter, you figured out how much you own and how much you owe. In this chapter you took the more difficult step of figuring out how much you are spending and saving. The result? You have already completed the first step of the Money Diet—**Getting On the Financial Scales**. Now that you have recorded your financial history, you can focus on the future. We are about to put your personalized Money Diet into action! The next step? **Setting Your Financial Goals!**

STEP TWO

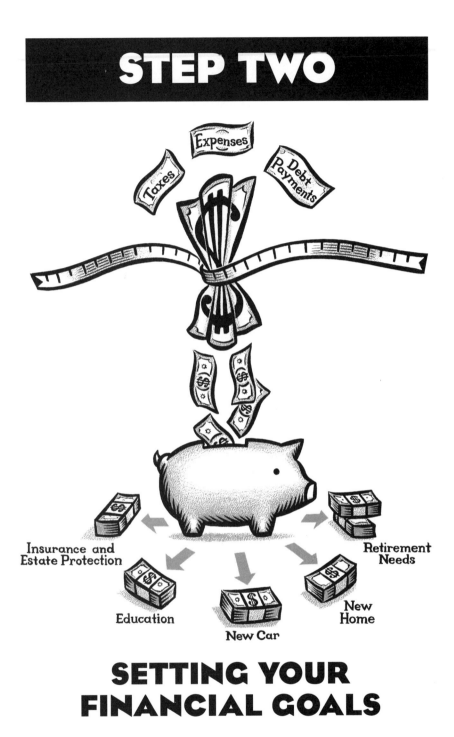

SETTING YOUR
FINANCIAL GOALS

CHAPTER FOUR

What's Your
Financial "Goal Weight"?

ONE OF THE MOST satisfying moments in a financial advisor's professional life is that first, in-depth meeting with a new client. In addition to the satisfaction of knowing that yet another person is willing to take a "leap of faith" and make the commitment to improve his financial life, there is the personal anticipation of perhaps developing a lifelong, close relationship with this new client. A financial planner simply cannot work closely with an individual, couple, or entire family over a period of time without having that relationship transcend pure business. A few years ago, however, as I waited for one new client to arrive, I found myself wishing I could be somewhere else entirely. I was about to meet with a well-known artist who had made it abundantly clear that a visit to me was dead last on his wish list.

As soon as Roland arrived, he told me that he hadn't wanted to make an appointment with me; he was doing so only because he loved his wife, Jacqueline, very much, and she had insisted he meet with me. Jacqueline had retained our firm because their finances were rapidly growing in both size and complexity, and she was too busy with her own career in advertising to pay attention to them. Roland, the painter, was very clear about his priorities in life, and financial planning was not one of them. His reason for avoiding dealing with their financial situation? He did not want to think about money for fear it would disrupt his creativity. But his participation was critical; I needed information about his retirement plans and investments and would have to pose questions to which only he knew the answers.

Despite Roland's reticence, the first part of the meeting actually went fairly smoothly, but when I asked him about his financial goals, his impatience with me became obvious. "My only goal is to paint!" he assured me. "I don't think about, and I don't care about, money!" But as we talked, it turned out that like the rest of us Roland did have goals and concerns—retirement in the near future, two elderly parents and two new grandchildren to consider, the probability that he would far outlive Jacqueline, complicated insurance issues to address, and an overall concern that he and his wife were losing money because neither one had the time or inclination to pay attention to managing it.

When I pulled all their financial information together, I discovered that almost all of their money was in bank and money market accounts, they still owned life insurance policies that they thought were canceled years ago, and the beneficiary of one of their IRAs was a trust that had been terminated the previous year. And the red ink on the fifteen-year cash flow projection I prepared made it graphically clear that if Roland and Jacqueline didn't immediately take action, they would run out of living expense funds and be stuck with nothing but their house within ten years after retirement.

I have found that nothing motivates a client to take action quicker than a glimpse into a future awash in red ink. (Later on in the Money Diet you, too, will have the chance to preview your own future.) Roland was no exception; once he saw just how disorganized their finances were and what major financial changes they would have to make if they wanted to meet their goals, he became an enthusiastic participant. The good news is that three years later, this artist's work is as good as ever, and he still has the time and the interest to check in regularly for an update on his family's finances.

The moral of my story? Actually, there are two. First, like Roland, you probably already have financial goals, even if you haven't ever articulated them. Second, pulling your head out of the sand and facing reality is not going to make your world fall apart. I'm not saying that setting goals and working to achieve them won't be painless, but it cannot be as bad as the gnawing anxiety of not really knowing whether you have a chance to get what you want in the future. Now that you have completed Step 1 of the Money Diet, **Getting On the Financial Scales**, you have the facts you need to take the next step— **Setting Your Financial Goals.**

What are financial goals? They are tangible (house, car) and intangible (education, retirement) things that will require you to come up with money in the future. They may involve fulfilling some lifelong dream (such as a career change or extended vacation), getting some necessary evil out of the way (braces for your five children), or the ability just to maintain things the way they have been (a comfortable retirement or disability income). What do these things have in common? You want or need them and you cannot pay for them in the course of everyday life, so the only way to achieve the goal is to *plan ahead*.

If you have never stopped to think seriously about how you picture your financial future, you are not alone. A recent study of people who actually hired financial planners found that at first almost half (43 percent) had not established financial goals. And this was the case even though something had prompted these people to call financial planners in the first place! Just think of how high that percentage would be if it included all those other Americans who have never hired a professional to help them with their finances. Even financial planners have difficulty thinking about their own goals because they are so busy dealing with everybody else's.

Obviously, managing your money better and planning ahead will help you achieve whatever goals you have in mind: getting your spending under control, stopping the fights with your spouse about money, ending your constant anxiety about money, knowing what to expect in the future, and getting your spouse and/or children more involved in your financial decisions. These are the wonderful psychic boosters that proper planning can provide. But in addition to (and sometimes conflicting with) financial goals are the goals that money can't buy. These personal goals might include spending more time with your family and friends, developing a hobby or interest you love, reducing your stress by taking a less demanding but lower-paying job, or changing to a career you really love instead of the one you hate every moment of the working day. This is where real conflicts arise.

Women in particular face this dilemma if they have children. I recently worked with a couple who wanted to look at what it would cost for the wife to quit working for a few years. She had already cut back her hours but wanted to assess the impact of quitting altogether. Stanley and Ashley had succeeded in accumulating a substantial nest egg during the years before the children arrived through a combination of frugal living, successful investing, and occasional gifts of money from Ashley's parents. Consequently, their goals of a comfortable retirement and four years of college education for each child could still be met even if Ashley took a few years off. But they also were committed to sending the children to a private high school because (after doing much research) they were unhappy with the quality of the local public school. This couple had to make the trade-off between their financial goal (education) and their non-financial goal (Ashley taking a few years off). They decided education was more important, so Ashley kept her job.

Remember in the preface when I said that decisions cannot be made just by the numbers or no one would ever have children, buy a nice house, or choose a low-paying career? But if you never take the time to figure out what your long-term goals are, be they financial or personal, *you will almost always fail to reach them.* Your short-term needs and wants will always take priority because, unlike long-term goals, you can feel and see them *right now.*

I have found, from both my own and my clients' experiences, that we often already know deep down that we are going to have to sacrifice some of those short-term gratifications we love so much once we set our long-term goals down on paper. That is usually one of the main reasons we put off doing so. It is also difficult to set goals when you don't have a clue what those goals should be. How much retirement income do most people need? How much will college cost in 2005? What amount is enough for your family to get by on if you die or become disabled? Whenever I ask new clients how much they need for each goal, I know that based on past experience, at least three out of four will say, "I have no idea. That's what I'm paying you to tell me!" And even if some clients know what coverage they want in one area, such as college tuition, they don't have the foggiest idea about the others, like disability income.

I wish *The Money Diet* could guarantee every reader that each financial goal is achievable. It can't. I can, however, guarantee that *simply by writing down your goals in **Setting Your Financial Goals** (page 42), you will increase your ability and willpower to meet them.* Just by thinking and putting pen to paper, you have started the planning process, and you will find that your spending and saving behavior may change (even if just a little) because you have given yourself an impetus to change your money habits. In the opinion of one client, this Willpower Worksheet is like the movie *Back to the Future,* where you can clearly visualize what you want for the future, and that vision prompts you to do things differently in the meantime to make sure it becomes reality. That is good news, because the sooner you plan for your goals, the better the chances are that you will be able to meet them.

Although the figures may vary, your range of goals is probably about the same as those of other people with the same family situation (marital status, age, number of children, etc.). Most of us would like to have a worry-free retirement, to provide up to four years of college for our children, to guarantee enough for our spouse and children (and perhaps our elderly parents) to live on if we die or become disabled. Except for education and specific purchases, such as a boat, most of your goals will depend upon your current income and expenses unless you want to drastically change your standard of living. Even the kind of house you want to buy is probably somewhat dependent upon your income and expenses. The amounts we will use in these exercises are here to help get you thinking about what is reasonable; these numbers and percentages are based on studies of family finances and are accepted as norms by the financial planning profession.

FIGURING OUT YOUR FINANCIAL GOALS

Let's look at **Setting Your Financial Goals** line by line. Before you start, you need to write down your Annual Income (before taxes) and

Setting Your Financial Goals

What you will need (in today's dollars)

A. Annual Income
(Before Taxes)

B. Annual Expenses
(Spending and Saving, p. 28, line H)

Goal	Based on Current Amount		Amount to Multiply by		You will need
C. Retirement	$ _____ (**B:** Annual Expenses)	×	0.8	=	$ _____
Example	$30,000	×	0.8	=	$24,000
D. Education (per child)	Private: $20,000/yr	×	no. of yrs. in college	=	$ _____
	Public: $9,800/yr	×	no. of yrs. in college	=	$ _____
E. Buy House	$ _____ (**A:** Annual Income)	×	2.5	=	$ _____
F. Death (children at home)	$ _____ (**B:** Annual Expenses)	×	0.7	=	$ _____
(no children at home)	$ _____ (**B:** Annual Expenses)	×	0.5	=	$ _____

continued on next page

Setting Your Financial Goals (cont.)

What you will need (in today's dollars)

Goal	Based on Current Amount		Amount to Multiply by		You will need
G. Disability	$ (B: Annual Expenses)	×	0.7	=	$
H. Other Goals (example)	$ $19,000 car	×	1	=	$ $19,000

Retirement plans, life and disability insurance, and scholarships for education can also help you meet your goals. Be sure and check to see what you already have.

Annual Expenses at the top of the worksheet. Why are these numbers important? They are the starting points for figuring out how ambitious your goals can be. Write your Annual Income (Before Taxes) on line A. Your Annual Expenses (**Spending and Saving**, page 28, line H) should be written on line B and also where indicated in the Based on Current Amount column.

Retirement Here, you multiply your current annual expenses by 0.8 (80 percent) to estimate the income you will need in today's dollars when you retire. This assumes that your living expenses will be less than they are now when you are working because you won't have commuting costs and your clothing and lunch bills will decline. Let's assume your current annual expenses are $30,000. To figure out your retirement income goal, you would multiply $30,000 times 0.8, for an answer of $24,000. Remember, expenses do *not* include income taxes. Write the answer on line C; this is your annual income needed at retirement.

Education This amount depends on how many children you have, whether you want private or public education for any or all of them, and how many years of college you want to provide for each. You can also include private-school costs prior to college, or even graduate-school costs if you would like. The current total cost of a private college is approximately $20,000 per year; that of a public college is approximately $9,800 per year. Multiply whichever cost you choose times the number of years in college times the number of children you have. What do you get? Your total education costs in today's dollars, assuming you or your child cannot qualify for any loans, scholarships, or work-study programs. (Before you panic, read chapter 10 to learn about all the financial aid for which you might qualify.) The easiest way to calculate this figure is to add up how many years of school (for all of your children) you are planning to pay for. To use Stanley and Ashley as an example, they plan to pay for eight years of school (four in high school and four in college) for two children. The total number of years they have to pay for is sixteen. Write your answer on line D.

House Of course, this purchase amount varies according to your personal tastes, the size of your down payment, prevailing interest rates when you buy, as well as the area of the country where you live. Generally, with a down payment of 20 percent, the most expensive house you can qualify to buy is about 2½ times your gross annual income before taxes. It used to be that this "2½ times rule" was an actual method mortgage lenders used to figure out how big a mortgage you could qualify for. As we all know, however, times have changed; we will look at mortgages in detail in chapter 11, "Buying and Selling Your Home." For now, if you do plan to buy a house in the future, and you do not yet have a specific price in mind, use this estimate of 2½ times your annual earnings. Write your answer on line E.

Death "Death" surely sounds like a strange goal, but the goal is actually to make sure that your family is adequately cared for if you die. You certainly do not want your family's fond memories of you to be mixed with sadness (or worse!) because your poor planning meant the family home had to be sold, or Mom had to go to work, or the kids had to drop out of college. The best way to preserve your memory is to make sure that no one suffers financially if you die. To figure out how much annual income your family may need in the event of your death, multiply your annual expenses by 0.7 (70 percent) if you have children living at home, or by 0.5 (50 percent) if your children have left home and if your spouse survives you. Your answers go on line F.

Disability "Disability" also is a strange goal, but the idea here is to make sure that you and your family will have an adequate income if you or your working spouse become disabled and cannot earn a living. Here you multiply your annual expenses times 0.7 (70 percent), and write your answers on line G.

You can see that I am assuming your family's expenses will go down if you die or become disabled, or when you retire, because that is what studies have shown usually occurs. One of the big unknowns here is medical expenses, and the percentages I use assume you have adequate medical insurance. These are numbers you should think about carefully, and when we get to the next chapter, "Smart Spending," you will be able to make them more specific because you can then identify the expenses you or your family would definitely *not* have in the events of retirement, disability, or death.

Other Goals There is also a section of the worksheet (line H) for Other Goals because most of us have one or more special dreams. A major vacation is one. Some people go on lavish vacations every year, and others take them only once or twice in their lifetime. If you are planning on taking a future vacation that is likely to be much more expensive than those you normally take, list it as a goal here. Many people are also planning to renovate or improve their houses instead of moving. If that's a goal, put it here. You may have your heart set on a vacation home; if so, this is the place to list it. Finally, we all periodically need to replace our cars if we own automobiles. Since the current average price of a car is around $19,000, most of us will need to budget for a new or used car sometime in the future.

Before you panic at the sight of the size of your goals, keep a few things in mind. First, we are at the beginning of the Money Diet process, and your perspective may change by the time you finish this book. You may decide to reduce or eliminate some goals, and you will certainly discover new ways to make your money go further so that you can improve your chances of achieving your dreams. Each worksheet you complete will strengthen your willpower to make needed changes. Also, as we'll determine, you probably have assets, insurance, or employee benefit plans that already take you partway toward your goals. Take, for instance, Social Security, which covers over 90 percent of the American population. Even though the program may not be able to continually increase benefits (and some critics question whether it can even meet current projections), it is safe to assume that Social Security will provide *some* benefits when you retire or if you die or become disabled. If you call 1-800-772-1213, you can order a personalized estimate of your Social Security benefits.

Another reason not to panic is that your goals may be smaller than the goals I have listed here; I've used percentages that are somewhat generous. If your goals are more modest, you may not have to do much cost-cutting. Finally, no one can predict the future. If you told me ten years ago, when I was anticipating a life in a reclining wheelchair, that I would be writing a book like this and appearing on the *Today* show, my whole family would have considered you temporarily insane. I cannot tell you how many times clients have come to see me and have seemed to be in very difficult financial situations, only to have some wonderful event change their lives. You can probably control more of your financial life than you think—whether it is how much you have in your checking account at the end of the month or the amount of money in your IRA when you retire—and the event that changes your life may well be a direct result of the changes you make in your money behavior. For example, I know a doctor who decided to switch positions so he would be eligible for the generous retirement and employee benefits available with the new job. The unexpected result? His research career has taken off, and he recently received a large grant to study a cutting-edge medical issue.

Now that you have taken the time to write your goals down on paper, you can forget about them because it is time to switch gears back to the present and move on to Step 3: **Developing Your Money Diet Plan**. But, as you read the rest of this book, I'll bet your goals will stay in your mind. This may be the first time in your life that you have actually written down your wishes and dreams, and you will almost certainly find that you start to think about your money differently. Now the fun starts, because we are going to look at all the different ways you can save more today so you will have more to spend later on these goals that mean so much to you.

STEP THREE

DEVELOPING YOUR
MONEY DIET PLAN

CHAPTER FIVE

Smart Spending

NOW THAT YOU have your goals down on paper, with dollar amounts beside them, it is easy to see the importance of trying to earmark every dollar you can for the future instead of spending it today. As **The Money Diet Method** shows, the ways to squeeze more savings out of your income are to spend less, pay less in taxes, and get out of debt. And the key to begin improving your financial health is to watch what and how much you spend, just as counting calories and cutting down on fat improves your physical health. "Smart spending" is the place to start developing your Money Diet plan.

If you are dreading this chapter because you have never followed a budget before or don't know the first thing about where to start, remember that you are not alone. And if you knew what most financial advisers know about some of their wealthiest clients, I guarantee you would (1) be shocked, (2) feel smug if you do budget, and (3) know that you are a part of a very elite group if you don't. Keep in mind that we are not talking about perfection here! If you know exactly where each of your dollars goes, I wonder whether you are enjoying life to the fullest. But there is a happy medium between blind spending and acting like a twentieth-century Ebenezer Scrooge. "Smart spending" is, quite simply, *consciously* making the decision to spend every time you do so, with an understanding that the value of what you get in return is worth the loss of those dollars for your future goals. In other words, you are getting your money's worth today *and* in the future. It's just like smart eating—trying to maximize taste at the same time you are eating foods that will safeguard your future health.

A couple of years ago, a newly divorced woman came to me for investment advice. Deborah felt overwhelmed because for the first time in her life she needed to pay attention to her money. As a part of her divorce agreement Deborah had received a cash settlement as well as modest monthly alimony payments. She came to me so that she could start to develop an investment strategy that would help her meet her goal of retiring in ten years.

After we talked about how much risk Deborah could afford to take and how much income she needed to live on, I did some quick calculations to show her what kind of investment return her nest egg would have to earn in order to meet her annual expenses, make her car payment, and pay her taxes. Unfortunately, we discovered that even the most brilliant money manager in the country could not pick investments that would, year after year, generate the level of income she thought she needed. I sent her home with a list of common living expenses (rent, utilities, food, clothing, travel, insurance, and so on). Deborah's homework assignment was to go through her checkbook, find out exactly how much she was spending on different things, and fill in the list.

About a week later, the call I was expecting came in—the call that most financial planners I know have received over and over again.

"I finally went through my checkbook, and I was shocked to find out how much I was spending," Deborah said. "I was almost too embarrassed to call you." I assured her that many people who go to a financial planner experience these same emotions, and that this level of discomfort was actually the start of very positive changes in her life. The dilemma Deborah faced was that after an entire lifetime of not having to think about money because first her parents and then her husband handled everything, she would quickly need to develop the skills to balance her budget. At the same time, our planning needed to take into account the fact that it was going to take her *up to a year* to learn these skills.

Why do I say "up to a year"? After working for years with clients to help them change their spending habits, I have come to the conclusion that for every year of your life, it takes a week to change your spending behavior. Why so long? The longer you have been doing something, the harder it is to change. If you think about how many times you have probably tried to diet and how long it took if you have actually succeeded in modifying your eating habits, you will know exactly what I mean. Obviously, some people can change more quickly, but if you use my rule of thumb, you will be much less likely to get discouraged. Deborah was almost fifty, so I told her not to expect to feel completely comfortable with her new budget for about a year. In addition, she faced the difficulty of trying to make major spending changes without the moral support (and watchful eye) of a spouse trying to do the same thing. We agreed that she should monitor her progress and update me regularly so that she felt accountable to someone besides herself.

The next day, an architect came in to see me with his expense "progress report" in hand, which showed where his money had gone for the previous few months. Andrew had first sought my help several months earlier, when it became clear that the New England economy was going to have a long-term effect on his personal finances. The firm's corporate clients were cutting back their building plans or even canceling projects altogether. What Andrew initially thought was going to be a short-term inconvenience looked as if it would be a major—and perhaps permanent—problem. The time had come for Andrew and his wife, Marie, to make a change in their lifestyle. In fact, they had already put it off for too long, hoping that things would turn around, and ending up spending much of what they had worked so hard to save over the years. Marie and Andrew were well known for their generosity to employees, charities, and their children. Unfortunately, this generosity was the primary source of their cash-flow problem—they were used to putting everyone else's financial needs before their own. And as a result, they were jeopardizing their own future by consuming too many "financial calories."

These are some examples of people becoming aware of the "smart spending" process, *learning to base their current spending on their long-term goals*. The idea is to save first and *then* spend what is left over, not vice versa. The same week I spoke to Deborah and Andrew I had lunch with a single attorney who had almost a year of "smart spending" under his belt. The previous year, William had added up his annual credit card charges for "nonessentials" such as vacations, entertainment, and clothing. He was shocked to find it totaled almost $30,000, or close to half his take-home salary! Even worse, he had no savings, although his most important goal was to retire in fifteen years. William was determined to change, and he did. He declared the next year would be a "no-frills year" and decided to cut his spending by $25,000, then invest his newfound savings after he had paid off his credit card balances.

What is the point of these three stories? First, many people will face the problem of having to live on a tight budget at some point during their lives. Others have to count pennies their entire lives if they want to meet their goals (ironically, because they get so much practice, these people often have better success at meeting their goals than do their wealthy counterparts). The best defense against financial tough times is to learn how to budget *before* you have to. You will always end up with more money in the long run than if you had waited to budget until you hit a cash crunch. Deborah, Andrew, Marie, and William each could have accumulated tens of thousands of dollars in savings during the years they paid little attention to their spending. And in these uncertain times no one's financial future is assured. With all of today's spending temptations, even if you have been frugal in the past, it is all too easy to catch the "spending virus," that state of mind enticing you to spend all of, or even more than, you earn. This state is similar to a period during which your eating habits suddenly get out of control due to stress or other factors and you end up with ten or twenty extra pounds for perhaps the first time in your life.

My second point is that change is not easy, and it does take time, so leave room in your budget for slipups. The worst thing you can do is to set unrealistic spending goals (similar to trying to stick to a 500-calorie-a-day diet); if you are like many people I know, you may give up completely and end up spending more than you were before you started! Keep in mind that in addition to your own resistance, you may face opposition from your friends, your children, or even your spouse if you do not embark on this Money Diet together.

Your family may resent the fact that their lifestyle is being downsized, you may feel subtle (or even overt) social pressure from your friends, or you may have such a generous heart that you can't say no to those you care about. Andrew and Marie, the couple facing massive spending cuts, worried about precisely these issues. It is always hard to put your financial future first because it seems so selfish, but in this instance you must. Spending less now means that you will be better able to take care of yourself in the future so you will not become a financial burden to others.

The third lesson from these spending stories is that smart spending *is* possible, even by someone who has never thought about budgeting for a day. Deborah and William were each able to make immediate, drastic spending reductions; they got their willpower by seeing negative numbers in their worksheets. Even Andrew and Marie managed to reduce their cash outflow somewhat, although their social and family pressures made it especially hard to do so. Fourth, your world will not fall apart when you spend less, and in my experience you will usually find that the pleasure of saving becomes an addiction that not only is good for you but feels good too. When your spending level is where it should be (and deep down inside you probably know where it should be), you will be amazed at how much relief you feel. Your anxiety will decrease, and you may even sleep better.

One client recently described to me the daily satisfaction she now gets from spending 50¢ less for breakfast by bringing her own apple to work instead of buying one in the cafeteria. Liz's family income is well over $200,000, and this change in her money behavior saves her just $125 a year in food expenses. But to hear Liz describe it, that $125 feels just as good as a $5,000 bonus. She also pointed out that by setting a "smart spending" tone at the beginning of each day she finds herself spending less elsewhere as well. Smart spending is just like dieting: Those first few cuts are easy (just like those first few pounds seem to melt away); then it gets harder and harder until habit sets in. And, just like dieting, if you blow it and spend too much at the beginning of a day or week, you are likely to give up trying for the rest of the day or week, too. You have to keep at it.

It may be that you are already in debt; if so, your problem is twofold. Not only will you need to cut back on your spending so that you won't get into deeper debt, but you will also need to figure out how to pay off your credit cards and other debts altogether (there are tricks for doing so in the next chapter). Whether you are in debt or not, the quickest way to improve your annual savings is "smart spending"—basing your overall spending on your goals and spending what is left over after you save for them.

HOW AMERICA SPENDS

In **America's Monthly Cash Flow** (below), you can see how the median American household spent its income in a recent year. This table is a fascinating snapshot of American life. What does it tell us? First,

America's Monthly Cash Flow

Average Values Per Household in 1992

	Annual Amount	Monthly Amount	% of Before-Tax Income
Before-Tax Income	$33,854	$2,821	
Taxes	4,008	334	12%
Total Expenses	**$29,846**	**$2,487**	**88%**
Housing*	$9,477	$790	28%
Food (total)	$4,273	$356	13%
• Food at Home	$2,643	$220	8%
• Food Out	$1,631	$136	5%
Clothing	$1,710	$143	5%
Transportation	$5,228	$436	15%
Health Care	$1,634	$136	5%
Insurance	$2,073	$173	6%
Other†	$4,097	$341	12%
Savings	$1,354	$112	4%

* Includes: shelter, utilities/fuels/services, and furnishings/equipment.

† Includes: entertainment, personal care, reading, education, cash contributions, alcoholic beverages, tobacco and other miscellaneous expenditures.

SOURCE: Bureau of Labor Statistics, Consumer Expenditure Study, and author's estimates.

From The Money Diet, by Ginger Applegarth.

let's figure out how much Americans are saving. We start with income and then take out taxes and expenses. What's left over is savings, which as you can see in this table was only 4 percent. Some numbers here are particularly fascinating, including the fact that we spend three times as much on transportation as we do on clothing. It is also an eye-opener to investigate further and learn that 40 percent of all food dollars are spent outside the home. Other Expenses includes things like vacation and entertainment, child care, charitable contributions, education, and other costs that are not specifically included in particular categories.

IDENTIFY YOUR SPENDING PATTERNS

Now let's take a look at how *your* spending stacks up with that of the median American household. I know from years of personal and professional experience how excruciating taking such a look can be, not only because there are so many categories you have to keep track of but because there are times when you just don't want to be that sensible. Clients have told me that keeping track of their expenses temporarily takes the fun out of spending, but such monitoring gets easier with time.

Before you get started, you need to have a heart-to-heart talk with yourself. Are you truly committed to looking at all the cash that flows through your hands? Ask yourself how long you will be willing to keep track of your expenses. I recommend you make a two-month commitment, since that is a manageable length of time. To make the exercise easier, plan to break those two months down into weekly segments. Then ask yourself again, "Will I do this?" If your answer is no, ask yourself, "How can I make myself do this?" To help yourself get started and keep going, you might build in some free or inexpensive bonus for every week you keep track of your expenses. Some rewards that I know have worked for others include a new compact disc or movie, a bottle of wine, and breakfast out on Sunday morning. In the beginning, the cost of your reward may offset the money you are saving, but it is worth it because you are learning spending discipline and, we hope, changing your behavior forever. I recommend you keep a small notebook just for the purpose of keeping track of your expenses; you can keep it in your pocket or purse to write expenses down, or use it to total up your ATM and charge expenditures, or both. As time goes on, this notebook will prove to be one of the most enlightening books you will ever read.

To evaluate your current expense patterns, you will need to take a look at where your money is going. The trick is to concentrate on either the past two months or the next two months. If you have been doing a fairly good job of writing down all your cash expenditures before you started this book, you may want to use my "go-back option." This means going back over the last two months and adding up all your expenses in the various categories in **Where Does Your Money Go?** (page 59). In fact, you already have done part of this in chapter 3, "Your Current Weight: What You Are Spending and Saving." Now we need to see *where* the money went. Be sure to include the monthly equivalent of any insurance premiums, estimated taxes, vacation bills, and other costs you pay for on a quarterly, semiannual, or annual basis. If your records for the last couple months aren't complete, use the "go-forward option" and keep track, for the next two months, of where your money goes, but do not try to save any yet. You want to see your *current* spending patterns (before you reform them!). You need to look at two full months because some expenses are not paid every month.

You may noticed that **Where Does Your Money Go?** focuses only on the "big picture," and some detail has been sacrificed. I usually recommend starting with the big picture first because so many people find it less intimidating than trying to compile every detail of your spending. You can add in any subcategories you find helpful. For example, under Transportation, you can add up all your car expenses in one general category or break out each type of expense—such as gas and oil, maintenance and repairs, car washes, automobile insurance, etc. (Do you see how confusing this can be?) At this stage, there is nothing to be gained by making things complicated and lots to be lost because you may just give up and then feel guilty.

The payoff for completing this exercise is that once you get a picture of your spending patterns in this Willpower Worksheet over a two-month period, you can take a look and identify your spending

Where Does Your Money Go?

	Month One	Month Two
Taxes		
Housing (including mortgage)		
Transportation		
Insurance		
Retirement Plans		
Health Care		
Food		
Vacation/Entertainment		
Clothing		
Gifts		
Unaccounted Cash		
Debt Payments (not mortgage)		
Alimony		
Child Support		
Other		
Other		
Total (Add all categories)	A.	B.

Add **A.** + **B.** = _____. Then, divide by 2 to find monthly average.

C. Monthly Average _____

Note: Do not forget to include expenses (such as insurance) that you pay on a quarterly, semi-annual, or annual basis. For those expenses, add up all the payments you make in a year and divide the total by 12 to get a monthly figure.

From *The Money Diet*, by Ginger Applegarth.

problem areas (and everybody has them!). Seeing these results should give you the willpower to spend less. You may also be able to figure out if you are likely to end up with any savings at the end of the year or if in fact you will have to go into debt just to pay your expenses. Sometimes this exercise shows such a large negative cash flow (i.e., expenses are much greater than income) that it shocks a client into making immediate, permanent budget cuts.

TRACK YOUR CASH

Of course, in any expense-tracking system, it is easy to total up all your checks and credit card receipts at the end of the week or month and put them in categories. What is the biggest problem here? Figuring out where all your ATM withdrawals and cashed checks went! If you just total up the amount of cash that passes through your hands in one month, it may render you temporarily speechless (the all-time record I have seen is a monthly average of $5,000 cash spent on "miscellaneous"). In a recent year, Americans used their ATM cards 7.2 billion times, averaging 600 million times a month. The average household used ATM cards 6.3 times per month, and the average amount per ATM withdrawal was $66. I have found that unaccounted-for cash expenses have gotten worse because of ATMs (and I confess I used to be one of the guiltiest parties in this regard). Years ago I used to advise clients with spending problems to make themselves go to their banks and write out checks for cash because actually cashing checks somehow makes that cash feel more like money than the cash you get from a machine. The problem with most people's hectic schedules these days is that my old advice is now virtually unworkable—few people have the time to go in and cash personal checks. So I now advise using an ATM instead of writing out checks for cash; you can put the receipt in your wallet and write down on the back of the receipt where you spend your cash every time you pull out your wallet. You can also use your budget notebook. You may feel foolish at first pulling out a pen to jot down your expenses in front of the salesclerk or cashier; I certainly did. But now I explain what I am doing when I get strange looks, and thus far I have won more than a few converts to this system.

SCHEDULE A WEEKLY REVIEW

If you have ever kept track of your expenses before, you are probably familiar with the temptation to slack off and stop writing everything down somewhere around the second or third week. It's exactly the same as "forgetting" to count calories once the thrill of losing those first few pounds has passed. That's why it is important to mentally break down the months to weeks and commit up front to a weekly review. Plan to set aside one hour a week to look back at how you spent your money during the previous seven days and to make plans for the upcoming week. I usually recommend doing this review on Saturday, Sunday, or Monday—whichever day feels like the first day of a new week to you. Of course, the ultimate goal of this exercise is to realize where you are spending more than you should (and remember that no one can define "more than you should" except you). But the short-term goal is *just keeping track*. Do this week by week, and it will become easier over time. You may see surprising, immediate benefits. For example, if you have children, you may often forget if and when you paid out allowances, money for work around the house, etc. You may end up double-paying from time to time. You now have proof of where your money goes, and you can quickly determine if you have already paid the paper carrier this month or whether the cry "You never buy me anything, but you buy Jennifer everything she asks for!" is accurate.

There are two reasons I recommend you start fresh every week. First, you have to keep track of your spending only one week at a time, and second, if you blew it last week, you can start with a clean slate this week. It's just like when you are counting calories; if you eat the hot fudge sundae at lunch, you give up trying until tomorrow. Starting fresh every week prevents long slides. As you tally up your expenses each week, you may be thrilled, or depressed, or both! It is very easy to spend $20 at 5 different places, though you might be able to keep yourself from spending $100 in one place. But saving $20 a week—which may simply mean that once a week you do not give in to a $20 temptation "just this once"—will result in spending $1,040 less this year. And that money can be used to pay off debts or be invested to meet your other financial goals.

IDENTIFY SPENDING PROBLEM AREAS

Once you start tracking your expenses, you may find that your problem areas are pretty obvious. I have found that problem areas for most people, regardless of their income, are restaurants and fast food, entertainment and vacations, clothing, gifts, and unaccounted cash. For example, it is easy to blow a whole year's savings by enjoying your vacation so much that you forget about financial reality. Turn to the Willpower Worksheet **Identifying Spending Problem Areas** (page 63), and let's look at each problem area in detail. Earlier in this chapter, I talked about getting a handle on your expenses with the "go-back option" (if your expense records are good) or the "go-forward option" (if you have not kept records). In **Identifying Spending Problem Areas,** take the last two months ("go back") or the next two months ("go forward") and write down how much you spent (will spend) in each of these categories.

What is a reasonable budget? It varies for each client I have—one may spend $100 a month on restaurants, another may spend $1,000 a month, and both consider these amounts "absolute minimums." A good way to set a budget amount is to first look at whether you are saving any money right now. If you are not or are setting aside only a small amount each year, your first step is to cut spending *everywhere* until you have a balanced budget and can save some money as well. Your next step is to compare your expenses as a percentage of your income to those in **America's Monthly Cash Flow** (page 56). As your income goes up, the percentage of income you spend on basics such as food, clothing, etc., should go down or at least stay the same. Finally, look at each category relative to the other. You may decide that you don't want to keep spending three times as much on clothing as you do on your vacation, for example.

Most people calculate different budget categories using different time frames. For example, you may think of clothing expenses as "$150 a month" but of food expenses as "$75 a week." You can set weekly or monthly budget goals for different spending categories. Some people I know even have daily budgets for certain categories such as restaurants and unaccounted cash. Remember that your overall goal is to come up with annual income, expense, savings, and

Identifying Spending Problem Areas

Problem Area for You (✓)	Spending Problem Area	Amount Spent (Month One)	Amount Spent (Month Two)	New Budget Amount
	Restaurants/Fast Food			
	Vacation/Entertainment			
	Clothing			
	Gifts			
	Unaccounted Cash			
	Other			

From *The Money Diet*, by Ginger Applegarth.

other figures, because you will want to review your Money Diet every year, and unusual expenses can make a particular week or month look good or bad. To motivate you and make keeping track of your spending as easy as possible, however, you should first total up your results once a week; these weekly results are then added together to get your monthly totals, and so on.

BUILD IN SPENDING STOPPERS

The next trick is to build in automatic "spending stoppers." After you sit down for an hour each week to total your expenses, think about what you will have to pay for in the coming week. Decide in advance exactly how you will use your money this week, go to the bank, withdraw the money, and *then take your ATM card out of your wallet.* Also, take all credit cards out of your wallet except one card that has to be paid on a monthly basis or one that you have vowed to pay off every month. (When I first did this, my wallet shrank and I could actually snap it shut for the first time ever.) You may already have credit cards with balances on them; put them away and try to use the one that has a zero balance if possible. If they all have balances, pick the one with the lowest outstanding balance and make a commitment to yourself that you will pay all new charges every month. Use checks instead of cash when possible so you can track how your money has been spent. If you are reluctant to pay by check or credit card because cashiers ask for personal information, remember that when paying by check you do not have to write a credit card number on the check. Nor do you have to write your address or telephone number on any credit card receipt. In fact, some states specifically prohibit the merchant from asking you to do these things because dishonest sales clerks might use your personal information to make unauthorized charges on your credit card or cash counterfeit checks on your account.

The best thing to do with your credit cards is to put them in a place where they are hard to get. My favorite Money Diet story, which I mentioned briefly in the preface, comes from a young woman in South Bend, Indiana, whom we profiled on the *Today* show. Melissa had run up about $1,500 in credit card debt, and her parents suggested she cut up all her cards. But she decided that rather than get rid of them altogether, she needed to teach herself restraint. This enterprising young woman put her credit cards in a leak-proof plastic bag and then froze the bag in a container of water! As she explained, if she ever wants to use her cards, she will have to wait several hours; she cannot put them in the microwave to speed up the thawing process without ruining the magnetic strips and melting the cards. The last time I spoke with her, she was pleased to report she has not had to thaw them out once.

Another good spending stopper when shopping is to decide how much you want to spend and what you are planning to spend it on. Take only cash; *leave your credit cards at home.* If you find the buy of a lifetime, you can always have it put "on hold," then drive home and pick up your credit card or check. But by this time, the urge to buy may pass. Clients have told me this is especially effective when shopping with children or teenagers; sometimes their offspring will forgo those new clothes if they have to return home and then come back to the mall with their parent. That new jacket your child "absolutely must have" becomes "too much of a pain" if it means another trip to the mall with Mom or Dad.

I realize this next bit of advice may sound painfully un-American, but try to avoid shopping for recreation unless you do so with empty pockets or you have set yourself a budget of one small item. Sometimes shopping becomes more than recreation. Experts say not to shop when you are depressed, but everybody I know falls prey to this temptation sometimes. Deborah, my newly divorced client who had to adjust to a budget for the first time in her life, found this spending stopper the most difficult recommendation to implement of the dozens I gave her.

Another spending stopper, especially for larger purchases, is to think of the amount of money you had to earn *before taxes* to pay for it. For example a $15,000 car could cost up to $25,000 in earnings. A good rule of thumb you can use is to multiply the purchase price by 1.65 to get your before-tax cost.

You have already identified your spending problem areas; now let us look at some spending stoppers for each of these potential budget leaks. Almost 40 percent of the average American family's food budget goes to restaurants and fast food, which is not only loaded with calories but usually not the most nutritious food either. Entertainment and vacations are easy overspending items because when you are on vacation the feeling of liberation that accompanies leisure often makes you feel especially free with your credit cards. When you do take a vacation, set a budget before you go and bring that amount of money in traveler's checks or cash. Just take one or two credit cards and an ATM card for emergencies, but vow not to use them without asking yourself whether you will still want that special memento of your trip when you get back to the real world. A common problem is the proliferation of outlet malls near vacation spots across the country. They are located there to tempt you at your weakest moment. You are on vacation anyway, and outlet malls are supposed to be so inexpensive that it can be easy to buy everything in sight. Reality does not hit until the credit card statements come a month later.

Everyone knows it is smart to buy clothes on sale, but often in our busy lives we just cannot do that. And if we do buy on sale, there is that tendency to overbuy because "it is too good a deal to pass up." So we end up spending *more* on sale items that we would have spent on regularly priced items. You can save money by making an inventory of your clothing, figuring out exactly what you need, and limiting your clothes spending to those things.

One way to use sales effectively is for holiday gifts. I recommend making a list of everybody you buy gifts for during the year and keeping the list in your wallet or budget notebook. When you are shopping, pull out the list and, if you see a good item on sale that someone on your list would like, buy it. This saves special shopping trips and you end up paying less than you would if you rushed out at the last minute. It's a good idea to have two "gift budgets"—one monthly budget for day-to-day gifts and one annual budget for holiday season gifts. Remember to keep a list of the holiday purchases you have already made in your budget notebook. I learned about this the hard way when I went into a spending frenzy before Christmas, forgetting that I had already bought presents. Then, the night before Christmas, when I pulled everything out and put it under the tree, I could not believe what I had done.

Children present special spending problems. When I mentioned kids as a problem area on the *Today* show, everyone laughed. I had to explain what I really meant: If you add up how much money you fork over to your children in a week's or month's time, you may be amazed. Give them an allowance and stick to it, and do not lend money. Your children need to learn now to earn their money before they spend it. If they don't learn this from you, it will be that much harder to learn it in the real world. If you make the Money Diet a family project, your children will be part of the process and learn by watching your example of managing the family's money. But most kids these days earn their own money, too, so they need help. Take some time and sit down with your kids to help them make a budget. If your child has a checking account, make sure that he or she balances it every month. I am still amazed when I see forty-five-year-old clients who are making $100,000 a year but have never learned how to balance a checkbook. They never had to because they always had enough money to pay their bills. They never looked at what they were spending, and they no doubt have forfeited thousands of dollars in potential savings over the years.

It is easy to see why the Money Diet will be successful only if all members of the household are involved. Your spouse *must* cooperate to make it work. Otherwise, his or her overspending may cancel out any savings you are achieving on your own. *You must talk about what you are planning to do with your family even if you forgo telling all the details of your new budget.* You may pay the monthly bills while your spouse takes care of day-to-day expenses; if so, I can guarantee that each of you has an idea or two about how the other could do a better job in cutting costs! Your children probably already know if you are having money difficulties; within reason, you should talk with them about this issue.

When we interviewed families on *Today* for the "Money Diet" series, we spoke with Robert and Ann, a couple with young children. Robert carried most of the credit cards, so it wasn't surprising that he was the one with a credit card spending problem. He adored Ann and wanted to buy her everything in the world. Robert bought her jewelry on the credit cards; she loved the jewelry but she hated the fact that they would be paying for it for months to come, with interest to boot. For Ann, the gift just was not worth the financial strain. Their solution? A moratorium on Robert's purchase of big presents for her and the removal of all credit cards from his wallet except the one with no monthly balance.

Remember that we are taking one day, week, and month at a time to change your spending behavior in different areas. If it is too hard to make monthly goals, make weekly goals. If a week is too long, make daily goals. And start small. If you are eating lunch out every day, try to each lunch out four times a week instead of five, and bring your lunch one day. Then, when that feels easy enough, cut down to three times a week. The goal is to make the painless cuts first. If you embark on this process gradually, you will fool yourself into thinking you are living just as well as ever because you will barely feel the changes.

Smart spending is not easy, especially if you have tried it in the past and have given up. But even if you try now and fail in the beginning, you are still on the right track. It is just like counting calories on a food diet; the longer you try, the easier it becomes and the more successful you are. Now that you know how to cut current spending, you will free up extra dollars to pay off all those debts you may have accumulated. Next on the Money Diet plan is getting rid of your financial fat and keeping it off—getting out (and staying out) of debt.

CHAPTER SIX

Getting Out
(and Staying Out) of Debt

THESE DAYS it seems as if everywhere you turn, the word *fat* comes up. Advertisements herald low-fat and fat-free products, magazine articles proclaim the evils of fat, and what are you on the lookout for when you survey yourself in the mirror? *Fat.* When you eat fatty foods, the short-term pleasure usually gives way to guilt, lethargy, and yet a few more excess pounds that seem impossible to shed.

Accumulating debt is exactly like eating too much fat and suffering the consequences. That's why getting out (and staying out) of debt is such an important part of developing your Money Diet plan. The temporary enjoyment of the fancy meals, new clothes, vacation trips, etc., soon disappears when the bills arrive and you don't have the money to pay them. To make up for your past excesses, you have to consume less, and doing so is at least as hard as cutting back on calories. Just as things beyond your control (medication, forced inactivity, metabolism) can make you gain weight, unexpected expenses or a drop in income can result in creating or increasing debt.

A big tax bill is often one of those unexpected expenses pushing people over the edge into debt. In my experience, self-employed people are especially prone to this debt creator. One of the hardest things about being self-employed is that since you are not sure what your taxable income for the year is until December 31 (or later, if you haven't kept track of your expenses), it is all too easy to get stuck with a big bill at tax time. And most people I know really have to scramble to come up with the money. A self-employed couple with small children was recently referred to me for exactly that reason. Despite making many of the right financial moves—buying enough insurance, putting money in retirement plans—they still were stuck every April 15 paying their taxes with a credit card advance.

If around tax time you have looked at credit card advertising, you will know that this is a common way of paying taxes; in fact, it's encouraged. When I assured this couple that their problem was by no means unique, they told me that it wasn't just the *fact* that they took the advances that was the problem but the *size* of the last one—$25,000—that really concerned them. This was exactly the credit limit of only one of their credit cards. Now, before you write Brad and Charlotte off as financial incompetents, it is important to see why the advance was so large. They were trying to do the right thing by contributing every tax-deductible dollar they could to their retirement plans, to the tune of almost $15,000 in the year in question. Essentially, more than half of Brad and Charlotte's short-term debt was racked up so they could deduct as much as possible on their tax return and also get the benefit of saving for the future. As parents of small children, they also found that day care and school tuition made balancing the budget impossible. Each year, they would dig themselves out from under last year's debt; then tax time would roll around and they would be stuck going into debt all over again. This couple was determined to get ahead of the credit game for the first time in their lives. They wanted to stop the cycle of accumulating and then working off their "financial fat."

Although the amount of Brad and Charlotte's advance seems high, the basic facts of the story are not that unusual. In fact our love affair with debt is long-standing. In 1960, our outstanding consumer credit (not including mortgages) averaged 18.5 percent of our disposable personal income. In 1992, it was about the same—17.9 percent. But although our debt load is not higher as a proportion of our income than it was thirty-five years ago, we are using credit more and more for convenience's sake. For example, total credit card spending was $201 billion in 1980. By 2000, that number is expected to rise to almost $900 billion. As we put more on credit cards, it becomes easier to be tempted to overextend ourselves. Some studies show that we spend up to 30 percent more if we "put it on plastic" instead of paying cash. I am not suggesting that using credit makes you a bad money manager (after all, only 3½ percent of people with credit cards get into serious trouble with them). But debt and interest payments are becoming an increasingly substantial part of our economy, and the problem is that we end up using current dollars to pay off the past instead of to save for the future. As of December 1993, we carried $297 billion of credit card debt, and there currently are over 1 billion credit cards floating around in Americans' pockets. And the problem is getting worse—by the year 2000, experts have projected that our credit card debt will almost double and the number of credit cards will increase by 30 percent. We simply have to stop mortgaging the future to pay for the past, but it's hard to develop the willpower to do so.

A client recently expressed the credit card dilemma to me in personal terms. After looking at her debt load and the amount of time it would take to pay it off, she realized that it would be at least three years before she could save even one penny for the future. As Barbara said, "It's as if there is a dance going on and I am always three steps behind everyone else." This is actually a very accurate description, because I know from personal experience that daily living and the expenses associated with it can seem to have a life of their own and can make you feel as if you are simply along for the ride.

Not all debt is inherently bad, and most people do need debt at some point in their lives. If you had to wait until you could pay cash for a home, you probably never would be able to buy one! The same is true with starting a business or buying real estate as an investment. Debt can also help tide you over when there is emergency dental work to be done or the water heater bursts. The problem with debt is that it can become the "financial flu." If you have a lot of it, you wake up in the morning feeling dragged down, and you find it difficult to focus on doing anything productive. It's hard to feel positive about life in general when you have the burden of big monthly payments stretching out for years to come. *Debt mortgages your future in order to pay for your past.* The only exception is when you take on a debt to make an investment that you anticipate will increase in value, such as a home or business.

When we talked about how the Money Diet works, we discussed what happens to your dollar from the moment you receive it until some part of it is available as savings. Remember, out of your income dollar comes the TED squeeze—Taxes, Expenses, and Debt payments. Those debt payments can put a real drag on the Money Diet because you end up with less money to save this year and less savings to invest and grow next year. Let's assume you get a $1,000 raise next year. If you are like most people, you immediately start daydreaming about what you are going to do with that money. But let's also assume you are carrying a $1,000 balance on your credit cards. Though you haven't even earned your raise yet, it will probably have to go to pay off your debt. To get your debts under control, you must know exactly how much and what kind of debt you have, examine your attitude about debt and how comfortable you feel having it, and come up with a workable plan to pay it off.

SECURED AND UNSECURED DEBT

There are two basic kinds of debt. First, there is *secured* or *collateralized* debt. This means that you have agreed with your lender that some asset you own—such as your house, your car, your furniture—will serve as collateral to secure a loan. If you fail to repay the loan, the lender can take the asset to satisfy the debt. The second kind of debt is *unsecured* or *uncollateralized*. In this case your borrowing is based purely on your promise to pay back the loan. Examples include line-of-credit loans, overdraft protection, credit cards, and demand loans (loans that you are required to pay back whenever the lender asks you to). In general, secured debt carries a lower interest rate because the lender is not risking as much by loaning you the money. After all, the lender can get your collateral in return if you default on your loan payments. Credit cards, which typically are unsecured, and other unsecured loans generally have a higher interest rate because the lender is less likely to recover the value of the loan and may have to spend more to do so if you do not make your payments. Keep in mind, however, that in some circumstances a lender can still go after your property if you do default on an unsecured loan.

The largest debt (secured or unsecured) you will likely ever have is a mortgage on a house; mortgages are always set up with your house as collateral because very few people can borrow that much money based simply on a signature and promise to repay. When you buy a home and take out a mortgage, it is called a first mortgage because your lender has the first dibs on your property if you do not make your monthly payments. Even if you refinance at some point, you will usually still end up replacing a first mortgage with a first mortgage. There are also home equity loans and home equity open-end loans, or revolving lines of credit, which, if you have a first mortgage, are considered second mortgages on your home. You may, for example, take out such a loan to remodel your kitchen, consolidate your credit card debts, or buy a new car. These loans are called second mortgages because if you default on all your home loans, the first mortgage holder has priority over the home equity or line-of-credit lender for repayment. I know of a situation where a house was foreclosed on and then sold; the sale price was less than the amounts due the first mortgage lender and home equity lender. The bank holding the home equity loan got only what was left over after the first mortgage was paid.

There are key differences between a home equity loan and an open-end line of credit. With a home equity loan, you borrow money for a fixed period of time, and if it has a fixed interest rate, you pay the same amount on it every month. With a home equity open-end line of credit, the amount of the loan and the amount of your monthly payments will depend on how you use the line. For convenience's sake, it is great to have a home equity open-end line of credit, but since you can draw against it simply by writing a check against the credit line, it requires self-discipline not to use it for frivolous things. I know of situations where home equity lines were used for vacations, clothes, and even a new dog!

The advantage to mortgages is that interest on the first mortgage on your house is virtually always tax-deductible, and the interest on the home equity loan or home equity line of credit is usually tax-deductible up to the first $100,000 of the loan amount (you should *always* check with your tax adviser to find out if you qualify for a deduction). Because the first mortgage lender is taking less of a risk than the second mortgage (home equity) lender, the interest rate on a first mortgage is likely to be lower than that of a second mortgage taken out at the same time. When you look in the financial pages of your newspaper, you will see that current interest rate quotes are lower on first mortgages than on second mortgages.

Other secured or collateralized debts include loans you may take out to purchase expensive consumer items such as cars and sometimes even furniture or television/stereo equipment. If these loans are secured, the lender has the right to repossess whatever it is you used the proceeds of the loan to buy. Unless the lender is offering you a special low interest rate as an incentive to purchase the item, this type of loan generally will have a higher interest rate than first or second mortgages taken out at the same time. Why? One reason is that your collateral immediately depreciates in value the minute you buy it and take it out of the store or showroom door. For example, the value of a new car can drop by as much as 10 percent the moment you drive it away.

Until credit protection laws were enacted, starting in the 1970s, lenders could go to extraordinary lengths to get money back if you defaulted or were late with payments. They could come to your home and repossess virtually everything in it—including your household pets! Even today, you could end up losing something (such as a TV) you have already paid for if you fall behind in payments on another purchase (such as a stereo). This would happen when your loan has a provision called an "add-on" clause; if you financed two different items from the same lender, you could end up losing both.

YOUR CURRENT DEBT LOAD

You have already tallied up all your debts in your **Detailed Net Worth Statement** (page 24). In **Your Current Debt Load** (page 75), write in all the important features of each debt you have, including the lender, current balance, interest rate, how the rate is charged, and whether the interest is tax-deductible. Take the time now to group

Your Current Debt Load

Lender	Current Balance	Interest Rate	Current Monthly Payments	How Interest Is Charged	Tax-Deductible Interest?	Date Loan Ends	Prepayment Penalties?
Mortgages/Home Equity Loans (Including Home Equity Loans)							
			+				
			+				
A. Total Current Monthly Mortgage Payments			A. =				
All Other Debt							
			+				
			+				
			+				
			+				
			+				
			+				
B. Total Other Monthly Debt Payments			B. =				
C. Total of All Monthly Debt Payments (A+B)			C. =				

Note: Refer to the charts Simplified Net Worth Statement (p. 22) or Detailed Net Worth Statement (p. 24) for your current loan information.

your debts into two categories—mortgage debt and consumer (all other) debt—because you will need this information in later chapters. Include your current monthly payment, when the loan will be paid off, and whether a penalty will be charged if you pay the loan off early. You may have to call your lender to get some of this information; for example, with credit cards you will have to call and ask how long it will take to pay off your balances if you continue to make the same monthly payment until that time. However, this sleuthing is well worth it in the long run. If you are like some of my clients, you will be amazed at how much debt you have and how long it will take to pay it off. And if you try to "starve" yourself by cutting living expenses too much, you will probably give up and incur even more debt—just like breaking down and eating the hot fudge sundae after starving yourself all day.

HOW INTEREST IS CHARGED

To find out how you are being charged interest, you will need to pull out your credit card bills and installment loan statements and the disclosure forms for any other loan contracts you have. Just looking at the initial interest rate stated in the contract does not give you the real picture; the actual interest rate you are charged may in fact be almost twice as much as the number stated in the contract, depending on how interest is computed. For example, let's assume you decide to borrow $500 for one year at 10 percent interest. If your lender calculates the interest on an "add-on" basis, your interest of $50 would be added on to your loan amount the day you borrow the money, so you are technically borrowing $550 from Day One. With this method of calculating interest, the effective annual rate on this loan would be 18 percent, not the 10 percent stated in the contract. Instead of "add-on" interest, your lending agreement may say that interest is computed based on the "discounted interest" method. This means that the interest you owe is deducted from the proceeds so that you end up with $450 in your pocket, instead of $500. In that case, the real interest rate is almost 20 percent. While you are checking how the interest rate is computed on each of your debts, look and see which balance is being used to compute interest charges, as well as when interest begins on any new charges. With some lines of credit and credit cards, there is a "grace period"—here, interest is not charged on new purchases until the end of the statement period. This means that, for example, if you charge something at the beginning of the month, receive a statement on the fifteenth of the month reflecting this new charge, and pay the entire balance when it is due at the end of the month, no interest is due on those new charges. Other lines of credit and credit cards start charging interest the day the charge is actually incurred.

PREPAYMENT PENALTIES

When you are looking at ways to reduce your debts quickly and minimize your total interest charges, you may decide to pay your debts off at a faster rate, even though this will temporarily reduce your annual savings. In that case, it is important to look at any prepayment penalties that may be incurred if you pay off some of the balances you listed in **Your Current Debt Load**. Home mortgages generally do not have prepayment penalties, but many consumer loans do. Check the language of your loan and credit card agreements carefully for something called the "Rule of 78s," which refers to the mathematical formula used. Unfortunately, if you see this term, it means that there are prepayment penalties. What happens is that most of the interest gets paid in the early months of the loan and less in the later months. On a one-year loan, this means that by the fourth month of the loan you will have paid over half the interest for the year. In contrast, a loan with interest computed on the "actuarial method" charges interest based on the loan balance as it declines, so interest is not loaded up in the early months and you avoid being penalized for paying it off early. I am embarrassed to admit that before I knew what to watch out for, I ended up with more than one "Rule of 78s" loan.

MINIMUM PAYMENT PROBLEMS

With some credit cards it can take as long as ten years to pay off a balance under the "minimum payment" provisions, where the required monthly payment declines as you reduce the loan balance. For example, let's assume you have a credit card with a balance of $5,000 at an interest rate of 18 percent. If your current minimum monthly payment is $40, even if you don't charge anything else on your card, it could take you up to ten years to pay off the $5,000 balance depending on how the interest rate is charged and how the monthly minimum payment due is determined. When I explained this to one client, he immediately canceled his vacation plans and used the money to get rid of his credit card debt.

If you are short of cash one month, you may be tempted to skip a payment altogether and make up for it in next month's payment. Don't. Your failure to pay may be recorded on your credit report and thus jeopardize your creditworthiness. In fact, late payments are the primary cause of negative information on your credit report.

DEBT REDUCTION STRATEGIES

Once you have completely filled in **Your Current Debt Load,** you can assess whether there are ways to (1) use savings on hand to pay down your loan balances, (2) increase the amount of principal that is being paid off each month and thereby reduce your interest, or (3) make more of your interest tax-deductible. In any event, try to never get caught in the "minimum payment" trap that, like the Duracell Rabbit, keeps your loan going and going and going . . .

■ Strategy: Pay down faster.

The best way to increase the rate at which your loans are being repaid is to make a commitment to add a certain amount to your current monthly payment. When you determined your financial weight (in chapters 2 and 3), you figured out how much savings you have on hand as well as what your current expenses are. Then, in chapter 5, you looked at ways to cut spending. What you save should go to pay down your loans. If you use savings on hand to pay down loan balances, make sure you leave enough in your savings as an emergency fund to cover three to six months of living expenses. This emergency fund can be used if there is a medical emergency, you lose your job, or some other catastrophe happens. You can design a payment strategy in **Prepaying Your Loans** (page 80) by committing to higher monthly loan payments. Be sure to choose the loans with non-deductible interest to prepay first. Another trick is to vow to yourself that when you receive any unexpected income—such as tax refunds, gifts, rebates, and awards—you will immediately use them to reduce your loan balance. One client told me that his tax refunds were the only way he stayed out of debt. He endorsed the refund check directly to MasterCard or VISA because he knew that if he deposited it in his checking account, he would never have the self-discipline to write out a check to the credit card company himself; it was too tempting to spend it all. If you can't bear to sign it *all* over, save a small amount for yourself and use the rest to pay down your debts. A young woman with several thousand dollars of credit card debt was positively beaming when she told me that she had won $200 in the lottery, saved $20 for herself and promptly sent the $180 to one of her creditors. She also shared a terrific idea on how to avoid being so overwhelmed by your debt load that you just give up trying to whittle it down. She picks $1,000 of her balance at a time, concentrates on paying that down, and tries to forget about the rest. While $100 may look like a drop in the bucket if your debts total $3,000, it makes a real impact on $1,000.

You may have noticed that I said to pay down *non-deductible* loans faster. Clients often ask about the advisability of using extra money to pay down their first mortgages, home equity loans, or home equity lines of credit, all of which usually carry tax-deductible interest. In theory, this sounds like a good idea, but I often do not recommend it in practice. Most people need as much liquidity as possible when they reach retirement, and it does not help if they have an expensive, paid-up house and not enough cash for their living expenses. The fact that home mortgage interest is tax-deductible makes these

Prepaying Your Loans

Loan	Current Balance	Your Current Payment Amount	Additional Payment Amount	Total NEW Payment Amount
VISA (example)	$5,000	$90	$10	$100
Totals	A.	B.	C.	D.

Current Balance	Your Current Payment Amount	Additional Payment Amount	New Payment Amount

loans the last type you should consider prepaying, assuming your interest rate is competitive. In chapter 8, "Developing a Winning Investment Strategy," you will find ways to make your dollars grow at a rate that should exceed the interest rate on your mortgage (unless you neglected to refinance while interest rates were low). You always have the flexibility to use investment assets to pay down your home loan balances, but in the meantime you can invest them or use them to meet other goals. By the way, this is also why I usually recommend that clients skip the fifteen-year mortgage and take the longest mortgage possible—so that they have as much cash and investments on hand as possible for goals such as retirement and education.

■ Strategy: Reduce the interest rate.

One of the easiest ways to reduce the interest rate on your loans is to shop around for lower-rate credit cards or lines of credit. But always check for a high interest rate on new purchases, a short or nonexistent grace period, or stiff penalties for late payments—these can make your "good deal" a bad one. You can also probably reduce your interest rate by converting an unsecured loan to a secured loan, for instance by consolidating your credit card bills with a home equity line of credit or home equity loan. In addition to a lower interest rate, the interest may be tax-deductible.

We had the lowest interest rates in decades in the early 1990s, so many people have already taken the opportunity to refinance their home mortgages to reduce their interest charges. It always makes sense to keep an eye on mortgage rates; you should consider refinancing if the current interest rate is 2 percent less than that of your existing mortgage and you plan to stay in your home for several years. Also, consider refinancing to lock in a fixed rate if you have a variable-rate mortgage with a high maximum interest "cap," if current rates are reasonable, and if you plan to stay put for a while. Your lender can prepare a "break-even" analysis for you, showing how many years you have to keep the new mortgage before you recoup your up-front closing costs such as title insurance, attorney's fees, points, etc. *Always obtain and study the "break-even" analysis for any proposed mortgage refinance before you sign to make sure it is worth doing.*

ARE YOU IN OVER YOUR HEAD?

Clients often ask me how they can tell when they are in over their heads. There are two general rules of thumb, depending on whether or not you have a mortgage. If you have a mortgage, you are in over your head if your total monthly debt payments are more than 38 percent of your monthly income before taxes. If you are mortgage-free, you have more debt than you can manage if your total monthly debt payments are more than 15 percent of your monthly income before taxes. **Are You Over Your Head in Debt?** (page 83) can help. Before you start, write down your *total annual income before taxes* from **Setting Your Financial Goals** (page 42), line A. This goes on line A of **Are You Over Your Head in Debt?** Divide this number by 12 and write your Total Monthly Income Before Taxes on line B. Multiply your answer on line B by 0.38 if you have a mortgage or 0.15 if you do not, to arrive at your Maximum Safe Debt Payment Load; write your result on line C. Compare this number with your Total of All Monthly Debt Payments (from **Your Current Debt Load**, page 75, line C) on line D here. If C is more than D, your debt load is within safe limits. If D is more than C, your debt load exceeds safe limits.

Many experts believe that you should always try to keep your consumer debt payments to less than 10 percent of your before-tax income, which is much less than the 15 percent mentioned above. Of course, if you are truly in over your head, you probably do not need percentages or ratios to tell you. You may already be worrying about your debts, skipping payments on some or all of them, making the absolute minimum payments required, and using up savings or taking credit card advances for things like food and clothing. You may even find that you avoid totaling up your loans or paying attention to what you are spending because you are afraid of the bad news. If you fit this description, the best thing you can do for yourself and your family is to get help right away.

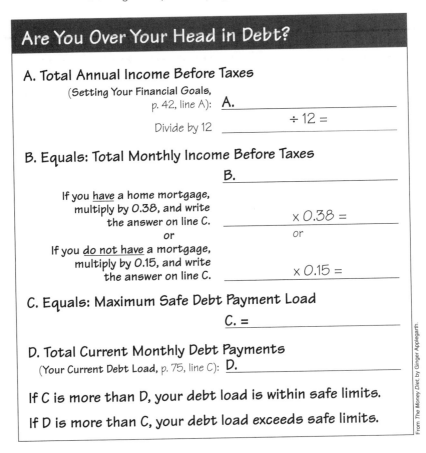

Are You Over Your Head in Debt?

A. Total Annual Income Before Taxes
(Setting Your Financial Goals,
p. 42, line A): **A.** _____

Divide by 12 _____ ÷ 12 = _____

B. Equals: Total Monthly Income Before Taxes

B. _____

If you *have* a home mortgage,
multiply by 0.38, and write
the answer on line C. _____ x 0.38 = _____

or *or*

If you *do not have* a mortgage,
multiply by 0.15, and write
the answer on line C. _____ x 0.15 = _____

C. Equals: Maximum Safe Debt Payment Load

C. = _____

D. Total Current Monthly Debt Payments
(Your Current Debt Load, p. 75, line C): **D.** _____

If C is more than D, your debt load is within safe limits.

If D is more than C, your debt load exceeds safe limits.

From The Money Diet, by Ginger Applegarth.

CONSOLIDATION LOANS

One option is to take a consolidation loan, which will allow you to combine all your non-mortgage loans and make one monthly payment (which is usually less than the total of all your existing loan payments). The disadvantage to these loans is that the repayment period may be much longer than the repayment periods of your current loans, so it is easy to compromise even more of your financial future by stretching out payments for years to come. Another option is to get in touch with the Consumer Credit Counseling Service (800-388-CCCS), which is a nonprofit organization funded by credit card companies to assist individuals who are overextended. A trained counselor will work with you to structure a repayment schedule you feel comfortable with, and then will notify all your creditors that you are participating in a CCCS repayment program so they will stop hounding you to pay up. The service's popularity is growing; the number of people using it jumped from 783,000 in 1991 to 919,000 in 1992, and the number of counseling sessions has been increasing each year. Do not be embarrassed because you think your debt situation is the worst the Consumer Credit Counseling Service has ever seen. The *average* client has ten credit cards, an annual household income of $22,000, and $18,000 worth of debts, which means that many clients have significantly higher debt loads than these averages. The only disadvantage of using the Consumer Credit Counseling Service is that your participation in the program is reported to the credit bureaus, so it may show up on your credit record. But since missed payments and defaults on loans are also reported, the report that you are using the CCCS is certainly the lesser of two evils.

BANKRUPTCY

A last resort is bankruptcy, and you should *never* take this step without adequate legal advice beforehand. The reason is that under the Fair Credit Reporting Act a bankruptcy will stay on your credit report for up to ten years. (All other negative information will stay on your record for up to seven years.) Bankruptcies do provide protection for you and your creditors—you have a way to start over, and your creditors may also be able to get at least some of their money back. There are generally two types of bankruptcy under federal law—a Chapter 13 proceeding and a Chapter 7 bankruptcy. If you have an ongoing monthly income, you may be able to file for a Chapter 13 proceeding, which is a repayment plan sanctioned by the court under which you agree to repay part or all of your debts over an agreed-upon period of time. A Chapter 7 bankruptcy, or total liquidation, means that everything you have is sold to pay your debts except for certain allowances (which vary by state) for various items. Good legal advice about Chapter 13 versus Chapter 7 bankruptcy is key: Every situation is different, and the decision is too complex (and too emotional) for you to make on your own.

REVIEWING YOUR CREDIT REPORT

Whether you have $1 or $1 million worth of debt, it is smart to obtain copies of your credit reports so you can make changes if any information is wrong. There are three principal credit bureaus to which you can write to obtain your credit report. They are:

Equifax Information Service Center
Attention: Consumer Department
P.O. Box 105873
Atlanta, GA 30348
1-800-685-1111

TransUnion Corporation
P.O. Box 390
Springville, PA 19064-0390
312-408-1400

TRW Credit Information
Consumer Assistance
P.O. Box 2350
Chatsworth, CA 91313-2350
1-800-682-7654

You should check your credit reports every couple of years—and certainly, at least six months before you apply for a mortgage—so that inaccurate information can be corrected before you are turned down for credit. Several years ago, the Federal Trade Commission's single biggest source of complaints was credit bureaus. In fact, one Consumers Union survey showed that 43 percent of all credit reports contain errors. You may have to pay a small fee for your credit report (usually under $10), but the law requires that this fee be waived if you have been turned down for credit in the last thirty days so that you can find out why. And, if you are or were married, you may be able to request that information regarding a joint account in your and your spouse's names be considered in determining your creditworthiness.

Many people are confused (and rightly so) about the effect that marriage or divorce might have on their creditworthiness. The simple explanation is that your loan contracts and credit card agreements are not affected by marriage or divorce. If the debt is in your name alone, it does not affect your current, future, or ex-spouse's individual credit rating. Likewise, if a debt is in both your name and your spouse's name, as far as the lender is concerned you are both still liable regardless of what your separation agreement says if you become divorced.

Unfortunately, for many people these days the after-effects of the last recession still show up on their credit reports in the form of late or missed loan payments, or even loan defaults and mortgage foreclosures. Here is a practical look at how your creditworthiness can be affected by your spouse.

Janice had to default on an automobile loan three years ago. She recently married Jerry, who has an unblemished credit record, and they have decided to look for a house. Janice is still paying off several credit balances that she ran up after the honeymoon. Jerry is not tarnished by Janice's poor credit record because the loans were never his responsibility, even though some of Janice's credit card charges were made during their marriage. All those loans were in her name only. Jerry could apply for a mortgage in his name only and his credit report would look fine. The problem is if he applies without Janice as co-borrower, he can't count any of her income for purposes of qualifying for the loan. They will have to settle for a much less expensive house than they could afford if Janice's income was counted.

During Greg and Tina's ten-year marriage, they bought a house together and Tina co-signed Greg's auto loan. Greg always handled the family finances, so Tina was shocked when she discovered that Greg had been running up huge balances on their joint credit cards and was months behind on the mortgage and the car loan. Greg then announced that he wanted a divorce. Under the terms of their divorce agreement, they canceled all their joint credit cards, and Greg agreed to take over responsibility for the loan on his car and the mortgage. Tina got the house, and that's what mattered, she thought.

Tina was subsequently shocked when the automobile lender sued her for repayment of the auto loan after Greg defaulted on it. The lender did not care what her divorce agreement said; the loan contract had her name on it. Tina's only recourse was to pay off the car loan and sue Greg to recover her costs. In order to pay off the car loan, Tina applied for a home equity loan. Even though she had made every mortgage payment on time since the divorce, she couldn't qualify for a loan because of Greg's delinquency in making payments on those loans for which she had joint responsibility. Tina had to borrow money from a relative to repay the auto loan, Greg was nowhere to be found, and her credit record would be blemished for years because of his actions.

It is not easy to get out of debt once you have dug yourself into a hole. And in today's economy, there is no guarantee that you will be able to avoid incurring debt in the future. Loans are not necessarily all bad—they allow you to buy things you could not otherwise have (such as a home), they give you flexibility in an emergency, and they may allow you to take advantage of unique investment opportunities. The key is to use common sense so that you do not overindulge in debt and compromise your financial future. By leaving as much as possible in your pocket after payment of taxes, expenses, and debts, you will increase your annual savings and make sure that you have more money to invest in the years to come to meet your goals. Getting out (and staying out) of debt is one of the best ways to increase your future financial stability.

CHAPTER SEVEN

Cutting Your
Tax Bill

IF ALL MY CLIENTS through the years have had one thing in common, it's the desire to pay as little as possible in taxes. It's hard enough to make a decent living, pay the bills, and try to set aside enough to meet your goals, but when Uncle Sam siphons off his share each year it can be downright painful. And of course there are also state income taxes, which for some people can end up being even higher than federal taxes. Even my most uncharitably minded clients would rather donate their tax money every year to worthy causes than write out checks for thousands of dollars to the Internal Revenue Service.

One client, however, stands out as being the most tax-phobic person I have ever encountered. Stephen had arranged his entire financial life around the issue of taxes—namely, he was doing every possible thing he could (no matter how time-consuming and paper-generating it was) to reduce his tax bill. He had already exhausted the patience of two CPAs and was finally referred to me by his lawyer so I could give him some big-picture common sense.

I knew we might be in for quite a long meeting when Stephen showed up with two large boxes stuffed to the gills with papers that were in no discernible order. He immediately launched into his "I hate the IRS and I don't want to pay them a penny" mantra. The one thing that became clear immediately, however, was that Stephen's attempts to pay less in taxes had created an even bigger problem: His finances were totally out of control. Stephen had invested in the wrong investments (too much in tax-free bonds and limited partnerships of dubious value). He had made large tax-deductible retirement contributions but not reduced his spending (so the size of his credit card debts at 19 percent interest had been growing and growing). And he was paying a succession of tax preparers (changing to a new adviser every year because no one was aggressive enough for his taste) to learn his complex financial situation and then generate tax returns that were dozens of pages long. The more Stephen tried to reduce his tax bill, the more miserable he became. It was time to take a fresh look at his tax situation in light of his entire financial situation so that decisions could be made for the right reasons—not just tax reasons.

The last thing I want to suggest is that you should give up trying to whittle down your tax bill. If doing so has seemed more difficult these last few years, you haven't been imagining it; many tax loopholes have been plugged, and now it takes harder work and more creative planning to come up with legitimate ways to reduce your tax bill. That's why when you are developing your Money Diet plan, cutting your tax bill is one of the first priorities. But it is all too easy to get so caught up with the details of saving tax dollars that you miss the big picture. You end up making financial decisions that save you little in taxes but create a record-keeping nightmare and perhaps actually cost you more money in the long run through unsuitable investments, unnecessary loan interest charges, extra tax preparation fees, and the cost of defending yourself at an IRS audit.

At the opposite extreme from doing too much is doing too little and doing it too late. If you are resigned to paying high taxes and don't take a fresh look at the tax laws every year, you are probably doing too little. If you are like a lot of people, you resolve to get your tax materials organized so you can figure out how to make (or put off making) some last-minute payments to save taxes. Then you get caught up in the holidays and realize on New Year's Day that it's too late and you missed your chance. Of course, the ultimate insult about income taxes is that they are due just after the shock of the holiday bills, when you are still scrambling to pay them off. All of your New

Year's money resolutions for *this* year seem to fall by the wayside when you end up faced with a huge tax bill from last year. Your plans to "save more this year" or "contribute more to your retirement plans" or "pay off your credit cards" disappear on April 15 when you are scrambling to pay the extra taxes you owe. All too often, you just give up and say you'll try to get your finances in order *next* year. Then the cycle starts all over again.

What does this have to do with the Money Diet? Plenty! Every dollar you pay in taxes means one less dollar for savings this year, so one less dollar is available to help you meet your goals. Remember the example of John and John Jr. in chapter 1, where John Jr. ended up with so much more money because he started saving earlier in life? That dollar you save in taxes this year could perhaps be worth several dollars by the time you spend it on a future goal. And if several dollars does not sound like much, what if you can save $100 or even $1,000 in taxes in a year? That may translate to several hundred or several thousand dollars at retirement or whenever you need it most.

When a new client walks in the door, one of the first things I do is sit down with her and ask her to rank her goals in order of importance. Most of the time, saving taxes is at the top of the list. Still, you do not have to go to a financial planner or tax professional to take advantage of some of the best tax strategies around. It may well be that *organizing* your records and *properly preparing* your tax returns will save taxes and increase your annual savings. There are actually two parts to cutting your tax bill. The first is making smart tax moves throughout the year, and the second is making sure you have included all of those smart moves on your tax return. If you do not itemize deductions but rather take the standard deduction each year, you may be limiting your possible tax moves. But chances are you can benefit from better organizing and preparing your return (at least in the time and aggravation you save yourself). And if you do itemize deductions, the possibilities are enormous for cutting your tax bill.

The goal of this chapter is not just to tell you how to pay as little in taxes as possible come April 15, but to show you how to do income tax *planning* throughout the year so you are not faced with an overwhelming task at tax time. This way you are not just reacting after the fact, and you can save every tax dollar possible to invest for your future goals. Another bonus with advance planning is that you can get your tax return done early. You will have plenty of time to figure out how to pay any tax that is due, or better yet, savor the fact that you will receive your refund early as well. Starting your tax return well before it is due gives you time to find the money for a last-minute retirement plan contribution if you qualify.

PHASE 1: TAX PLANNING
THROUGHOUT THE YEAR

There are two ways to plan for taxes throughout the year—controlling when certain inevitable things happen and taking purely voluntary steps. Surprisingly enough, most tax-planning tips are fairly simple; the catch is that you have to act on them before December 31 in order to take advantage of them. That means starting well before holiday season to make sure you have enough time to carefully think through actions before you take them. All too often I see clients who have made last-minute decisions that turn out to cost more than the taxes they save. For example, one client ransacked his house to find all the unneeded clothing, furniture, and other items to donate to charity before the end of the year. In his rush to get to Goodwill before it closed on December 31, Barry threw in a couple of his old wallets without first checking their contents. After all, they had been sitting in the back of his sock drawer for at least three years. A week later, Barry suddenly woke up in the middle of the night to realize that not only had he donated his key to his safe-deposit box (which would cost him several hundred dollars in bank fees to have drilled open) but also the $500 cash he had decided several years ago to keep on hand in case of emergencies, after his bank's ATM machine had shut down over the July 4 weekend.

STEP 1: TIME YOUR INCOME AND DEDUCTIONS

Here are some ways you may be able to control your tax bill through controlling exactly when you receive or pay money:

- **Defer earned income until next year (if you expect your taxable income to be the same as or lower than this year's) or take the income this year (if your tax bracket will be greater next year).** For example, if you are self-employed, you can delay sending out invoices to make sure they don't get paid this year. If you get a bonus, you can always ask your employer to pay it in January of next year (although your company may have tax reasons of its own to pay you before the end of the year). **Common Income Tax Categories** (page 93) has a list of types of income.

- **Sell investments that will produce a gain next year, and sell those that will produce a loss this year.** This way, you are deferring the taxes on your gain until next year's tax return, and you can claim your loss on this year's. You can also offset gains from good investments with losses from poor investments. But don't ever sell an investment just to get a gain or loss; you should have a sound investment reason for doing so.

- **Look at all the deductions you might be able to itemize and try to lump them into either this year or next year.** For example, the dentist's bill can be paid in December or January. **Common Income Tax Categories** lists the various deductions you may be able to "time." You can pay your state income taxes before the end of the year, pay January's mortgage payment in December, or defer these and other payments until next year.

- **Write off worthless investments and debts you will never be able to collect.**

Common Income Tax Categories

Income

Wages and Salaries	
Tips	
Scholarships and Fellowships	
Interest	
Dividends	
Pension, Annuity, or IRA Income	
Unemployment Compensation	
Social Security & Railroad Retirement Benefits	
Self-Employment Income	
Partnership Income	
Rents and Royalties	
State and Local Tax Refunds	
Capital Gains	
Gain from Sale of House	
Alimony	

Adjustments to Income

IRA Contributions	
Keogh Contributions	
Alimony Paid	

Itemized Deductions

Taxes	
Home Mortgage Interest and Points	
Charitable Contributions	
Moving Expenses for Business Purposes	
Unreimbursed Employee Expenses	
Medical/Dental Expenses	
Investment Interest Expense	
Personal Casualty Losses	
Gambling Losses	

Tax Credits

Earned Income	
Credit for Child and Dependent Care Expenses	
Credit for the Elderly or Disabled	

From *The Money Diet* by Ginger Applegarth.

STEP 2: TAKE VOLUNTARY ACTION

In addition to controlling when certain inevitable income and expense items are received or spent, there are other tax planning steps that you do not ever have to take (but it's smart if you do):

- **Make tax-deductible contributions to all the retirement plans you can.** This is discussed in great detail in chapter 9, "Planning for a Comfortable Retirement," but virtually every adult in the United States can invest some money in a retirement plan and pay no income taxes on that contribution. In addition to the tax deduction, you can save on future taxes because your plan's earnings and growth do not get taxed until you take the money out. Here timing is important, too, because with some plans the money has to be contributed by December 31; with others you have until April 15 or when you file your tax return.

- **Invest in tax-deferred and tax-exempt investments.** Again, we discuss these investments in chapter 8, "Developing a Winning Investment Strategy," but you can put money in bonds whose interest is free from federal and sometimes state taxes, and annuities shelter your investment growth and earnings until you take the money out. But remember, any tax strategy you take should be based on a sound investment strategy.

- **Convert non-deductible interest to tax-deductible interest.** You may remember reading about this in the last chapter, but converting your credit card and auto loans to a home equity loan or first mortgage may make the interest tax-deductible.

- **Keep track of your cash expenditures and mileage driven for business or charitable reasons (especially if you are self-employed).** For example, miles driven for business are currently deductible at $.25 a mile, and if you drive for the church group or Cub Scout outing you can deduct $.12 a mile.

PHASE 2:

DOING YOUR TAXES

Once January 1 arrives, it's time to focus on getting your tax return finished and in the hands of the IRS. (Because all states have different tax laws, we are focusing on your federal taxes here. However, most states use the same numbers and logic, although some deductions and income items may be different.) Whether you fill in every line yourself or pay someone else to do your taxes, you should know the process that takes you from the top lines of your tax return to those at the bottom that show whether you owe the IRS or it owes you. There are five things to figure out in the process: your Filing Status, Number of Exemptions, Total Income, Total Deductions, and Amount of Taxes Due or Refundable to You. Let's look at these steps one by one so you can come up with the best answers you possibly can to reduce your tax bill.

STEP 1: FIGURING OUT YOUR FILING STATUS

Your filing status is based on whether you choose to file the return by yourself or to join in with somebody else. The choices are "single," "head of household," "married filing jointly," and "married filing separately." Why do you care? The amount of taxes you have to pay on the same income varies according to filing status, that's why. For example, Daniel's taxable income was $25,000 for 1993. If his filing status was "married filing jointly" or "head of household," his tax would have been $3,754. If he was "single," the tax would have been $4,134. And if Daniel had chosen "married filing separately," his tax would have been $4,609. Single people with no dependents don't have a choice about filing status, but everyone else does. If you are a single parent with a child, you almost always want to file as head of household if you qualify, because that will save you taxes. You can qualify as head of household sometimes even if your child is not technically a dependent, as long as she lives with you. If you are married, most of the time you should file jointly with your spouse unless one of you makes most of the money, only one of you incurs most of the medical deductions, or your combined income is over about $110,000. In those cases, it might make sense to file separately, so make sure you or your tax preparer runs the numbers both ways just to confirm you are using the filing status that will save you the most in taxes.

STEP 2: MAXIMIZING EXEMPTIONS

The next item—exemptions—is really confusing. Exemptions are valuable because they provide extra reductions to your taxable income, which means that your tax will be lower. Exemptions are based on whom you are supporting, and you want to take every one for which you qualify. That's because every exemption you take reduces your taxable income (for 1994 taxes, the amount per exemption was $2,450). You can always take one exemption for yourself, and you get to take two on your return if you are married at any point during the year and are filing jointly with your spouse. I recently took a random poll of fifty people and asked each of them whether you could take an exemption for someone if he or she is not related to you. Forty-eight said no, and two said yes. Believe it or not, those two people are right! The IRS has five rules, and you can take an exemption for a close relative who is *not* living with you (such as an elderly parent for whom you are providing over half the support) or a nonrelative who *is* living with you (such as your daughter's boyfriend, who is too lazy to get a job). Confused? So is everyone else, so call the IRS or your tax preparer for clarification if you think you might be entitled to more exemptions.

STEP 3: TOTALING INCOME

The next step is to total up all your income. Adding up your income is usually fairly straightforward, but there is a lot of income that you may not even realize is taxable until the IRS notifies you otherwise.

This includes employer-provided term life insurance premium costs for policies with over a $50,000 death benefit, the value of certain company discounts (your company will tell you which), some employee plans for child care, a portion of your use of a company car, a Fulbright scholarship or other scholarship, Publishers Clearing House winnings, gambling income, and some other income sources. (In fact, one of the ways that the government goes after illegal gamblers is having the IRS convict them of not reporting their gambling income.)

The refund you got last year on your federal taxes is not taxable (although your state tax refund is), but this is a good time to check and make sure that you actually received your federal (and/or state) tax refund from last year. Pull out your last year's return to see how much you were supposed to get, and check your records to determine whether you have received it. If you never received a check, call the IRS toll-free at 800-829-1040. Every year, thousands of people do not ever get their refunds because they have moved, or the envelopes became illegible, or the Postal Service could not deliver them for some reason (one reason: the recipient returned the letter unopened thinking it was a tax notice!). In September 1993, the IRS was looking for at least 96,000 taxpayers whose 1992 refund checks were returned as undeliverable by the post office. Those checks totaled over *$50 million*.

It is very tempting to hide some of your income and not report it for tax purposes, but think long and hard before you fudge your income figure. While the IRS may be willing to concede a deduction or two that is ambiguous, income is clear-cut—either you got it or you didn't. Remember that almost all income is already reported to the IRS anyway by the person or company that paid you (including all interest and dividends), so it makes sense to be honest. Also, the IRS takes a closer look if some or all of your income is from work as a waitress, plumber, taxi driver, or any other occupation where you might receive cash payments. Penalties are so stiff that it is definitely *not* worth taking a chance getting caught underreporting your income just to save on taxes.

STEP 4: CLAIMING DEDUCTIONS

When we talked about tax-planning tips to use during the year, we covered the importance of timing when deductions are incurred and claimed. **Common Income Tax Categories** lists all of the possible deductions available; using the tips in phase 1, you may have been able to increase the amounts you can write off for this year. If you look at this list, you can see why keeping track of receipts and cash expenditures is so important.

Everybody gets a certain dollar amount of deductions against taxable income free of charge. You have to compare your total actual itemized deductions with the amount the government will give you automatically (called the standard deduction). You get to choose to take the greater of your total itemized deductions or the standard deduction. For the 1994 tax year, the standard deduction ranged from $6,350 for a married couple filing jointly to $3,800 for a single taxpayer. You get a higher standard deduction if you are blind or sixty-five or older, but no other handicaps are taken into account. There is one great concession that the federal government allows—if you turn sixty-five on January 1 of *this* year, the IRS actually pretends that you turned sixty-five *last* year so you can claim an extra deduction. What a birthday gift!

One of the most frequent questions I get is "Should I claim deductions even if I don't have receipts for them?" A resounding yes is always my answer. My rule of thumb is that if the deduction is clear-cut and legitimate, even if you do not have the receipt when you file your return, take it. If you are audited, you can always go to the trouble of getting a copy of the credit card receipt or canceled check; and I have learned from my clients' experiences that the IRS may accept your word even if you cannot produce a receipt. But if the deduction is in a gray area and you don't know whether the IRS will accept it, think twice before claiming it with no substantiation.

You want to keep track of all your deductions throughout the year, and this is why I *always* recommend keeping track of your cash transactions because so many of us use cash to pay for things that may be deductible. These deductible cash items may include co-payments at the doctor's office, supplies if you are self-employed, medicines and prescriptions, glasses, taxi fares for business or medical appointments, etc. Keeping track of your cash is *crucial* if you are self-employed, because so much of what you spend is out-of-pocket—taxi fares, meals, postage, etc. Other deductibles items you probably pay for by check include interest on a mortgage up to $1 million used to buy a first or second home and interest on home equity loans of up to $100,000 (both are subject to some limitations). You can also deduct medical expenses paid on behalf of your family that are over 7.5 percent of your adjusted gross income—and this *includes* parents and others as long as you are claiming them as dependents. Don't forget charitable donations (and remember to include the value of all the stuff you donated to the church rummage sale!). Keep in mind that you now need an actual receipt (not just a canceled check) if a single donation is over $250. Also, luckily, whatever you paid your tax preparer last year may be deductible this year. And most taxes, including state, local, and real estate taxes, are deductible (except Social Security and federal taxes).

When clients ask whether they should take such deductions as home office expenses, they are invariably raising the issue of IRS audits. A letter or visit from the IRS is a dreaded event; I know that whenever I get a letter from "Internal Revenue Service" as return addressee, a chill always runs down my spine, even though my tax records are crystal clear. Certain income and deduction items on your return will increase the chance of being audited. These items include unusually high deductions, a home office deduction, addition or subtraction errors, a major jump (or drop) in income, limited partnership losses, and self-employment income. Your location can also be a factor: If you live in Philadelphia, your chance of being audited is 0.31 percent; in San Francisco, it is 1.30 percent (only the IRS knows why for sure).

STEP 5: FIGURING YOUR TAXES

Now you are at the point where you can figure what your taxes are. In fact, if you cannot calculate your taxes and you've figured your deductions, you can even send your tax return in with every line completed down to the line for taxes due, and the IRS will figure them out for you! This is *not,* however, a way to avoid paying your tax now, because you still have to pay at least as much as you are going to owe (once the IRS figures out how much that is). Any amount you overpay will be returned to you as a refund. And always file a return even if you do not have the money to pay any taxes due; you may save a bundle in interest and penalty charges. The IRS is becoming more flexible about working out repayment schedules if you can't afford to pay everything you owe now, and you may even be able to negotiate down the total amount due.

MAKING TAX SEASON EASIER

We have talked about what you can do between January and December to minimize taxes and then covered the steps involved in doing your taxes. But what can you do to make the job of getting your tax return in on time easier? Whether you plan to complete your return on your own or go for help, here are some steps that will simplify the process.

■ Start early.

My first recommendation is to start early (even January 1 if you want an excuse to skip the football bowl games!) by doing last year's taxes and by planning for the year to come. Make a note of the deductions you might be able to claim for the upcoming year; refer to **Common Income Tax Categories** and decide *now* how you are going to keep track of any deductible expenses you will pay for in cash. And remember, when you need tax advice, *ask.* A lot of help is free for the asking from the IRS.

Before you delve into this year's return, pull out your most recent tax return. Did you receive a big refund on your federal and/or state taxes? Do you expect to get one again this year? If so, vow to change your withholding allowance so that in the future you are not giving the government an interest-free loan of your hard-earned money.

Many people have extra money withheld for taxes as a way to force themselves to save, but they lose interest on this money for up to fifteen months (that's because the extra money you have withheld in January will not be refunded to you until you file your tax return a year or more later). A better idea is to have this amount automatically deposited into a savings or investment account—you can have it withheld from your paycheck just as taxes are withheld or you can have it transferred from your checking account to your savings account each month. Others end up having extra money withheld because they don't write down enough "withholding allowances" when they complete their employee withholding form at work. You can claim up to ten withholding allowances without raising the IRS's suspicions, and as long as you don't end up with a "balance due" on your tax return you'll be in good standing with the IRS.

■ Get organized.

For many people, the hardest part of doing their taxes is getting organized, especially if they have not been systematically keeping track of all those tax-related papers throughout the year. Even people who pay someone else to prepare their taxes *still* have to go through this less-than-pleasant process. Organizing means digging through all your papers for the last year, pulling out any that could possibly be relevant to your taxes, and grouping them according to category— salary, interest paid, medical expenses, etc. Of course, if you were setting aside tax-related papers all through the year in your **Money Diet Quick Filing System** tax folder (or even a large envelope), you'll find this task "payback" time for all your efforts. I usually recommend that clients defer making a decision about where to go to get tax help until they get their papers organized. Why? As one client with a very simple return told me a couple of years ago, "By the time I ruined a few Sundays getting all my receipts together and filling out that tax organizer document my accountant gave me, I decided I might as well finish the job myself instead of paying someone else."

- ■ Set up a plan of attack.

The way to get organized is to set up a plan of attack. Do not try to do everything in one day or even in one weekend. You should have received your various tax information slips (salary, dividends, interest, self-employment income, etc.) by the first part of February, so most people should be able to start organizing by that time. If you haven't received one or more of these slips, now's the time to call and find out where they are—perhaps a former employer does not have your new address. I recommend that you divide your "tax attack" into three different days (or two, if you are using outside help). On the first day you will get organized, the second day you will complete the return, and the third day you will check the return for accuracy before you mail it or submit it by electronic filing. This last step is critical even if you have had the most expensive tax help in the world. Why? You know more about your own situation than anyone else, and if there is a mistake on your return, the IRS can penalize *you*. It may be that you will notice that your preparer misread your handwriting, or perhaps reviewing the return will jog your memory and you will realize you forgot to put in some big deduction or income item. Of course, you are also trying to minimize mistakes; the IRS can charge you up to 25 percent in interest and penalties on such mistakes, and state income tax penalties can be onerous as well.

A plan of attack does *not* mean that you have to spend all day, each day, on your taxes. The point is to give yourself a break between each of the steps so that you can clear your head and avoid mistakes. In fact, I recommend not filling out your return on the same weekend that you get all your papers organized or checking your return the same day you complete it.

- ■ Target your information search.

The prospect of sorting through a box full of receipts and documents is a daunting task; I usually take every opportunity to procrastinate, and you probably do too. One way to procrastinate in a useful way is to look at a list of that year's possible income and deduction items

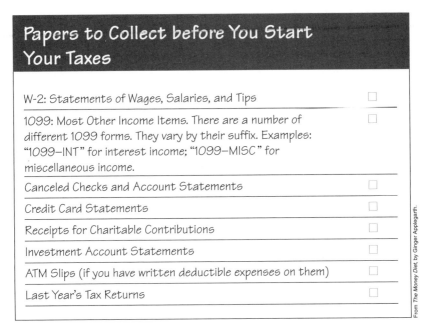

Papers to Collect before You Start Your Taxes

W-2: Statements of Wages, Salaries, and Tips	☐
1099: Most Other Income Items. There are a number of different 1099 forms. They vary by their suffix. Examples: "1099–INT" for interest income; "1099–MISC" for miscellaneous income.	☐
Canceled Checks and Account Statements	☐
Credit Card Statements	☐
Receipts for Charitable Contributions	☐
Investment Account Statements	☐
ATM Slips (if you have written deductible expenses on them)	☐
Last Year's Tax Returns	☐

From *The Money Diet*, by Ginger Applegarth.

(which the IRS seems to change every year). Then you can refer to that list as you go through your papers. **Common Income Tax Categories** includes the most common long-standing income-taxable and income-deductible categories, but because tax laws are not carved in stone, it is always a good idea to check a list for the current year. You can call 1-800-829-3676 and ask for IRS Publication 17 (*Your Federal Income Tax*). An up-to-date list is also included in your tax preparation forms, thoughtfully mailed by the IRS just in time to ruin the new year. Some of the items on this list may appear obvious, but I cannot tell you how many people (including me) have missed deductions because they did not know that something was deductible or misplaced a credit card receipt or canceled check. (Of course, you can always go back and file an amended return, but many people hate the tax process so much or fear an audit so much that they don't think it's worth the time or aggravation of filing an amended return. In truth, an audit may not be all that unpleasant if you've been honest on your return, but we'll get to that shortly.)

A list of the papers you need to review and organize is in **Papers to Collect before You Start Your Taxes** (above). These papers include

W-2s, 1099s, checks, investment statements, ATM slips (if you have written deductible expenses on them), credit card statements, cash receipts for deductible items, and receipts for cash or non-cash contributions (clothing, etc.) to charities, as well as last year's tax return. Of course, if you have been keeping track of all of your income and expenses for the last tax year on your computer, your task will be made easier. If you are using an outside tax preparer, you can use the "organizer" (the form to list tax information) provided by that preparer, or the organizer in any of the income tax guides you will find in most bookstores, or my decidedly low-tech method. Over the years, the tax organizer solution I have developed (and used for quite a few clients) is this: one envelope for each of the categories listed in **Common Income Tax Categories** (page 93). I keep the checks, receipts, and documents inside and write the totals on the envelopes.

■ Get rid of the clutter.

At the same time, this is a great opportunity to get rid of all your old checks, papers, and other documents that have been cluttering your basement. These include your ATM receipts for the last year unless you have actually written down cash expenditures on them that you can deduct. Remember my recommendation to track your cash on your ATM receipts so you can see where you are spending your money? Here is where it pays off by perhaps saving you hundreds of dollars in taxes. I accumulated fifteen years' worth of old checking account statements and tax returns and moved them to four different houses along the way, just in case I got audited or needed an old check. Then I learned the rule of thumb that you can get rid of your old checking account statements after three years and your old tax returns after seven years. The exception? You should *always* keep the tax return for any year in which you bought or sold any residences; at some point, you are going to need those returns if you sell and have to declare a capital gain. Many years ago clients sold their large house and "downsized" to a less expensive condo when they retired. Rose and Henry had made the mistake of throwing out their old tax returns—including those for the three years in which they had bought and sold homes. The problem was that Rose and Henry had started living in a place of their own in 1946. Trying to re-create each of their buying and selling transactions became a logistical nightmare, and they know they ended up paying much more tax than they should have because it was impossible to substantiate many capital improvements and sales expenses.

TO USE (OR NOT TO USE) OUTSIDE HELP?

Next, you need to decide who is going to do your return (along with that return, you should expect good tax advice for the coming year as well). I always tell clients that if they really do not like doing their tax returns, they shouldn't force themselves to go it alone. (For one thing, you may miss deductions and make mistakes.) Taxes are painful enough, so be nice to yourself while you are going through the process. Many people feel they cannot afford tax advice, but there is a wealth of information available for free or at a modest cost from the IRS, your local library or college, and professional tax preparers. In my experience, if you use a tax preparer, you usually will save more in tax dollars than you have to shell out in preparer fees.

About half of all taxpayers do their own returns, and half rely on outside help. How do you know if you need tax help? My rule of thumb is that if you have questions about your income, deductions, etc., that you can't answer after looking through the tax information booklet the IRS mails with your blank tax forms, you need help. This does not mean you have to go to the most expensive tax specialist around, but you do need some kind of help. If you have used outside help in the past, you may want to continue using it this year even if your situation is not complicated, if only because you have limited experience doing your own taxes. If you do not know which tax forms should be used and you cannot understand the forms even when you study them, you need help. Here are some specific situations where you probably need help:

- if you are self-employed or have a small business

- if you own investment real estate

- if you own limited partnerships

- if you have bought or sold your house or refinanced your mortgage this year

- if you have moved your residence for business reasons

- if you have bought or sold substantial amounts of securities

- if you are taking IRA or annuity distributions this year

- if you married or divorced during the year

This "outside help" can range from having a preparer complete your entire return for you to giving what you have done a "once-over" (as a professional okay) to merely answering questions by telephone.

■ Option 1: Do it yourself.

Your first option, rather than consulting an outside expert, is just doing your taxes yourself, especially if you are already using a computer to keep track of your personal finances. Most of the home accounting computer packages now have easy tie-ins to tax preparation software, so you can take all the checkbook, credit card, and investment information you have entered for the year, transfer it to the compatible tax preparation software program, and have your taxes completed in just a few hours. The tax forms are even printed by the software! There is nothing wrong with doing your tax return yourself, and millions of people do. But I do not *ever* recommend that you plan to prepare your taxes as a way to learn how to use the computer or even to learn a new computer program unless you are completely computer-literate. This is because you will have two frustrations at once—doing your taxes and learning how to use a computer. Too many clients have told me that they ended up having to file an extension because it took them so long by computer!

Unless your tax return is simple and straightforward, I *still* recommend that you have it checked by a tax preparer or service; when you do this, be sure to include all supporting documentation for verification. And it goes without saying that if you are planning to prepare your taxes by yourself, make sure you order any necessary additional forms in January or February so that you will not have a long wait before you can send in your tax return.

■ Option 2: Take advantage of free help.

I never thought I would be writing this, but the first place to start, believe it or not, can be the IRS. Why? It's all for free! You can call and ask questions over the telephone. You can call and ask them to send out their various publications that explain how to fill out the forms and what forms should be used (and then you can call them and ask them what the bulletins really mean). You can even get free help *in person* at their taxpayer assistance locations around the United States. These are the almost 10,000 VITA (Volunteer Income Tax Assistance) walk-in sites, with over 50,000 volunteers who have been thoroughly trained in all aspects of tax preparation. In 1993, the VITA program helped almost 2 million people. The only caveat to relying on the IRS for help is that it will not accept any liability if that advice is wrong. Another free resource to consider is some of the major tax preparation services such as H & R Block, who will answer questions by telephone and will even review your self-prepared tax return without charge.

- Option 3: Pay for help.

One (usually) low-cost option is a taxpayer preparation service. Most people know the name of the largest service, which is H & R Block. In 1992, H & R Block prepared 12 percent of all U.S. tax returns at an average fee of about $60. There are a number of other large tax preparation services, however, such as Jackson Hewitt, and you can check in your Yellow Pages for a listing of those near you. You will also find regional and local tax preparation services listed.

Another source many people are familiar with is CPAs, or Certified Public Accountants, professionally trained accountants who have passed a comprehensive exam and have met minimum experience requirements. CPAs are generally best suited to taxpayers with more complex income tax situations, but many people with simple returns also go to CPAs because they feel more comfortable with them. One of the advantages of a CPA is that if you get audited, the CPA will represent you before the IRS, meaning that you do not have to go to the audit (more on this later). Most major tax preparation services will send someone with you to the IRS, but they cannot actually represent you unless that individual is a CPA, an enrolled agent, or an attorney. An enrolled agent is a good source of tax assistance and is often less expensive than a CPA; to earn this title the individual either has five years' experience with the IRS or has passed a comprehensive exam. An enrolled agent can represent you to the IRS and may provide a less expensive alternative to CPAs. Many financial planners and local accounting/bookkeeping services also advertise tax assistance and preparation.

Wherever you go for tax preparation help, it is very important to check credentials and experience. Make sure your tax adviser has experience working with people who have incomes and tax issues similar to yours. Look for ways that their expertise can be checked in some way, by asking about degrees, years of experience, references, etc. Also ask whether the tax preparer will go with you (or in your place) if you get audited. You can find a list of questions in chapter 16, "Choosing Your Financial Advisers."

If you are going to use outside help, it is usually smart to develop a relationship with your tax preparer *before* you are ready to send in your taxes. Try to schedule a meeting with him early in the tax preparation process so you get guidance in completing this year's return. In addition, your preparer can help you come up with a tax strategy to make sure that you utilize every legal opportunity to reduce your future taxes—and increase the dollars going into your pocket. Whenever you are dealing with tax preparers, the earlier you seek help the better. After all, they are only human, and as April 15 draws closer and the workload mounts, their error rates increase.

■ Your last resort: Get an extension.

If the tax completion process becomes too confusing to deal with before April 15, you can always get an automatic extension until August 15. You *must,* however, file the form to request an extension by April 15. Some people think filing for an extension is a great strategy to avoid paying their taxes until August 15. Unfortunately, this is simply not the case. You still have to estimate and send a check for your total tax due for the year along with your application for an extension; otherwise, you could end up paying a big penalty as well as interest. If you have a compelling reason why your taxes cannot be finished by the automatic extension deadline of August 15, you can request an additional extension; some friends of mine had to go this route when most of their financial documentation was destroyed in a house fire. The risk, of course, is that doing your taxes may become like any dreaded job; the longer you put off doing it, the harder it is to do. If you ever find yourself starting to have trouble getting your taxes done on time, get help right away so you can avoid ending up in tax limbo.

PHASE 3:

AFTER YOUR RETURN IS COMPLETED

ELECTRONIC FILING

When your tax return is completed, there is one more decision to make—whether to mail it or use electronic filing. Electronic filing has become more popular each year since it was introduced by the IRS, and almost 15 million taxpayers chose this method of sending in their tax forms for 1993, up from 25,000 in 1986, the first year the IRS made the service available. With electronic filing, your tax information is entered into a computer and transmitted via modem to the IRS (and many state tax departments). Of course, you still receive a paper copy of the tax return for your files. The primary advantage is that you will receive any refund due you about three weeks faster than you would have if you had mailed in your return. The primary disadvantage is cost, which can range from as little as $5 upward to $50 or more depending on how much profit the tax preparer is trying to make. If you decide to use electronic filing, shop around for the best price. Many tax preparers will give you a discount on the electronic filing fee if you also have your taxes prepared by them.

LOANS AGAINST REFUNDS

If you come down to the line on your return that says "Amount to be refunded to you" and you see good news, you will of course want that money in your hands as soon as possible. A number of tax preparation services and consumer loan companies advertise that they will lend you most of the refund amount right away; in return you agree to have your refund check sent directly to the lender. The fees for this service can be staggering. *Check the terms of any such loan carefully.* Remember that you are receiving your refund only a few weeks earlier than you would have otherwise and then decide if the fees are worth it.

AUDITS

You followed all of the steps listed here, sent in your return and a check for any taxes due on time, and this year's tax preparation experience has now faded to a mere unpleasant memory. Then, all of a sudden, you get an audit notice from the IRS. Should you panic? As long as you have been honest, the answer is no. Usually, your audit will cover only a small part of your return. If your tax preparer can represent you, this will help because he or she is familiar with your return. Most experts agree that you should avoid going to your own audit unless the IRS insists upon your presence. This way, you will not stick your foot in your mouth by divulging information about an unrelated part of your return (which then becomes fair game for the auditor to challenge), and the tax professional representing you can stall answers until you two have had a chance to confer and decide on your response.

Taxes are a certain fact of life, as Benjamin Franklin said so many years ago. But they do not have to *rule* your life. The trick is to be organized, plan ahead, and get help when you need it. With good tax planning, more of your income will end up in your pocket instead of the government's, increasing the ways in which the Money Diet can work for you. It pays to become tax smart, so that *you* have control over your taxes instead of the IRS.

CHAPTER EIGHT

Developing a Winning Investment Strategy

SOMETIMES BEING a financial planner is like being a psychotherapist. A great deal of what we often find ourselves doing is listening to clients describe how money is making their lives miserable, absolving them of their guilt about not doing a better job on their own with their money, and then showing them how to improve their financial lives. Nothing illustrates this better than my recent experience with someone who came to see me because his success at saving was actually becoming a liability. Chris had insisted on doing so much research into the best investments for his hard-earned money that he became overwhelmed and incapable of making any decisions. Then he was so upset by his lack of decision-making that he threw himself into even more meticulous research, trying to find the best deal. And the more Chris knew, the more he realized he did *not* know. Chris's paralysis by analysis was driving him crazy.

Here's what happened. After spending several years building up money market accounts of $80,000, Chris decided last year that it was time to become educated and make some investment decisions. He ordered a subscription to a research service and several financial publications to get current financial information about his proposed investments. He read all the prospectuses and highlighted the important parts of each. Chris's research became almost an obsession, with prospectuses piling up under his bed because they became an important part of his nighttime reading. The problem was, the more he read and the more questions he asked, the more confused Chris became. All this newfound gain in financial knowledge was useful for his own edification, but it was completely worthless when it came to having that $80,000 earn more than money market interest rates. Because of his "paralysis by analysis," Chris missed one of the biggest stock market surges in recent history.

Investing is one of the basic tenets of the Money Diet and is a major factor in any successful financial plan. You will recall from chapter 1 ("How the Money Diet Works") that the only ways to meet your goals are to save money every year and to invest that money as wisely as possible. Following a well-thought-out investment strategy is like following a balanced diet—you become more financially fit and feel better in the process. But the psychological hurdles associated with investing are similar to those associated with dieting in another way. You can collect the details of every diet plan under the sun, but until you *do* something, the pounds stay in exactly the same place.

People often tell me that investing is their goal, but just like a diet, investing is really a means to an end. Of course, many of us receive pleasure and satisfaction from investing well (and keep ourselves up at night with worry when we are not doing so well), but apart from emotional satisfaction or dissatisfaction, the whole purpose of investing is to make your pot of assets grow so that you can do the things you want to do in the future.

There is nothing people love more than free financial advice, and there is nothing they think they should learn more about than investments. This applies to people regardless of their level of income, level of education, or amount of assets. In fact, if you heard some of the questions that lawyers, doctors, and millionaires ask me about their own finances (one example: What is the difference between a stock and a bond?), you would certainly feel better about your own. Like most people, they are too tired and stressed out by the time the weekend rolls around to make any headway in their own financial planning. The result? Large sums of money can sit idle, losing the battle against inflation.

Even the best advice in the world is not good enough to make you pick up the phone and take action. You have to understand an expert's advice, agree that it makes sense for you, and be willing to face the consequences of a bad decision. It's the same as dieting, where you have to know what to (and what not to) eat, decide that you can stick to the diet, commit to exercising regularly, and be willing to face the consequences of perhaps being hungry at times and having to forgo certain calorie-laden foods you love. Because this is hard, a lot of us have a few extra pounds, and a lot of us are avoiding making investment decisions with large sums of money. According to the Investment Company Institute, in 1991 over half our financial assets, or $500 billion, was in money market mutual funds. (I call these "pretend investments" because you pretend to yourself that you have actually made an investment decision, but you are just parking your money where it may not even keep up with inflation.)

It is not a surprise that investing is the one area of financial planning on which we tend to focus most of our energies. Quite simply, it is a lot more fun to think about making money from investments than it is to make a decision about buying more life insurance, or getting a will, or figuring out what you should be paying in estimated taxes, or figuring out how to earn or save more. But investing also involves decisions that can make or break your future plans, so it's easy to "pretend invest" month after month or year after year. I have had clients come through my door who become physically panicked when confronted with an investment decision as routine as where you put this year's IRA contribution.

Another reason we focus most of our attention on investing is that, unlike other areas of financial planning, the results are measurable. We can pull out our investment statements and see how much the account has gone up or down in the last year so we have some way to measure our success or failure. We may also think a lot about investing because everyone seems to be talking about it: Whenever I am at a party and am asked what I do for a living, my response seems to open the floor up to every investing success story in the room (and surprising admissions of failure as well). Even the nightly news reports reflect this; every day we receive economic news of one sort or another and learn whether the Dow-Jones Industrial Average (which only 19 percent of adults in a recent survey could correct identify) has gone up or down by how many points. Many people have little idea what this business information means, except that if the stock market went up, it must be good; if the stock market went down, it must be bad. But good for whom? And what impact does this have over the long run on *your* financial situation?

Many of us do not have much money to invest to start with, so it's hard to take a chance on losing some or all of it. In 1991, families headed by an individual between the ages of forty-five and fifty-four had median assets of $2,300, excluding home equity. If you have just $2,300 to invest, you may think it is not worth it to pay much attention to where that money goes. In reality, you need to pay more attention than ever because you have less money to start with. Investing smart does not mean that you will get a 20 percent return year after year. Very few professional money managers can achieve this kind of spectacular return; according to one study, two-thirds of professional money managers have failed to meet the return of the Standard and Poor's 500, an index of stock market performance that has averaged just over 10 percent over the last seventy years. Some money managers deliberately chose to take less risk than stocks and opt for a safer (and usually lower) return by investing in bonds, but many just picked the wrong stocks for their clients. And if many professional money managers who do this for a living cannot achieve these high returns, how well can we expect an amateur, working on his own, to do? Instead of setting yourself up for failure by setting a high investment rate of return as a target, "investing smart" means getting the highest return you can while still taking your tolerance for risk into account.

I have a client whose annual income is $20,000; George plans to retire in a few years and needs to increase his assets as quickly as possible. But George is uncomfortable taking the risk that his investments will go down in value substantially. He knows he will not be able to sleep at night if all his money is tied up in investments that *could* generate a 15 percent gain but could just as easily generate a 15 percent loss. After discussing his situation in detail, George and I decided that he could live with the possibility of modest (less than 5 percent) losses. We then agreed on a portfolio of investments that I believed had the greatest chance to grow given his risk tolerance. The place for you to start your investment strategy, then, is with risk tolerance.

RISK

Whenever we think about investments, we think of the risk of investing as the chance that the investment will go down in price. But this is only one of two basic kinds of risk you face when planning for your future. Of course, many investments can go down in price, so investment risk is a concern. The price of your investment portfolio may drop to $40,000 from $50,000. We can become so obsessed with avoiding a decrease in price at all costs, however, that we invest very conservatively and expose ourselves to the more pervasive kind of risk—purchasing-power risk. By purchasing-power risk I mean the *I* word: *inflation*.

Early in my career, I worked in the trust department of a bank and had the opportunity to see the effect of inflation on different kinds of portfolios. All too often, I found myself commiserating with elderly clients who were so afraid of investment risk (the chance that the value of their investment would go down) that they left themselves completely open to purchasing-power risk (the likelihood that the value of their investment would be slowly but surely wiped out by inflation).

Inflation, which averaged 5.1 percent in the 1980s and has averaged 3.1 percent since the 1920s, means that every year your dollar is worth less in terms of what it can buy. Even at a fairly low inflation rate—say 3 percent—the dollar you invest today is worth 75¢ in ten years. We see the perils of inflation most painfully with retirees on fixed incomes. As a client said to me recently about her mother, "When my father died twenty years ago, she had a very generous retirement income. Now she cannot even make ends meet without our help." The reason for this hardship is that her mother's income has come almost entirely from interest on a bond portfolio and a pension that guaranteed a certain level of income and did not increase with inflation. Virtually nothing was invested in the stock market, which historically has beaten inflation by 7 percent or more a year over the long run.

RETURN

"Return" is an interesting name for what should be the end result of investing. "Investing for return" does not just mean that you get your money back but that it pays you income or increases in value, or both. You hope to get a positive investment return this year so that next year your money will be worth more than it is now. Still, it is easy to get so focused on one small aspect of investment return that you miss the bigger picture. There are two kinds of investment return—*yield* (the income you get on your investments, such as interest or dividends) and *appreciation* (the increase in the price of your investments, such as when you buy 100 shares of XYZ stock for $1,500, and a year later the price has gone up to $1,700). Yield and appreciation together are *total return*. It is important to always keep *total return* in mind. Otherwise, you may think that your XYZ stock is doing terribly because you're getting only $20 a year in dividends (income), which is a yield of just over 1 percent. But you are also getting $200 growth in the price (appreciation), which comes to a gain of 13 percent. The total investment return on that particular investment would be over 14 percent—making it an excellent investment to have! Different kinds of investments emphasize the two types of return. Fixed-income investments generate income, and stock investments can provide appreciation, or income, or both. In general, when you invest, the fewer the guarantees you have, the higher the potential for overall return. The key is to figure out exactly how much risk you can take and then make sure that that amount of risk is reflected in your portfolio. Later in this chapter we will discuss how to invest based on your risk tolerance.

TYPES OF INVESTMENTS

FIXED-INCOME INVESTMENTS

There are two basic categories of investments—*fixed-income* and *equity* investments. With *fixed-income* investments, you are essentially loaning your money to a company or a government organization, and they guarantee to pay you a certain percentage of interest every year. Then, at the end of the loan period (sometimes called a "term"—such as with a ten-year bond), you get your money back. Because you are being offered some guarantees in the form of yield or income, there is usually no appreciation or gain in the price of the investment because the borrower promises only to return your money ("principal") at the end of the term. For example, let's say I buy a $1,000 certificate of deposit for a one-year term at 5 percent interest. I receive interest of $50, and I get my $1,000 back at the end of the year.

How Have Different Investments Performed? (page 119) shows the average annual returns for different types of investments over more than seven decades. Long-Term Corporate Bonds, Long-Term Government Bonds, Intermediate-Term Government Bonds, and U.S. Treasury Bills are all fixed-income investments. Money market accounts, bank accounts, and certificates of deposit also fall into this category. If you refer to the chart, you will see that fixed-income investments ranged between 3.7 percent and 5.6 percent during the period from the 1920s to the early 1990s, compared with the average inflation rate of 3.1 percent. If you followed investments in the 1980s, you may be surprised at these historically low returns because many of us got spoiled when bond returns in the 1980s were often in the double digits. Unfortunately, this high performance is unusual and cannot be expected to continue. Keep in mind that the more guarantees you are given, the lower the appreciation and overall investment return is likely to be.

One of the hardest problems an investment adviser faces is when a client announces, "I need twelve percent guaranteed and my income must go up with inflation." (In other words, the investor is saying the

How Have Different Investments Performed?

Average Annual Returns for the Decades

	1920s	1930s	1940s	1950s	1960s	1970s	1980s	1990s	LT Average
Small Company Stocks	-4.5%	1.4%	20.7%	16.9%	15.5%	11.5%	15.8%	14.1%	12.4%
Blue Chip Stocks	19.2%	0.0%	9.2%	19.4%	7.8%	5.9%	17.5%	10.6%	10.3%
LT Corporate Bonds*	5.2%	6.9%	2.7%	1.0%	1.7%	6.2%	13.0%	12.2%	5.6%
LT Gov't. Bonds*	5.0%	4.9%	3.2%	-0.1%	1.4%	5.5%	12.6%	12.8%	5.0%
Inter-Term Gov't.	4.2%	4.6%	1.8%	1.3%	3.5%	7.0%	11.9%	10.9%	5.3%
U.S. Treasury Bills	3.7%	0.6%	0.4%	1.9%	3.9%	6.3%	8.9%	4.9%	3.7%
Inflation	-1.0%	-2.0%	5.4%	2.2%	2.5%	7.4%	5.1%	3.7%	3.1%

*LT= Long Term

SOURCE: *Stocks, Bonds, Bills, Inflation*, Ibbotson Associates (12/31/93)

value of his investments must go up every year as well, because he wants 12 percent of a steadily increasing number.) Unfortunately, filling such a client order is virtually impossible. You just can't have it both ways—high income *and* substantial growth in the price—year after year. With a food diet, you have to plan your menu around the fact that different foods have certain basic characteristics (such as calories, carbohydrates, and fat content) that you just cannot change. It is the same thing with the Money Diet: The more investment guarantees you get, the lower the total return you can expect over the long run.

EQUITY INVESTMENTS

The second major category of investments are *equity* investments—investments in the stock of corporations. With stocks in corporations, you gain a share of ownership (equity) by buying a piece of the company, but this means that you also assume the risk that your share may either increase or decrease in value depending on the market and/or company conditions. With stocks, you get ownership and no guarantees; with bonds, you get just the opposite. Stocks do not come with a guarantee that you will get all your initial investment back. Stocks may pay dividends, which are considered income. Often, the stocks that pay the highest dividends grow very little in value— that is, the price per share does not go up, so you cannot sell your stock for more than you bought it. With those stocks, you own shares of well-established companies that are no longer expected to experience rapid growth and are paying out a larger portion of their profits in dividends. Other stocks (usually those of smaller, growing companies) may rise rapidly in value but pay virtually no dividends. And, of course, some stocks will both decline in price and not pay any dividends. The riskiest types of equity investments are stocks of small companies.

Over the long run, stocks as a category have a substantially higher return than fixed-income investments. Since 1920, stocks have averaged a return 5 to 7 percent greater than that of fixed-income investments. And, over the last fifty years, bonds have barely kept pace with inflation while stocks have outpaced inflation by about 8 percent annually.

OTHER TYPES OF INVESTMENTS

Of course, there are other investment categories as well. Investment real estate runs the gamut from apartment buildings to undeveloped land to time-shares. The major advantage of real estate is that prices can appreciate rapidly; the disadvantage is that real estate is very "illiquid," meaning that if you need to raise cash quickly, you may have to sell your investment at a loss (if you can sell it at all). In the 1970s, "hard assets" such as gold had some spectacular returns, but they lost favor with investors when their performance lagged behind traditional investments such as stocks and bonds. And, of course, you may still own a limited partnership or two that you bought back before tax laws changed in the mid-1980s and wiped out most of their tax benefits. With a limited partnership, you invest in a business venture and your potential loss is limited to the amount you put in. In return, some of the business venture's income, growth in value, and/or tax deductions or credits get passed on to you. Unless you are a sophisticated investor with plenty of money already in the fixed-income and equity markets, you are probably better off sticking to the basics. As a rule, no more than 10 percent of your investment assets should be in real estate, precious metals such as gold, artwork, antiques, collectibles, livestock, or limited partnerships concentrating in these areas. In fact, I have found that most investors can accomplish their goals by investing in bonds and stocks.

If you look at the generation that started investing in 1940, and you wonder who started out rich in the 1940s and who is rich today, you will see that their investment success depends on *where* they invested their money back then. This is why it is so important to invest in the stock market over the long run. Let's take my grandfather as a hypothetical example of how making different types of investments produces very different results. After my grandfather retired, he spent many hours each day poring over the financial pages, and he prided himself on his investment abilities. Let's assume that his investment performance matched the return of the stock market as a whole (since the majority of all professional money managers fail to outperform the stock market, "average" is quite good). We will also assume that he hedged his bets by buying one of each of all the stocks and bonds available, so his portfolio was a small version of the whole investment market. If he had one dollar in 1940 and put it in long-term government bonds, it would have been worth $8.84 in 1994. If he had taken even less risk and had invested the dollar in U.S. Treasury bills, it would have been worth $7.92 in 1994. But if he were savvy (and lucky!) and put it in the stock market, it would have been worth $266.16 in 1994.

It is very clear that for the long term, you are better off taking more investment risk so you can avoid purchasing power risk—that is, the risk that inflation will grow faster than your nest egg. In fact, I have often said that the only good thing about the falling interest rates of the late 1980s and early 1990s is that people finally have started moving their money out of bank accounts and into investments that might produce a higher return. After a lifetime of investing only in CDs, bonds, and money market accounts, one of the families we profiled on the *Today* show decided to move some money into medium-risk investments with no guaranteed income but with potential for income and growth. Why? Interest rates had dropped so much that when their CDs matured and needed to be reinvested, the new interest rate was substantially lower than their old rate. Investing in something that is not 100 percent guaranteed was a huge step for Dorothy and Tony, and they were smart to reposition only a little money at a time until they felt comfortable committing more. With interest rates so low, though, and a life expectancy of thirty or more years beyond their planned early retirement date, Dorothy and Tony realized they had to invest to *beat* inflation.

MUTUAL FUNDS

You may have noticed I haven't mentioned mutual funds. That's because mutual funds are not a whole separate category of investments, but a *way* of holding stock, bonds, and other investments. With a mutual fund you pool your money with many other investors, and the manager of the mutual fund buys many different stocks, bonds, and other investments. Some mutual funds even have stocks and bonds in their portfolios at the same time. Mutual funds have a couple of key advantages. First, because of economies of scale, the investment manager of a mutual fund can buy large blocks of stocks or bonds (or other types of investments) more cheaply than you could on your own. Second, mutual funds allow small investors to diversify in a way they never could before. With an investment as low as $500, you might be able to own as many as 1,000 different stocks (though of course you would own just a tiny piece of each one).

The popularity of mutual funds has skyrocketed in recent years. In 1960 only 161 mutual funds existed, but by 1990 there were over 3,000. Most of the growth in mutual funds has occurred since 1980. There were 12.1 million mutual fund accounts in 1980; that number had grown to almost 62 million accounts in 1990. And the assets in those accounts grew from $564 million in 1980 to $3.1 billion by 1990. This reflects a fundamental shift in the way Americans are investing their money. As the Federal Reserve Board's statistics show, more and more of us are taking money out of savings accounts and banking institutions and moving it into the stock market and mutual funds. And in the long run, that is the smart thing to do if you want to beat inflation and improve your chances of meeting your financial goals.

Because mutual funds are not a separate category of investments, their values vary according to the underlying assets within each mutual fund. That is why it is very important to look at a particular mutual fund's *objective*—what it is trying to accomplish—before you buy. **Anatomy of a Mutual Fund** (page 124) gives you an idea of different mutual funds' objectives, the investments that typically might be in those funds, and the relative risk and return of placing money in these funds. Clients complain to me—and rightly so—that a mutual fund's *name* often has little to do with the objective, and that many funds have similar names. This is why it is so important to know a mutual fund's portfolio and objective before you buy.

Anatomy of a Mutual Fund

The following chart is provided to help you compare mutual funds.

Type of Mutual Fund	Typical Investments	Goals of Fund Manager	Risk and Returns
Money Market Fund	Money Markets	Income	Low
Bond Fund	Bonds	High Income Little or no Growth	Low to Moderate
Balanced Fund	Stocks and Bonds	Moderate Income Moderate Growth	Moderate
Equity Income Fund	Income Stocks	High Income Moderate Growth	Moderate
Asset Allocation Fund	Cash, Bonds, and Stocks	Some Income Moderate Growth	Moderate
Growth and Income Fund	Income Stocks Growth Stocks	Some Income Higher Growth	Higher
Growth Fund	High Growth Stocks	High Growth Low Income	Higher
Small Company Fund	Stocks Smaller than S&P 500's	High Growth Low Income	Higher to Highest
International Funds	Stocks from Other Countries	High Growth Low Income	Highest
Global Fund	Stocks from U.S. & International Companies	High Growth Low Income	Higher
Aggressive Growth Funds	High Growth Stocks, Riskier Strategies	Very High Growth Low Income	Highest
Precious Metals and Other Specialty Funds	Stocks from a Narrow Industry	Very High Growth Probably Low Income	Highest

SOURCE: Warner A. Henderson, Applegarth Henderson Advisors, Inc.

From *The Money Diet*, by Ginger Applegarth.

YOUR INVESTMENT STRATEGY

Before you design your own investment strategy, you first have to establish where you stand right now. **Your Current Investment Strategy** (page 126) allows you to analyze the investment assets you currently have and to see how much you have invested in each of the different categories. In the **Simplified Net Worth Statement** (page 22), you added up your investment assets under Bank Accounts (line A), Investments (line B), and Retirement Plans (line C). Write the total of these three categories on line A at the top of **Your Current Investment Strategy** to make sure you include everything in this exercise. Then you need to divide your various investments into the three categories of Fixed-Income, Equity, and Other (such as investment real estate and limited partnerships). Do not include equity in your home as an investment here, because you probably aren't planning to use it to meet your goals, and you cannot reposition it into the Fixed-Income or Equity category without selling it or borrowing against your home and paying interest.

By following the steps in **Your Current Investment Strategy,** you will see what percentage of your total investment assets is in each of the different categories. (Be sure to separate your retirement plan investments out into these categories.) When you figure out your total in each category, divide each total by the number you wrote on line A. Now you have the percentage of your total investment portfolio held in each of the three categories. Some clients find they have every penny in one particular category and some clients don't have a penny in any category at all, so don't be discouraged if your investments look a little lopsided or modest.

The next step in developing an investment strategy is to figure out what you need your money for and when you need it. Take a look at **Setting Your Financial Goals** (page 42). If you were not overwhelmed by the size of these amounts when you listed them, you probably are now that you can compare them to the total of all of your investment assets, on line A of **Your Current Investment Strategy.** How much money you hope to have versus what you have now is the best proof I can give of why you *have* to take some investment risk in order to

Your Current Investment Strategy

Your Total Investment Assets
Add lines A, B, and C, **Simplified Net Worth Statement,** p. 22.

Total: **A.** _____

Fixed-Income Investments
You get interest or dividends, but virtually no appreciation of the investment. Your risk of losing money is low, and return is generally low.

Bank Accounts _____

Certificates of Deposit _____

Bonds/ Bond Mutual Funds _____

Government Securities _____

Life Insurance Cash Value _____

Total Fixed: **B.** _____

% Fixed **C. =** $\dfrac{\text{Total Fixed (B)}}{\text{Total Investments (A)}}$ = _____

Equity Investments
You may receive dividends plus appreciation of the investment. Your risk of losing money is generally higher, but your return is also generally higher.

Stocks _____

Stock Mutual Funds _____

Total Equity: **D.** _____

% Equity **E. =** $\dfrac{\text{Total Equity (D)}}{\text{Total Investments (A)}}$ = _____

Other Investments
You may receive income and/or appreciation of the investment. This category tends to be riskier than fixed-income and equity categories.

Investment Real Estate _____

Limited Partnerships _____

Gold/Silver/Metals _____

Other _____

Total Other: **F.** _____

% Other **G. =** $\dfrac{\text{Total Other (F)}}{\text{Total Investments (A)}}$ = _____

From *The Money Diet,* by Ginger Applegarth.

achieve your goals. If you have a long time until you will need access to your investment, you should have more money in the stock market to try to outpace inflation. But with a smart investment strategy, you can make sure you get as much return as possible for the risk you do take. This return can be achieved by investing in different categories and by not buying overly risky investments within these categories.

You may have been surprised that *all* your assets (including retirement assets) have been included in **Your Current Investment Strategy.** This is because all your goals are linked, just as every aspect of the Money Diet affects every other aspect. You cannot save for retirement without checking what you have saved for funding the kids' college education or buying a new car. An overall investment strategy is like a balanced diet: Each food or investment group contributes essential elements to your overall health. Without the right balance, you are liable to run out of energy (in a food diet) or money (in a money diet) to accomplish your goals.

SMART INVESTING PRINCIPLES

Some basic principles can guide you in minimizing much of the risk in your investment portfolio while maximizing your potential return. These principles may seem foreign to you because they are sometimes different from advice given in the financial media and because they contradict the "three stocks you should buy now" advice of financial magazines. (As a contributing editor of *Worth,* I obviously am a fan of personal finance magazines, but before you take any "micro" financial advice you need to understand the big picture of investing.) Nonetheless, as you will see, these smart investing principles can be quite useful:

- asset allocation
- diversification
- determining your tolerance for risk
- research
- paying attention to taxes
- remembering that you are smart enough

- dollar cost averaging
- avoiding panic when the price drops
- reviewing and rebalancing your portfolio annually

Following these nine strategic principles (as explained below) will help you develop—and maintain—a solid investment portfolio.

■ Step 1: Asset allocation

Asset allocation is a technical term used to describe the process we've begun in this chapter: deciding how much of your money you should put in different types of investments and then making your decisions about particular investments accordingly. The term became quite popular after the stock market "correction" (fancy word for "crash") of 1987, when people who had all their money invested in stocks may have lost 20 percent or more of their portfolio's value in just a few days. But smart investment managers have used this principle of asset allocation for years. In fact, studies have shown that how well an investment portfolio does over time has a lot more to do with the *types* or categories of investments in the portfolio than with *when* the investments were purchased or *which* specific investments were purchased. According to Ibbotson Associates' studies of how investments have performed over time, 94 percent of a particular portfolio's total return (income and growth in value) is based upon *what categories* of investments (fixed income and equity) are in the portfolio, and only 4 percent can be attributed to *which specific* stock or mutual fund was bought. Only 2 percent of the return comes from buying or selling at a particular time. Of course, this flies in the face of the importance of such traditional advice as "Buy XYZ stock today and sell it as soon as the price goes up ten dollars." But in a way, this news should be very liberating for the average investor because it means you do not have to worry so much about keeping track of individual stocks or mutual funds on a daily basis, and you do not have to agonize when prices are going down. In fact, if you are the average investor, you should stick to mutual funds and not have stocks to worry about anyway. You'll see why when we get to step 2, investment diversification.

Asset allocation also involves breaking down your fixed income and equity holdings. For example, your equity portfolio might include investments in large companies, small companies, and international companies. Large companies, also known as "blue chips," are well-known, mature companies. Small companies are less well known, attempting to grow to become blue chips, and international companies are headquartered outside the United States. The fixed-income portion of your portfolio should include bond investments that pay off over different time periods (short-term, long-term, etc.) and that are of different types (government, corporate). Allocating your assets is like going to the grocery story and buying lots of different kinds of foods to have the variety you need to help you stay on your diet. It's much harder to stick to your diet when you eat just grapefruit, or whatever, all day every day.

In fact, as you read about different investments from now on, keep the categories we've discussed in mind and note how the investment's *category* affects the financial results. For example, whether the investment is XYZ corporate bond or ABC corporate bond, if the interest rates go up, the value of either bond will probably drop. It's just like with food—no matter what kind of cheese you buy, it will probably have more fat than fruit does. The best example of how little advice about specific stocks can mean is the regular *Wall Street Journal* dartboard game, in which a *Journal* staffer goes out in the hall and throws darts at a dartboard listing a variety of different stocks. Wherever the dart lands, *Journal* staffers invest some imaginary money. This "model portfolio" of random darts is pitted against portfolios of stocks picked by investment experts around the country. At the end of a six-month period, the dartboard portfolio's return is compared with the experts' portfolios. The dartboard often beats the experts!

■ Step 2: Diversification

This one sounds as simple as "drink your milk," because telling you to diversify your investments is like telling you not to put all of your eggs in one basket. Diversification sounds like asset allocation, but diversification means buying a number of different investments in each asset allocation category. For example, let's assume your asset allocation strategy is to have 40 percent in large company stocks, which in your case means $6,000. Instead of just buying ABC and XYZ stocks for $3,000 each, you can reduce your risk by buying smaller amounts of a number of different stocks, thus reducing your losses if one drops in price or significantly cuts its dividend payments. Studies have shown that a diversified portfolio fluctuates less in value because investments that do particularly well or poorly over a short period of time are counterbalanced by others that may be doing just the opposite. From the example I just gave, you can see how hard it is to diversify if you don't have a lot of money to invest. That's why, in general, I recommend that clients achieve diversification by using no-load mutual funds. "No-load" means "no commission," although having to pay a commission should never be the sole reason to avoid a particular investment. Some of the long-term top-performing mutual funds (such as Fidelity Magellan) have commissions.

Mutual funds are not just for the small investor; many advisers recommend them for seven-figure portfolios as well. In fact, at my firm we manage investment accounts whose worth ranges from $250,000 to several million dollars using mutual funds.

If you are going to try some "do-it-yourself" investing, the best way to set up an account is to open one at a discount brokerage firm such as Charles Schwab or at a no-load mutual fund company such as Scudder (Fidelity, the industry giant, serves as both). If you plan to skip mutual funds and pick your own stocks or bonds, you should have at least twenty individual holdings to achieve real diversification. No single stock or bond investment should constitute more than 5 percent of your portfolio.

Diversification can also include using *index,* or passive, funds. This method of investing is becoming increasingly popular, because with an index fund you basically "buy the benchmark." A benchmark is the average of all the investments in one particular category. For example, you can buy a mutual fund that invests in every stock in the Standard and Poor's 500 Index, or every bond in the Lehman Brothers Corporate Bond Index. The advantage of index funds is that their expenses are much lower than those of other funds that have to pay for investment managers and research staffs to make buying and selling decisions. The only drawback to index funds is that you will never do better than the benchmark (for example, the Standard and Poor's 500) because the index fund's holdings are identical to the benchmark—just smaller. However, since the majority of all money managers fail to beat the Standard and Poor's 500, I think achieving the benchmark is quite good. We often use a combination of actively managed and index mutual funds in our clients' portfolios as a way to keep their expenses down. Expenses in index mutual funds are up to 80 percent less than the average fund, which has an investment manager making buying and selling decisions. Expenses in the average mutual fund run 1.4 percent a year. (Some are *much* higher, so always check commission rates when you buy *or* sell, as well as expense ratios.)

Experts usually recommend that you keep an amount equal to three to six months' expenses in bank or money market accounts in case of emergencies.

■ Step 3: Determining your tolerance for risk

One of the hardest things about investing is determining your tolerance for risk. It's comforting to know that just by following the eight other steps here you will reduce your risk. But you still need to know how much risk you can tolerate. If there were no inflation, and you already had every dollar you needed to meet your goals, you could play it 100 percent safe and put all your money in fixed-income investments with guaranteed income and safety of principal. Alas, inflation is a fact of life, and virtually everyone I know needs to invest to *beat* inflation because the cost of their goal will increase over time and they don't have all the money they need in today's dollars.

It is important to look at risk in relation to time. As a rule, the riskier the investment, the more the price will fluctuate up and down in the short term. If you will need to sell a particular investment next year so you can pay for the new car or freshman year of college for your child, you obviously don't want to take much of a chance that the price will drop in that time period, so it would be unwise to put that money in the stock market. Money market accounts and CDs make sense for those funds. But on the other hand, if you have ten years to invest until the money is needed, it doesn't matter how much the price fluctuates in the next few years as long as it is much higher when the time comes to sell it. For longer-term investment time horizons, a good portion of your money should be in the stock market.

Suggested Investment Portfolios (page 133) gives you some possible asset allocation strategies for your particular situation. This table is based on the number of years you have until retirement, because that is the one event we all must plan for, unless we die first. It also assumes that you have a diversified portfolio with mutual funds or at least twenty individual investments. If there are other goals that you need to pay for in the next ten years, more of those funds should be invested in fixed-income assets than the percentages shown here.

Suggested Investment Portfolios is predicated on the ability to take moderate risk. With moderate risk, you are willing to accept some fluctuation (called *volatility*) in your portfolio because you know that as a rule, equities will outperform fixed income in the long run. However, you probably do not feel comfortable with too much fluctuation, so some of your money stays in fixed income to stabilize the portfolio's price. If you are *conservative* (you cannot bear to lose any value in your portfolio), more should go in fixed income and less in equities than is shown in **Suggested Investment Portfolios.** Bear in mind, however, that by minimizing your potential short-term loss of value you are increasing the possibility you will barely keep pace with inflation and will end up short of what you need for your goals. If you are *aggressive,* you are willing to take the risk of price fluctuations. In that case you should put more in equities than is indicated in the table. You stand to lose more if you sell in the near term, because the prices may go down, but you stand to gain more in the long term because you are putting more of your portfolio in the category of investments (equities) that historically has done better than fixed-income investments.

Suggested Investment Portfolios

(Based on Years to Retirement; Moderate Risk)

Years until Retirement	0	1–5	6–10	11–15	16–20	20+
TYPE OF INVESTMENT						
Equities						
Small Co. Stocks	8%	10%	14%	17%	20%	23%
International Stocks	7%	10%	13%	16%	20%	22%
Large Co. Stocks	45%	45%	43%	42%	40%	40%
Fixed Income						
Bonds, CDs, etc.	30%	25%	20%	15%	10%	5%
Money Market/Checking	10%	10%	10%	10%	10%	10%

Note: This assumes all of your money is to be used for retirement. If you have other goals that will be funded in the next 10 years, more of your money should be put in fixed income than the percentages shown here. This also assumes that you have a diversified portfolio with mutual funds or at least 20 individual investments.

From *The Money Diet*, by Ginger Applegarth.

■ Step 4: Research

Once you have come up with your asset allocation strategy, have decided to diversify, and know your risk tolerance, you can invest by using one or more of the commercially available investment services such as Morningstar or Value Line. These can usually be found in your local library, or you can order your own subscription. For the average investor, I prefer the recommendations by investment services to those of individual financial columnists because recommendations by the services represent a consensus of opinion instead of the views of just one person. The main problem with certain investment services is that they make recommendations solely based on past performance, which is no guarantee of the future. Whatever you do, be careful when following the advice of *anyone* who will benefit from your purchase or sale (such as a stockbroker, financial planner who sells products, mutual funds salesperson, etc.). More and more, banks are selling mutual funds, but as a recent *Consumer Reports* survey shows, you cannot be assured of accurate advice even from banks. Only six of the forty bank salespeople contacted were accurate in how they described various mutual fund investments, and many of the others violated Securities and Exchange Commission (SEC) rules by quoting "guaranteed" returns and giving other incorrect information. Do not be misled into thinking that just because you go to the bank, your investment is insured like your bank account is under the FDIC. With mutual funds, there are no guaranteed investment returns, your account is not insured against loss of principal, and you have to make sure that the fund that you are buying takes your risk tolerance into consideration.

■ Step 5: Paying attention to taxes

The goal here is to pay attention to the effect of taxes on the investments you choose but not to be ruled simply by whether or not an investment is tax-exempt. A client once came to see me and mentioned she had invested in something that promised a 4.3 percent tax-free return. It sounded like a great deal, but it turned out not to be so because her tax bracket was so low. For the same amount of investment risk, she could have achieved a 9 percent before-tax return with another choice. If this client's tax bracket was 30 percent (and hers was even less), she would have ended up with 6 percent after-tax return by choosing the taxable investment. **Taxable or Tax-Exempt?** (page 135) shows how you can figure out whether tax-free investments make sense for you. And be sure to find out from which taxes (federal, state, local) the investment is exempt.

■ Step 6: Remembering that you are smart enough

Do not ever buy an investment you do not understand. Most people do not need complicated investments such as stock options, puts and calls, futures, etc. Usually, these end up in a client's portfolio because an overzealous stockbroker has put them there or because the client has taken on the management of his or her investment account as a

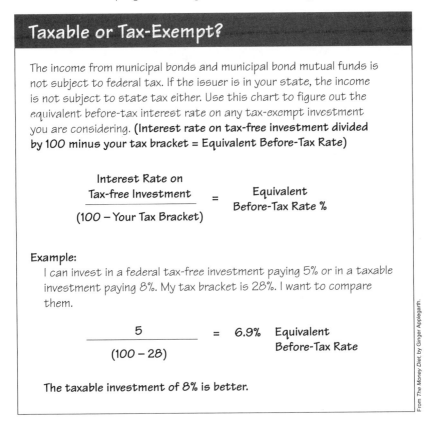

Taxable or Tax-Exempt?

The income from municipal bonds and municipal bond mutual funds is not subject to federal tax. If the issuer is in your state, the income is not subject to state tax either. Use this chart to figure out the equivalent before-tax interest rate on any tax-exempt investment you are considering. (**Interest rate on tax-free investment divided by 100 minus your tax bracket = Equivalent Before-Tax Rate**)

$$\frac{\text{Interest Rate on Tax-free Investment}}{(100 - \text{Your Tax Bracket})} = \text{Equivalent Before-Tax Rate \%}$$

Example:

I can invest in a federal tax-free investment paying 5% or in a taxable investment paying 8%. My tax bracket is 28%. I want to compare them.

$$\frac{5}{(100 - 28)} = 6.9\% \text{ Equivalent Before-Tax Rate}$$

The taxable investment of 8% is better.

hobby. (Of course, it is fine to make investments your hobby, but make sure that you are not shooting yourself in the foot by doing so.) Also, remember that you do not owe a salesperson anything; I have seen some of the worst investments bought because the client felt somehow obligated to an eager salesperson who called every week for a year. I also recommend that you never buy an investment over the phone. Insist on a face-to-face meeting with anyone who will be making money if you agree to invest.

■ Step 7: Dollar cost averaging

Dollar cost averaging means that instead of putting all of your money in the stock or bond market at one time, you spread it out over a year or two. At my firm, we typically invest a client's money over a one-year period, putting in an equal amount each quarter. This strategy works very well for investing on a monthly basis as well. Dollar cost averaging avoids the problem of putting all your money in the stock market when it is high and having it drop 20 percent, the way it did in October 1987. You avoid investing when the cost per share is excessively high or excessively low; studies show that you are more likely to reduce your risk in the long run with this strategy than if you invest your money all at once. It is also better for your heart—and your sanity level—to be investing on a dollar cost averaging basis.

■ Step 8: Avoiding panic when the price drops

One of the worst things you can do is panic and sell an investment just because it has gone down in value. When you purchase an investment, remember that you are not trying to "time the market" (predict which way an investment's price will go in the short term) and that in most cases you should plan to hold on to it for at least two or three years. The worst thing you can do is sell when the going gets tough. For example, during the month of October 1987, the stock market lost over 20 percent. But if you had put money in the stock market at the beginning of 1987 and sold out at the end of the year, you would have still *earned* 5.2 percent. If you had dumped your stock investments when the market crashed in October, you would have lost 20 percent for that month alone. In fact, if you left the same money in until the end of 1993, you would have earned an annual average return of 14.1 percent.

■ Step 9: Reviewing and rebalancing your portfolio annually

Because you are investing in different types of investments, one part of your portfolio is likely to do better than another part each year. Some years the international stock portion will perform better, and other years the bond portion will do better, etc. This means that you need to rebalance your portfolio at least once a year by going back and completing **Your Current Investment Strategy** (page 126) again. We will cover this in more detail in chapter 17, "Scheduling Regular Financial Checkups," but I mention it here just to remind you that investment strategies are not static; they do need to be reviewed periodically, even though you are not trying to guess where the stock and bond markets are going.

Let's use one of my clients as an example of how these nine smart investing principles and steps are used in real life. Ellen came to see me because she had recently inherited a sum of money and didn't know what to do with it. Based on her goal of retiring in fifteen years, we came up with an asset allocation strategy (Step 1) similar to the one in **Suggested Investment Portfolios** (page 133). She agreed with me that no-load mutual funds should be used to give her enough diversification (Step 2). We discussed Ellen's tolerance for risk; like many investors, she started out "conservative" but then realized that *conservative* meant she probably could not meet her goal. We agreed on a "moderate" risk strategy (Step 3). I did the initial investment research for her, but, as any investor should do *even* with an adviser on call, she reviewed my research to learn about what I was recommending (Step 4). We looked at Ellen's tax bracket and decided it was not worthwhile investing in tax-exempts (Step 5). We arrived at our investing decisions *together*—Ellen did not simply take my advice; she made sure her preferences were included in our choices (Step 6). We agreed to invest her money quarterly over a twelve-month period (Step 7). The prices of some investments *did* drop temporarily, and Ellen did not panic and insist I sell (Step 8). Finally, we review her portfolio together regularly and make sure that she continues to have the right asset allocation (Step 9). With these steps, Ellen has reduced her risk and maximized her potential return. Unless she had been very lucky doing so, Ellen's original plan of reading a few magazines, picking a few stocks and bonds, and then investing all of her money at once would have been much riskier.

SUMMING UP

Developing an investment strategy is one of the keys to securing your financial future and making the Money Diet work. A good investment strategy is like a healthy diet: More of your "calories" are digested and turned into energy so that you can do the things you want to do. And the worst thing you can do about your investments is not to do anything at all. Take action now! You simply cannot afford to wait. By following the basic Money Diet plan of asset allocation, diversification, dollar cost averaging, etc., you can develop an investment strategy that will take you much further toward meeting your goals than if you just bought investments in a haphazard fashion. If you follow my advice, you have already taken wiser investment steps than many of the money managers who do this for a living. You do not have to be rich to invest with the Money Diet, just smart.

CHAPTER NINE

Planning for
a Comfortable Retirement

A COUPLE YEARS AGO, a friend stopped me after a meeting we had both attended and asked to speak with me on an urgent private matter. She appeared anxious—even a bit uncomfortable—and I half expected to hear that some terrible financial catastrophe had suddenly befallen her and she needed my advice. My instincts were partially correct: She certainly was facing a terrible financial catastrophe, but luckily it had not yet occurred. What had happened to cause such concern? My friend had just turned forty, and with devastating clarity, she had suddenly started to view her future differently. As she explained, she had always assumed that some "knight on a white horse" would ride into her life to take care of her in her old age. My friend had never worried for a moment about the future, believing that because of her active social life sooner or later she would marry and share her life—and her future financial burdens—with someone else. But she turned forty, looked around, and realized that she had spent every penny she had ever made since she got out of school and no knights were waiting in the wings to rescue her from a nasty fall. As she said to me, "I have already accumulated a lifetime of great memories, but not a dime for retirement. And I want to retire in twenty years. What do I do?"

I wish I could say that this scenario is unusual, but unfortunately it is all too common, even though the reasons for financial planning procrastination can vary widely. The story is the same whether the speaker is male or female, single or married, with or without children. All too often, we are so busy living day-to-day that we barely notice the passage of years until something happens to wake us up. It might be a "milestone age" of thirty-five, forty, forty-five, fifty, or even older, or it might be the retirement or death of someone close to us. We suddenly realize that we do not want to keep working this hard for the rest of our lives, and retirement feels as if it is just around the corner. As my friend explained with painful clarity, "I can barely afford to live on my salary as it is. What will I do when this income stops?"

More than any other aspect of financial planning, an inadequately funded retirement resembles the hidden costs of an unhealthy diet. We are not talking about just excess calories here, but also the cholesterol and fat that build up in your system and cause major health problems as you grow older. You keep eating the same way day after day, with no warning about the damage you are causing to your system until suddenly you find yourself in the middle of a medical crisis with a lifetime of poor eating habits as the number one suspect. The same is true with planning for retirement: You can spend everything you make today (or even save a little for retirement along the way) and not feel a single warning twinge that you are setting yourself up for future financial disaster unless you start changing your consumption habits *now*.

PROBLEM 1: WE ARE NOT SAVING ENOUGH

If you have not paid much attention to retirement, you are not alone, but that does not exempt you from worrying about life after employment. A recent study estimates that three-quarters of Americans over the age of twenty will have *less than half* of what they need to live on at retirement. Other statistics show that being older does not automatically mean that you are in good financial shape. One-third of consumers aged forty and above have put away less than $30,000 for retirement; $30,000 is barely enough to cover expenses for one year, much less for twenty or more retirement years! And one-third of baby boomers between the ages of twenty-nine and forty-seven have not even started to save for retirement at all. Yet in 1994 only 54 percent of consumers surveyed said they were willing to spend less in order to save more for retirement. Over the last twenty-five years, inflation has averaged 5.9 percent. Let's say you are sixty-five and want to retire today with $20,000 annual income in addition to Social Security to cover expenses. Let's further assume that inflation will be at least 1 percent *less* than it was for the last twenty-five years and that you will live until age eighty-five. *To meet your goal, you would need to have $340,000 in the bank today.* This assumes your living expenses go up every year during retirement (due to inflation) and you spend every dollar you have by the end of the twenty years.

PROBLEM 2:
WE THINK WE ARE IN GOOD SHAPE

Despite the grim statistics above, as many as three-quarters of us expect our retirement to be as comfortable as or even more comfortable than that of our parents. We don't realize exactly how bad our financial health is because we can't see how much we have jeopardized our financial future by "consuming" too much (spending) and accumulating so much "fat" (debt). A poor food diet usually results in disease and/or death; a poor money diet results in the "disease" of having to live on a greatly reduced income and/or "death"—running out of money altogether.

We know generally that we need more money for retirement, but "retirement" is a moving target: It is so far away in the future, and our finances may fluctuate so much by then, how can we possibly plan since we have no idea how much we will need? It is also easy to make retirement our very last priority because it is so much more distant than replacing the old car, writing out tuition checks, or trading up houses. Like Scarlett O'Hara, we tend to take the attitude "I'll think about that tomorrow." But unfortunately, eventually "tomorrow" becomes "today," and retirement is likely to be the goal that we are stuck living with the longest. The bottom line is that for the last years of our lives we will suffer the long-term effects of not adequately preparing in advance.

In chapter 1, "How the Money Diet Works," we discussed the fact that every year you put off beginning to save, the harder it is and the more money it takes to meet your goal. Thanks to the time value of money, the sooner you start to save, the more your money will grow; it has all those extra years to do so even when you do not add another penny. Remember my example of John Sr. and John Jr. in chapter 1? John Jr. started saving in an IRA when he was twenty-five, and John Sr. started at age forty-five. Purely because of the time value of money, John Jr. ended up with over $700,000 more than his father did. Many of us are starting to save so late that we will have to work many more years than we would like just to meet our retirement income goal. So before you get your heart set on retiring at fifty-five or sixty, you should take a long hard look at whether you will be able to do so.

WHY WE NEED MORE THAN OUR PARENTS DID

There are a number of reasons why we need a substantial retirement nest egg. One of the most important is that we are living longer than ever before. If you plan to retire at age fifty-five and live to do so, the odds are you will be alive until age eighty-three. If you retire at sixty, your life expectancy is to eighty-four years. If you wait to retire until age seventy, chances are you will live to age eighty-six. And if you and your spouse are the same age, the actuarial experts tell us that one of you is likely to be alive four to six years later than the ages mentioned here.

In addition to living longer, we are retiring earlier and have fewer years to build up retirement assets. A Gallup survey of 1,000 workers between the ages of thirty and fifty showed that more than half of those polled expected to retire at age sixty or younger, with fewer expecting to retire at age sixty-five and only 6 percent at older than age sixty-five. Adding to the "living-longer" and "retiring-earlier" pressures of funding retirement is that fact that we expect a much higher standard of living at retirement than our parents did—a retirement that includes travel, entertainment, and perhaps even a return to school. Then, of course, there is inflation, which can insidiously reduce the purchasing power of your retirement nest egg every year. The combination of living longer, retiring earlier, and expecting a higher standard of living all make it imperative that we start to plan for retirement as early as possible.

Starting to plan early is often derailed by education costs. In my experience people often tend to start planning for retirement when their kids are out of college. But we are having children later and later in life, so education expenses are finished that much later, and only then can we focus on our own retirement needs. These needs get delayed just as we delay starting a diet until the big work project is finished, or until after the holidays, or until things are not so stressful at home.

At the same time that we are living longer, retiring earlier, and expecting more out of retirement, we are getting less and less retirement help from employers. At this point, only 39 percent of American workers have traditional retirement plans that pay a fixed monthly sum at retirement. More and more employers are moving to plans that encourage—or even require—employees to invest more of their own money while employers invest fewer corporate dollars. And we can't count on Social Security to make up the shortfall.

Social Security is a double-edged sword. It has certainly improved living conditions for retired American workers since it was enacted about sixty years ago, but it has tended to make us complacent because we have been raised to expect that Social Security benefits will increase with inflation throughout our lives. Unfortunately, we can no longer expect Social Security to continue increasing as it has in the past, because there are fewer American workers to support each retiree than there were ten or twenty years ago. And few people can afford to live on Social Security alone; the average monthly retirement check was $653 in 1993. We are stuck making Social Security contributions, but the younger we are the more pessimistic we are about Social Security as a good investment. A Harris poll for *Business Week* in 1990 showed that 90 percent of people aged thirty to thirty-nine do not believe they will get Social Security benefits that will equal what they have paid in. The amount you need to sock away in addition to Social Security may be staggeringly high. As I said before, if you were to need $20,000 a year on top of Social Security to retire, and didn't care that nothing would be left for your heirs, you would need to have $340,000 in the bank on the day you retire.

The solution to these retirement woes is to save more and invest better. In diet terms, this is like eating less and eating healthier. There are three ways to increase the likelihood of meeting your goal: You can reduce the amount you want to have as annual income when you retire, you can save more on an annual basis until you retire, and you can invest to get a greater investment return between now and the time you die. Notice that I did not say the time you *retire*, but the time you *die*. This is because you need to invest wisely *throughout* your retirement in order to maintain your purchasing power. The worst thing you can do is move everything into bank accounts or certificates of deposit the day you retire. Otherwise, unless you are very wealthy, you will almost certainly run out of money before you die because of inflation.

As a New York City taxi driver who had amassed a million-dollar net worth driving a cab told me, "My father always said not to wait until you are hungry to go to the store, so I started saving for my retirement when I was twenty-five years old." In other words, don't wait until you are near retirement to start planning, because the longer you wait, the worse off you will be.

FIGURING OUT HOW MUCH YOU NEED

One of the most difficult things about planning for retirement is that how much you need is a continually moving target. (After all, depending on your activity level, your body needs different amounts of calories and nutrients.) One of the biggest unknowns is inflation. If you change your assumption about future inflation by just 1 percent (in other words, assuming 5 percent instead of 4 percent), your projected "need" will be thousands of dollars more or less by the time you retire. Of course, the amount needed varies from person to person; your need is generally based on your current living expenses. In chapter 3 ("Your Current Weight: What You Are Spending and Saving") you calculated your current living expenses, and in chapter 5 ("Smart Spending") I hope you found ways to reduce those expenses. An acceptable rule of thumb is that your retirement income need is 80 percent of your current normal expenses. This is a general rule, because each person's situation is different. Retirees do not just sit home and wait to die; they are traveling, entertaining, and perhaps spending lots of money on medical care. In fact, the joke in my family is that instead of slowing down, my parents' travel and entertaining schedule quadrupled the day my father retired because he owned his own business and could never really get away until he sold it. Studies show that a fair number of retirees are still providing financial support for their children and/or grandchildren. The largest single amount needed for retirement income is housing, and your housing expenses will vary depending on whether your mortgage will be paid off by retirement or whether you plan to rent.

In **How Much More Do You Need for Retirement?** (page 146), you can figure out how much additional retirement income you will likely need in today's dollars after taking into consideration all your expected sources of retirement income. For many people retirement is too far off in the future to be motivated to start planning for it now. But the longer you wait, the harder it will be to meet your goal. This Willpower Worksheet can give you the motivation and willpower to begin planning now.

Be forewarned that the chart will probably show you need to come up with a great deal of income year after year in retirement. If you retire today and just want to live on income alone (without using up any principal), your nest egg must be as much as twenty times the amount of your annual income need. So, if you want to live on income alone and save all your money for your children, $400,000 worth of assets that can generate income and/or grow in value will be required to give you $20,000 for living expenses (assuming you earn an 8 percent return, pay 3 percent in taxes, and have 5 percent left over on your investment income). Thankfully, however, most of us are covered by Social Security, and for now we should assume we will receive our full benefits at retirement. Otherwise, the amount of assets you would have to come up with would be so astronomical that

How Much More Do You Need for Retirement?

Note: All numbers are in today's dollars. This chart uses annual, not monthly, numbers.

Part One: Total Assets You Need

A. Your Current Living Expenses (Spending and Saving, p. 28, line H)	A	
B. Less: Expected Annual Reductions in Living Expenses with the Money Diet	B.–	
C. Equals: Anticipated Annual Living Expenses	C.=	
Times:	×	0.80
D. Equals: Annual Living Expenses at Retirement	D.=	
E. Less: Approximate Social Security Benefit (Social Security Retirement Benefits, p. 149) ———— × 12 = Annual Benefit	E.–	
F. Less: Approximate Annual Pension and Other Income*	F. –	
G. Equals: Additional Income You Will Need to Provide with Assets Note: If line G is negative, that shows you do not need additional income. Stop here (and congratulations!).	G.=	
Times:	×	16
H. Equals: Assets You Must Have to Provide the Additional Income Needed	H.=	

Part Two: Assets You Have

I. Your Existing Investment Assets (Simplified Net Worth Statement, p. 22)

line A (Bank Accounts)	
line B (Investments)	+
line C (Retirement Plans) †	+
line D (House)‡ minus line I (Mortgage) House:_____ – Mortgages:_____ = House Equity:_____	
line G (Other Assets) §	+
Your Total Existing Investment Assets	I. =

continued on next page

From The Money Diet, by Ginger Applegarth.

How Much More Do You Need for Retirement? (cont.)

Part Three: Figuring Your Shortfall or Surplus

H. Assets You Must Provide (see above, line H)	H.
I. Less: Your Existing Investment Assets	I. —
J. Equals: Your Asset Shortfall (in today's dollars; if "I" is less than "H")	J. =
K. Equals: Your Asset Surplus (in today's dollars; if "I" is more than "H")	K. =

* Include estimated retirement plan income here. Some retirement plan statements give you two estimates — the lump-sum amount you can take out at retirement and the annual income you will have if you leave the money in the plan. If you include the income benefit here, do not list the lump-sum values of these plans in Retirement Plans on Line I, or else you will double-count the plan benefits. Also include any other source of ongoing income such as rent received, part-time job earnings, etc.

† Include plans that will pay you a lump sum at retirement. Do not include any annual income benefit from these plans on line F or else you will double-count the plan benefits.

‡ Include your house equity only if you plan to sell it at retirement. Your house equity is the amount you would have after paying off any mortgages on it.

§ Include only assets you are willing to sell for cash at retirement.

From The Money Diet, by Ginger Applegarth.

you might be tempted to give up on retirement planning altogether. To figure out how much you need for retirement, start by writing down your current annual living expenses on line A of **How Much More Do You Need for Retirement?**, which is line H from **Spending and Saving** (page 28). Then estimate how much you will be able to save in living expenses by following the Money Diet. Write this on line B. Subtract line B from line A; the result on line C is your anticipated annual living expenses if you stick to your financial plan. The next step is to multiply your current living expenses by 0.80 to take into account the fact that expenses will likely decline when you stop working. Write the result on line D. Keep in mind that if you are married, you and your spouse should be combining your incomes and benefits to find out where your household stands.

To finish **How Much More Do You Need for Retirement?** you need to refer to **Social Security Retirement Benefits** (page 149), which shows the approximate monthly payments in 1995 for a worker retiring at age sixty-five who has had steady earnings. Find the approximate Social Security benefit for the income nearest yours, multiply it by 12 to get the annual benefit, and write it on line E of **How Much More Do You Need for Retirement?** Line F is where your other retirement plans and miscellaneous income such as rent start to kick in. Pull out all your company retirement plan booklets and statements, as well as those for any IRAs or other plans you have on your own, and review them carefully. Do any state that they provide an annual income instead of a lump-sum amount when you retire? (This would most likely be the case if you are part of a large employer-sponsored retirement plan.) If you have a plan that does provide an annual income, write the amount on line F. Your statement may have "current year" and "future at retirement" values; use current-year values because you are comparing it with your need in today's dollars.

Some retirement plan statements give you *two* estimates—the lump-sum amount you can take out at retirement and the monthly or annual income you will have if you leave the money in the plan. If you include the income benefit on line F, do not list the lump-sum benefit on line I or else you will double-count your benefits.

Now, to calculate the additional income that must be generated by your assets each year, subtract your Approximate Social Security

Social Security Retirement Benefits

Monthly Benefits

Your Age	Your Family	Your Earnings in 1994				
		$20,000	$30,000	$40,000	$50,000	$59,000 or more
45	You	793	1,065	1,200	1,327	1,428
	You and your spouse[1]	1,188	1,597	1,800	1,992	2,142
55	You	793	1,064	1,180	1,269	1,328
	You and your spouse[1]	1,188	1,595	1,770	1,903	1,992
65	You	767	1,018	1,098	1,150	1,170
	You and your spouse[1]	1,151	1,527	1,648	1,724	1,754

[1] Your spouse is assumed to be the same age as you. Your spouse may qualify for a higher retirement benefit based on his or her own work record.

Note: These figures are calculated in today's dollars. They assume your earnings are steady and you work until full retirement age.

To find the correct amount, select the age nearest yours and move right until you reach the column for the salary nearest yours. If you are younger than 45, use the numbers for age 45, to provide a conservative estimate of benefits that will be available to you.

SOURCE: Social Security and author's estimates, based on previous years.

From *The Money Diet*, by Ginger Applegarth.

Benefit (line E) and Approximate Annual Pension and Other Income (line F) from Living Expenses at Retirement (line D). Write the answer on line G. Be careful when doing this calculation because some retirement projections from employers include Social Security benefits, and you have to make sure that you do not count them twice. This Additional Income You Will Need to Provide with Assets (line G) is the basis for figuring out how much money you will need on hand when you retire. Multiply your answer on line G by 16; write the result on line H. Why 16? If you were to retire today at age sixty-five and live for twenty years, you would need to have about $16 in the bank for every dollar of retirement income you need. This assumes that (1) inflation is just under 5 percent, (2) modest taxes would be due on your investment income, (3) you would use up all your money by age eighty-five, and (4) your annual living expenses will not exceed inflation but will keep pace with it.

If line G is a negative number, that's a *good* sign that you do not need additional income. Congratulations! You can stop here and not complete the rest of the charts. But be sure and reevaluate your situation every year so you can be aware if your situation changes.

Total up all your existing assets that can be used for retirement, and write the answer on line I. You have already listed your assets in your **Simplified Net Worth Statement** (page 22). Write them in the spaces provided for them at line I. Include your home equity (house value less any mortgages) only if you plan to sell your house at retirement. For Other Assets, list only those items that can be sold for cash at retirement. Subtract what you have (line I) from what you need (line H). If what you have is less than what you need, write the dollar amount of Your Asset Shortfall (line J). If you have more assets than the amount you need for retirement, write the surplus on line K.

Several years ago, a divorced plumber in his early sixties came to see me about retirement planning. When we reviewed Warren's expenses, we agreed that he would need about 80 percent of his current annual expenses of $24,000 once he retired, and that his expenses would probably increase with inflation every year. Warren anticipated receiving $10,000 in annual Society Security benefits once he retired. He also was entitled to a $3,000 pension per year from his union. We decided that Warren needed to come up with just under $100,000 to generate the $6,200 additional annual income he wanted. He already had about $60,000 in an IRA account and another $50,000 in savings accounts. Fortunately, Warren had just enough assets to meet his income need, in today's dollars; I told him, however, that for now up to half of his money needed to be invested in stock mutual funds so he would have some inflation protection. After all, his life expectancy was over twenty years!

You may have noticed that I keep saying "the amount that is required in today's dollars." We are assuming that Social Security benefits, pension income, and growth on your existing assets keep pace with inflation, so as your expenses go up, your income will too. This is why you need to start planning today for your future retirement.

As an example, let's assume Rick is about to retire today at age sixty-five and that he expects his living expenses to be $30,000 a year. Social Security pays $10,000, and his pension pays $10,000, so he has to come up with $10,000 on his own from his investments, IRAs and 401(k) plans. Rick expects that his living expenses will rise every year for the rest of his life (about twenty years), and he figures they will rise about 4 percent a year due to inflation. If the future unfolds exactly as Rick anticipates it will and inflation stays at 4 percent, Rick has *exactly* enough money on hand to carry him through those twenty years. He will have to use up some of his principal each year to live on and invest what's left to help pay for future years, and he will run out of money right around the time he dies. But let's further assume that inflation averages 5 percent a year instead of 4 percent. The result? Rick has to use up more of his principal every year than he anticipated, so he will probably run out of his own money well before the time he dies. He will have only his Social Security and pension income—a one-third reduction in Rick's standard of living. Inflation and how well your investments will do are the great unknowns of retirement planning. This is why we use "today's dollars"; we just can't predict the future, but we have to make *some* assumptions about it.

CUTTING THE SHORTFALL

■ Spend less at retirement.

If you have a retirement shortfall and are shocked by how big the shortfall is, you are not alone. What are some of the ways to cut your shortfall? First, you can decide that when you retire you will live on less than 80 percent of your current living expenses. When one of my clients saw that she would not have the money to live at 80 percent of her current expenses, she decided that, when the time comes, with careful economizing she could cut back to 70 percent of her pre-retirement expenses.

■ Save more before retirement.

The second way to cut your retirement shortfall is to save more. You still assume your expenses will be 80 percent of their pre-retirement level, but you make a commitment to save more in the meantime so you will have a bigger nest egg when you retire. When I ask clients whether they would prefer to cut back on spending so they can save more now or cut back on spending when they retire, clients often decide to save more now so they can live better later. (And since no one knows what the future may hold, this is a wise move anyway.) The added benefit of cutting back now is that you are developing self-discipline to live on less, so it will be easier to cut back even more at retirement if needed. It's like changing your eating habits a little at a time; a lot of small steps over time are much easier to do (and therefore you have a greater chance of success) than one drastic change all at once.

■ Invest better.

Investing for a higher rate of return is the third way to cut your shortfall. We talked about investing better in chapter 8, "Developing a Winning Investment Strategy." I counsel many financially savvy clients who have left their retirement plan money in fixed-income, low-return investments for years because they were worried about losing money or didn't feel they had the time to research investments. Your retirement money is usually a long-term investment; much of it should be in equities.

■ Generate additional income.

A fourth way to cut your shortfall is to start thinking now about how you might be able to bring in other sources of income at retirement. For example, you might decide to follow my lead and purchase a two-family house so that you can live in one part of the home, rent out the other, and have an ongoing and increasing stream of rental income at retirement.

■ Save smarter with retirement plans.

Finally, you can cut your shortfall by saving *smarter*; "saving smarter" means saving within retirement plans or other tax-deferred investments such as annuities whenever possible. Why does this matter? Simply put, the IRS gives most retirement plans tax-favored status. In many cases, your contributions are directly deducted from your taxable income so you do not have to pay taxes on money you put in your plans, and any tax on those contributions as well as on the growth and income they earn is deferred until you take the money out during retirement. Think of it as taking your retirement money and putting it in a separate account; further imagine that the IRS is pretending you never had the money until you start to take it out.

If you look at **Who Is Smarter?** (page 154) you can see what a good idea it is to invest in tax-deductible/tax-deferred retirement plans. Let's assume that you are brilliant with money and that I am stupid but that we are both in a 30 percent (federal and state combined) tax bracket and qualify to make tax-deductible retirement plan contributions. We are each planning to put $2,000 of our earned income into savings this year. You are brilliant and make a retirement plan contribution of $2,000; I am not brilliant and just use a regular savings account. Your $2,000 of income goes straight into your retirement plan without any taxes taken out, so your account has $2,000 in it. I, however, earn $2,000 of income and pay taxes of $600, so I have only $1,400 to put in the account this year. Next year, let's say that your $2,000 earns a 10 percent return; at the end of the first full year of investing, you have $2,200 in the bank. Even if my $1,400 earns a 10 percent return, however, and I have $140 of income, I have to pay taxes on the income, so I end up with only about $1,500 in the bank. In just one year, you are already ahead by about $700 *simply by putting your $2,000 into a retirement plan.* If you look at retirement funds as the ultimate tax shelter, you can see that you are automatically getting a 20 percent, 30 percent, or even 40 percent investment return in the first year simply because you did not have to pay taxes until years later when you take the money out.

Who Is Smarter?

$2,000 Income to Invest, 30% Tax Bracket

	Smart (in Retirement Plan)	Stupid (in a Regular Account)
Initial Investment	$2,000	$2,000
Less: Taxes Paid	0	600
	$2,000	$1,400
10% Earnings	$200	$140
Less: Taxes Paid	0	40
Total in Account at End of One Year	$2,200*	$1,500

* "Smart" will have to pay taxes on this money when he takes it out of the retirement plan, but by deferring taxes he can have much more money to invest until that time.

From The Money Diet, by Ginger Applegarth.

TYPES OF RETIREMENT PLANS

PENSION PLANS

There are various types of retirement plans, and you may actually be eligible for more than one at the same time. If you work for someone else, your employer may be contributing money to a standard pension plan every year. There are two basic types of pension plans. A *defined benefit* plan guarantees you a monthly income at retirement, and a *defined contribution* plan guarantees that the employer will put an amount equal to a certain percentage of your income into the retirement plan every year. Sometimes companies like to have more flexibility and do not want to contribute in years that are not profitable, so they may set up profit-sharing plans where a certain percentage of any annual profits are put in their retirement plans. The government limits the percentage of contributions on your behalf, but generally you or your employer cannot contribute more than $30,000 a year to all of your retirement plans combined.

401(K) AND 403(B) PLANS

As a result of corporate "down-sizing" and cost reductions, traditional pension plans are rapidly being replaced by retirement plans that require or encourage contributions on your part and allow you to make investment decisions about your money. The most common of these is the 401(k) plan, often called a thrift or savings plan. Each year you can contribute, before tax, the lesser of 15 percent of your income or about $9,500 (this dollar amount will increase every year with inflation, starting in 1995). With a typical 401(k) plan, your contributions may be matched to some extent by your employer, so that the more money you put in, the more money your employer puts in. Typically, you also have the right to make investment decisions about your money—the contributions from both you *and* your employer. A variation of the 401(k) plan for nonprofit organizations such as hospitals and universities is the 403(b) plan, or a tax-sheltered annuity. The 403(b) plan limits on your contributions are similar to those on the 401(k)—15 percent up to about $9,500, deducted directly from your pay. (Clients sometimes ask the significance of the numbers *401* and *403* and of the letters *k* or *b*. The numbers refer to sections of the Internal Revenue Code, and the letters refer to paragraphs in those sections.)

KEOGH AND SEP (SIMPLIFIED EMPLOYEE PENSION) PLANS

If you are self-employed, you can set up a Keogh Plan, which allows you each year to put into the plan the lesser of 25 percent of your income or $30,000. With a Simplified Employee Pension (SEP) plan, employers can contribute to their employees' IRA plans. Self-employed individuals can set up SEPs as well, but obviously they make all the contributions, since they are both employer and employee! The annual employer or self-employed contribution limit for a SEP is the lesser of 15 percent of your annual earnings or $30,000.

INDIVIDUAL RETIREMENT ACCOUNTS (IRAS)

The most well known and most often used retirement plan is the IRA, or Individual Retirement Account. Even if you participate in another retirement plan, chances are you can make at least a partially tax-deductible contribution to an IRA this year. In fact, half of all working Americans are eligible for a fully deductible IRA. The deadline is April 15 to make the previous year's deduction, so you usually hear a lot of advertising around that time of year. Here is how it works: Every working person can put the lesser of 100 percent of their earned income or $2,000 into an IRA. The contribution is tax-deductible as long as the worker or the spouse (if married) does not participate in any other retirement plan. And even if you do participate, you may still be able to make a tax-deductible IRA contribution, depending on your income level.

If you look at **Can You Take an IRA Deduction?** (page 157), you can determine whether or not you qualify. Let's assume that you do participate in another plan. If you are single and earn under $25,000, you can put $2,000 in an IRA and deduct the entire amount. If you earn between $25,000 and $35,000, the amount you can put in on a tax-deductible basis goes down. After $35,000, you cannot put in anything and deduct it if you are single. The same principle works if you are married (and filing jointly) and either you or your spouse participates in another retirement plan, except that your combined income has to be $40,000 before you lose the ability to each deduct a full $2,000 IRA contribution. The amount you can deduct goes down between $40,000 and $50,000, so that by the time you reach $50,000 of income, neither of you can deduct any of your contributions. If you are married and your spouse does not work, you can also make a tax-deductible contribution of $250 to a spousal IRA for that person as long as you don't participate in another plan and your income limits make you eligible for a deductible IRA too. In fact, you can split the money between each of your IRAs any way you like (such as 50/50) as long as no more than $2,000 goes to either account. The catch in determining deductibility is that you or your spouse

Can You Take an IRA Deduction?

1. If you (or your spouse, if married) do not participate in any other retirement plans, you can each deduct ALL of your contributions.

2. If you (or your spouse) are covered by another plan, here is the maximum amount you can each deduct, depending on your income.

Single Income	Joint Income	Maximum IRA Deduction
Up to $25,000	Up to $40,000	$2,000
26,000	41,000	1,800
27,000	42,000	1,600
28,000	43,000	1,400
29,000	44,000	1,200
30,000	45,000	1,000
31,000	46,000	800
32,000	47,000	600
33,000	48,000	400
34,000	49,000	200
35,000	50,000	0

SOURCE: Internal Revenue Service, Publication 590, 1992

From *The Money Diet*, by Ginger Applegarth.

(if you are married) cannot be a participant in any other retirement plan; you are a "participant" if you or your employer is setting aside money for you in any of the other plans mentioned here.

SOME ADVICE FOR RETIREMENT CONTRIBUTIONS

Of course, if you can afford to, you should try to put away more than $2,000 annually toward your retirement, so it is smart to learn which kinds of plans you can use to make tax-deductible contributions. Here are some general rules so that you can *minimize* your income taxes and *maximize* your retirement plan contributions and investment return.

First, go back and make a quick review of the worksheets covering your goals, your current net worth, and your spending and saving habits. Keep in mind that the Money Diet is a balance of all these different aspects of your financial life. But, more than any other goal, saving for retirement has a "built-in bonus" because of the tax deductions and tax deferral. That's why I recommend you put every penny you can live without in the next few years into retirement plans on a pre-tax basis. Figure out how much you could deduct on this year's tax return and make sure you put at least that much into a retirement plan this year.

Second, make your contributions as early in the year as possible so you get the benefit of tax-sheltered income and growth for as long as possible. For example, Cynthia has until April 15, 1996 (when she files her 1995 return), to make a $2,000 IRA contribution and deduct it for her 1995 tax return. She can put that $2,000 into her IRA anytime between January 1, 1994, and April 15, 1995—more than a year later. If she has the money on hand, why not make the contribution in January 1994? That way she can get fifteen more months of tax-sheltered growth and income on her money than if she waits until the last minute over a year later.

Third, make sure you contribute to any employer-matching plans *before* you put into plans that don't receive matching contributions. This only makes sense; if, for example, your employer agrees to put in $500 if you contribute $1,000 to your 401(k), it is much more advantageous to do that than to open up an IRA and put in $1,000 where there will be no matching contribution from your employer.

Fourth, keep in mind that conventional wisdom says you should be saving 5 to 10 percent of your income each year for retirement in order to ensure that you will have enough money to last as long as you live. Only rarely do I see clients who can meet their retirement goals without saving at a greater rate than they currently are saving. If need be, you should think about borrowing to make retirement plan contributions. Many people ask me if they should do this. My answer is that if you know you will be able to pay the money back within the next six to twelve months, it is definitely worth borrowing to make retirement plan contributions. The interest you pay on the borrowed money for those months will probably be more than offset by your tax savings. After all, you may be saving 20 or 30 or 40 percent in taxes! But you should also consider borrowing under other circumstances, even if it will take you longer to pay the loan back. This is where financial planning stops being "by the numbers" and starts operating based on your money behavior. Here's some advice that will no doubt be controversial, but I have seen it work time after time, so it's worth considering. If you have been having trouble saving, and you tend to run up balances on your credit cards, and you have not set aside anything for retirement, think about borrowing from any source—even if it is a high-interest-rate credit card—so that you will be able to put some money into a retirement plan this year and deduct it from your taxes. You will be starting to change your money behavior; by socking it away for retirement, you are saying that *you will not touch that money, period.* Many clients come to see me with $500 in their checking accounts and no savings—but with thousands of dollars in retirement plans. Somehow they manage to get by year after year without touching that retirement money; the tax penalty for doing so before age fifty-nine and a half is a great deterrent. That retirement plan money was "out of sight, out of mind," and somehow the clients learned to live without it. The trick is to commit yourself to paying off the loan taken from your credit card, line of credit, or other source. By vowing to pay off the credit card or other bill over a short period of time and by using up some of your credit limit, *you will be forced to spend less.* What you are doing, however, is crucial to your long-term financial well-being because you are changing your savings behavior. You will probably like the feeling of saving money, especially if you have never done so before, and the extra interest you may pay is well worth it if it helps you start to change your habits.

Finally, think about making a non-deductible IRA contribution. Even if you cannot deduct any of it, you can make a $2,000 contribution this year if you earned at least $2,000 (or the full amount of your income if you made less than $2,000). The advantage of a non-deductible IRA is that despite the fact that you cannot write off your contribution on your tax return, none of the income and growth in that IRA will be taxable until you reach retirement and start to take the money out.

The primary disadvantage to non-deductible contributions is that there is a substantial amount of bookkeeping involved; you have to split your IRAs between "deductible" and "non-deductible" categories and keep track of the contributions, earnings, and growth in each.

An alternative to a non-deductible IRA that avoids the bookkeeping problem but still keeps the investment earnings safe from taxes is to use an annuity. An annuity is a special type of investment to which you contribute money—either before taxes as part of an IRA (or other retirement plan), or after taxes if you are doing it on your own. Once the money is in the annuity, the income and growth is sheltered from tax until you take the money out at retirement. This is how an annuity acts like a non-deductible IRA, and you may find it easier to use.

RULES FOR RETIREMENT PLAN INVESTING

Because you will be investing your retirement plan money for a long time, you do not have to worry as much about short-term ups and downs of the stock market and interest rates. It's like a diet, where you stop focusing on your weight fluctuations day to day (because you know your weight will go up and down) and concentrate on how much you will lose in the long run.

You would think that because Americans are socking away retirement plan money in places where they cannot touch it, they would be investing for long-term growth, but much of the time this is just not the case. More and more retirement plans are requiring employees to make their own investment decisions, and part of the problem is the lack of employee education about those choices. According to one study, 19 percent of 401(k) participants received no investment education at all, and another 20 percent received investment education only when they first enrolled in these plans. The result? Seventy percent of all 401(k) investments are placed in fixed income—the *worst* way to go when it comes to long-term growth in your account! Of course, any savings account will do better than a poorly managed stock mutual fund that loses money over time. But remember my recommendation to diversify with mutual funds. Historically, over the long term, the stock category has far outperformed the fixed-income category of investments, so keep that in mind before you put all your retirement funds into CDs or savings accounts.

As we discussed in chapter 8, "Developing a Winning Investment Strategy," it is critical to look at your retirement plan investments within the context of all your other investments. After all, you can't just decide what to eat for dinner without taking into consideration what you've already had for breakfast, lunch, and between-meal snacks. If you look at how Americans have invested their IRA money from the period of 1981 to 1991, you see that they *are* starting to make better long-term investment decisions with their IRAs by putting their money in the stock market. In 1981, 54 percent of IRA money was in savings institutions, but by 1991 that percentage had dropped to 13 percent. We are getting the "invest for growth" message, but it took several years of record low interest rates to convince people to move their money out of savings accounts and CDs!

Here are some basic rules of successful retirement investing:

First, forget the rule of thumb that tells you to subtract your age from one hundred to arrive at the amount you should have invested in the stock market. That rule of thumb was devised when people were not living as long as they do now, and you need to make sure that you have as much inflation protection as possible. Second, people tend to look at their retirement plan accounts as being separate from their other investments, and they think these accounts require a separate investment strategy. *This is absolutely not true.* You need to look at all your investments together and make sure that your retirement plan funds are coordinated with all your other investments. For example, many people are tempted to put their $2,000 annual IRA money into a certificate of deposit or a bond fund. If you've put most of your other retirement and non-retirement investments in CDs, Treasury or savings bonds, or bond funds, and you have few or no stocks or stock mutual funds in your portfolio, you need to invest a large part of your retirement plan money in the stock market.

Third, do not ever put your retirement plan money into cash reserves or a money market fund thinking that you will invest it later. If you have to do so because there's no time before the deadline to research your investment options, *vow that you will move the money within the next thirty days.* In my experience, people take a long time to get around to making investment changes in their retirement plans. They tend to leave their contributions where they first put them and move them around less frequently than they do their other investments.

Fourth, your retirement plan money will probably stay where it is for the long term or at least until you are fifty-nine and a half—and often until you are seventy and a half or older and you *have* to start taking the money out. Therefore, plan to invest a substantial part of this money for long-term growth through stocks or stock mutual funds even when you are in your fifties and sixties. You want to focus on your long-term financial health, not just the next few months.

Fifth, especially with IRAs, where you are not making a large contribution, make sure you are paying as low a commission as possible—preferably none—because you want every single dollar you contribute to go directly into your investment. Also be careful of surrender charges if you decide to get out of an investment within the first few years. This is particularly true with annuities. Just because it says "no sales charge" on the brochure does not mean that you are going to avoid a penalty if you take your money out and put it somewhere else. You may well get charged a sales charge, except that it is called a *surrender* charge! For example, a client asked me to review the prospectus for an annuity that she had read about. If Edith had invested and then taken out her money just one year later, her annuity would have been assessed a 6 percent surrender charge—in her case, several thousand dollars.

If you have opened retirement accounts on your own, be aware that you are probably *not* stuck eternally with the bank, stock brokerage firm, or mutual fund company you originally chose. It is usually quite possible to move your IRA, Keogh, or SEP (if you are self-employed) money from one institution to another. The institution to which you are moving your retirement plan money will handle most of the paperwork for you, and you do not have to pay any taxes if the move is done correctly. Just make sure no transfer checks are made out to you directly.

RETIREMENT PLAN BENEFICIARY DESIGNATIONS

If you are married, for estate tax reasons you probably want your spouse to be listed as the primary beneficiary on your retirement plans. Otherwise, the day you die those proceeds will probably be entirely subject to income tax, so that if you have a $100,000 retirement plan, $30,000 or $40,000 might *immediately* disappear in taxes. By naming your spouse as the beneficiary, he has the option to roll this money into his own IRA and defer paying taxes until distributions are made. If you are divorced, I would suggest you immediately check to see who is listed as beneficiary on your plans. You may still have Spouse Number One listed, which could cause major problems if you have remarried and have assumed that everything would automatically go to Spouse Number Two.

RETIREMENT AND COMPETING NEEDS

But what do you do when you have competing goals, especially education versus retirement? More than any other area, retirement requires a "pact between the generations." You must secure for yourself a basic standard of retirement living before you invest a penny in college or other education for your children. When I say a basic standard of living, I am not talking about expensive boats, second homes, and global trips, but an income that will keep you from going into debt just to cover your basic needs (and loans are much harder to get once your earned income drops). You are not doing anyone any favors if you bankrupt your future in order to provide an expensive college education for your child or children, and then they have to turn around and support you.

A friend of mine who is a widow and could not fund both college and retirement had a long talk with her son before he went off to school. Their "pact between generations" was that Joanne would pay for her son's college tuition and that Jonathan would make modest monthly payments to her when she retired. Joanne also took out an inexpensive term insurance policy on Jonathan's life so that she would have a retirement income if he died before he was able to make these monthly payments to her. Rather then reduce their relationship to monetary terms, this understanding allowed Jonathan to enjoy his college years without the guilt of knowing every dollar he spent was coming out of his mother's retirement funds.

Recently, some new and creative methods for obtaining retirement income have been developed. For example, if you own your home, you may want to look into a reverse mortgage, where income is paid to you for as long as you live in your house. The amount of income is based on the value of your house. This payment can be a lump-sum payment, an ongoing monthly income, or a line of credit. The money has to be repaid only when you die or move out of your home (the lender takes the deed to the house and sells it). Reverse mortgages from reputable companies always have provisions that prevent you from owing more than the value of your home when it comes time to sell. Keep in mind, however, that interest rates usually are variable and that an increase in the interest rate might reduce your monthly payment. The FHA is insuring some of these loans, and as reverse mortgages become more and more popular they will be a readily available retirement income option for many people who find themselves house-rich and cash-poor as they grow older.

One of the most important tenets of the Money Diet is to take care of your own basic needs first. When you are receiving oxygen instructions on an airplane, you are always told to put the mask on your own face first before putting masks on your children so that you will be able to assist them without running out of air. This is true of retirement planning as well, because you must make sure you have a basic standard of living for yourself. With careful planning, you shouldn't have to forgo college educations for your children, but you may decide to forgo some of your expensive spending habits today so that you can have a comfortable retirement income tomorrow. The worst situation imaginable would be to reach retirement and end up in straitened circumstances that are also *straightened* circumstances, where you are straightening up to face the reality of an uncomfortably low income. Planning for a secure retirement means starting today with the Willpower Worksheets as motivation to make the changes required so that you can enjoy your later years. After all, with any good diet you have to sacrifice today to have a better tomorrow. That's exactly what *The Money Diet* proposes.

CHAPTER TEN

Planning for Your Children's Education

I MIGHT AS well warn you up front that some of my recommendations in this chapter will be controversial—in fact, I may even make an enemy or two. What I am about to say may sound antithetical to the American way of life, which for many years has been based on the idea of education at all costs. Many of us will be concerned about paying for college tuition during our lifetimes; with the American economy in its current state, education more and more is becoming a family affair with grandparents, aunts, uncles, and other relatives pooling their funds to help deserving children. The problem is that too many of us are jeopardizing our own retirement in order to put every penny we can toward college education. It's like "crash dieting" to meet some short-term goal, such as fitting into that bathing suit, but jeopardizing your long-term health in the process.

This is not the way many of us were raised. We learned (as we watched our parents do) to sacrifice almost anything to give our children a chance to get ahead with a college education. But college costs have risen much faster than inflation, and employers are not providing retirement plans that are as generous as they were in the past. The combination means that many of us may have to make a choice between paying for our children's education or paying for a secure retirement for ourselves. A 1993 survey showed that the median amount parents expect to spend on a child's college costs is almost $50,000. But the median amount these parents had saved was less than $6,000. Parents face the double whammy of funding education shortfalls and retirement shortfalls at the same time. The "education or retirement" dilemma is by far the most common financial planning issue clients ask me to help them address. We have already talked about how a good investment strategy is like a balanced diet; but in addition to balancing investments, there must also be the balancing of goals. Fortunately, for both retirement and education, there are government and private programs (Social Security; company pensions; and government, college, and special financial aid) to make the balancing a little easier.

During our lifetime, we have seen a fundamental shift in the way we view our generational responsibilities. As we talked about in the preface, our grandparents may have sacrificed everything so that our parents could have a better education and a better way of life. In return, our parents supported them in their old age. The problem is that this is just not happening anymore. I have seen too many retirement-age people in my office who have spent every penny on their children's private college and graduate school expenses, with disastrous financial and emotional results. The parents feel resentful and guilty because they have spent everything on their children, and the children feel resentful and guilty because they see their parents struggling at the same time they themselves are struggling. There can be bad feeling on all sides if the children do not (by their parents' standards) take full advantage of their college education or immediately get on a proven career track. Many times once education costs are over, parents realize exactly how little they have left to use for their own retirement and how early in their retirement they may have to turn to their children for help. I am not talking about giving up your responsibility to pay for your children's education so that you can have the vacation home or the boat, but *you must make sure that you will have a basic retirement income in addition to Social Security before you put a penny toward college.*

The problem is that education has become so costly that it is often one of the top three most expensive goals in our lifetime, along with retirement and buying a home. I know many people who end up paying more for their children's educations than they do for their homes. Education assistance programs often assume that we will use up virtually all our assets on our children. But smart individuals will protect themselves at the same time they are saving and investing for their children's education.

No matter what your financial situation is, planning for education costs *as a family* is an invaluable way to teach money values to your children. Your children should not expect you to foot the entire tuition bill yourself—if you do, you may *still* be paying off education loans after you retire! It only stands to reason that if a student knows he is paying for part of that 8 A.M. class or the books for the history project, he will take school more seriously, cut fewer classes, and get better grades.

I know a family of six—two parents and four children—who made it a *family* goal to provide a college education for whichever children wanted to go. In fact, in my opinion, these parents win top prize when it comes to raising kids with the right attitude about financial responsibility. From the time the children were young, they knew that they would be expected to work part-time through high school and contribute part of their college money themselves. In return, the parents sacrificed many of the comforts of the usual middle-class lifestyle because they made it a commitment to help out as much as they could. At the same time, these parents were aware that they needed to protect their own retirement, so they were making full contributions to all the retirement plans they could afford. When I asked them to sum up how they managed to accomplish all this, they said that they decided early on that there were two ways to pay for college: "You can either have your pain now or have it later." Remembering the time value of money, they said that the pain of scrimping and saving was easier before the college expenses hit because what they set aside would grow in value and the money set aside would have less overall impact on their standard of living. Also, they said it was easier to develop frugal spending habits early in their married life rather than later on. They figured that a dollar taken out of the budget when their children were very small would hurt less than the $1.50 or $2.00 (increased due to inflation) when the kids reached college age. Of the four children, three have graduated from college, and the fourth has a college education waiting for him when he is ready to go. The three who graduated from college took their studies very seriously, and it showed in their excellent grades.

Even wealthy families who can pay for college many times over, with money to spare, can use the education financing experience as a way to instill in their children a good work ethic and an understanding of the value of money. The worst thing you can do for your child is what, on the surface, looks like the *best* thing you can do—forking up every penny of tuition, room and board, books, and extras. When I hear a wealthy parent express concern about "making it too easy" for their offspring, I know this is a parent whose heart is in the right place when it comes to raising responsible children.

One couple in particular comes to mind, and their solution to the "problem" of having a lot of money (a problem we all would love to endure!) is one I have recommended over and over again to subsequent clients. This family's wealth was acquired not by inheritance but by business savvy and years of hard work. When it came time for college, Lenny and Jill paid for tuition, books, and other costs payable directly to the school, but the children were expected to work during the summers and holidays and use their earnings for any personal expenses. I'll never forget these parents marveling at the fact that their son made ATM withdrawals of $10 or $20 at a time to make his money last as long as possible (and always at ATMs that levied no service charges).

Another reason it is difficult to save for college is that these days we start paying for education costs for our children at a much younger age. For example, in 1970, only 37 percent of three- to five-year-olds were enrolled in nursery schools (which almost always charge tuition, some as high as $10,000 a year!). By 1991, that number had jumped to 56 percent. Moreover, with continuing concerns about public education, more and more parents are opting to use some of their valuable education dollars for private elementary and/or secondary school tuitions.

Like any other financial goal, planning for education costs is a multistep process. In chapter 4, "What's Your Financial 'Goal Weight'?," your amount for education may have been in the tens of thousands of dollars. The bad news is that those numbers are in *to-*

day's dollars; your actual need will probably increase with inflation (and then some). Most people cannot afford to "pay as you go" the year their child becomes a college freshman; how many of us have $15,000 or more left over after expenses, taxes, and loan payments? The way to meet any goal is to break it down into monthly or annual savings goals, and then to see what other scholarship, loan, and work-study funds may be available to reduce the amount you actually will have to provide.

HOW MUCH WILL COLLEGE COST?

Now that you are in a panic, relax! A substantial percentage of students receive financial aid in the form of grants, loans, and work-study earnings. Let's start by looking at how much college will likely cost in the future. The amounts are staggering. For the 1993–94 school year, the average cost for one year at a public college was $8,700, and the average private college cost was $17,800. According to conservative estimates, the total cost of a public four-year college education for a child born today will be over $100,000. Private college education weighs in at over $200,000, and an Ivy League degree has a projected price tag of $300,000 or more. These estimates include tuition, books, room and board, and other costs. **How Much Will College Cost?** (page 170) shows you what a college education is likely to cost your child by the time he or she is a freshman, assuming a 6 percent annual increase. The amounts are staggering. If you are starting from ground zero today with nothing set aside for education, these amounts look impossible to achieve. The good news is that you are likely to get a substantial amount of financial aid.

APPLYING FOR FINANCIAL AID

Let's first look at how much financial aid you are likely to get, based on today's rules (keep in mind that they are likely to change in the future). The federal program analysis to assess financial aid is done on a standardized basis nationwide using formulas that are specifically

How Much Will College Cost?*

(Rounded to the nearest $100)

Age in 1994	Year Entering College	Total Costs (Public)	Total Costs (Private)
Under 12 mo.	2012	$113,300	$236,200
1	2011	$106,900	$222,800
2	2010	$100,900	$210,200
3	2009	$95,200	$198,300
4	2008	$89,800	$187,100
5	2007	$84,700	$176,500
6	2006	$79,900	$166,500
7	2005	$75,400	$157,100
8	2004	$71,100	$148,200
9	2003	$67,100	$139,800
10	2002	$63,300	$131,900
11	2001	$59,700	$124,400
12	2000	$56,300	$117,400
13	1999	$53,100	$110,700
14	1998	$50,100	$104,500
15	1997	$47,300	$98,600
16	1996	$44,600	$93,000
17	1995	$42,100	$87,700

* Assumes 6% annual increase in total college costs; child enters college at age 18 and attends for 4 years. Based on costs for 1993–94 academic year.

From *The Money Diet*, by Ginger Applegarth.

regulated—believe it or not—by Congress. The Congressional Methodology (Need Analysis) developed in 1986 and the Federal Methodology enacted in 1993–94 use a uniform formula and set of factors for all college students in the United States. Usually taken into consideration are parental and child income, age of the parents, number of siblings, how many children are in college and dates of attendance, family medical costs, the value of certain assets, and an allowance for living expenses. (Depending on your income, some of this information is not required.) The good news here is that Congress recognizes how important it is to save for your own retirement; the value of your retirement plans is usually not included when considering how much money you must put toward your children's college education. In addition, the cash value of your life insurance, the value of any deferred annuities, the value of your home equity, personal property, and cars are not included in the Federal Methodology calculation.

You can qualify for federal grants, scholarships, or work-study programs by filling out forms and submitting them to organizations that process these forms and coordinate the calculation of your "Expected Family Contribution." To make the process simpler, you now have to complete only one form to be considered for federal aid, the Free Application for Federal Student Aid (FAFSA). The FAFSA is used at all the colleges to which your child is applying. The same form is often used for state-level aid and college-specific aid, discussed later in this chapter. Also, the U.S. Department of Education has made applying for federal aid simpler because families with adjusted gross incomes of $50,000 or less who do not file an IRS 1040 (in other words, they use the simplified income tax forms) do not have to provide details about all their assets.

There are a variety of types of financial aid. The best, of course, is a grant, because grants do not have to be repaid. Loans do have to be repaid, as do some scholarships. Work-study money may be available; in this case your child can get a job in college and earn money to put toward tuition or other expenses. These different types of aid may or may not be need-blind, depending on the type of aid you receive.

SOURCES OF FINANCIAL AID

There are four primary sources of financial aid—federal, state, college, and private. The federal aid programs are usually the most generous. **Federal Aid Programs for Education** (page 173) lists these federal programs. First, the federal Pell Grant is based solely on federal eligibility criteria and does not have to be repaid. If you are eligible for a federal Pell Grant, more is allocated if your child is a full-time student or is obtaining a more expensive education. For the 1993–94 school year the range of money available was between $400 and $2,300. In 1991, 23 percent of college freshman obtained federal Pell Grants; the average award in 1993 was $1,846.

The second type of financial aid is the federal Supplemental Educational Opportunity Grant (SEOG). This grant provides up to $4,000 a year and also does not have to be repaid. It is available only to undergraduates, and although the money comes mostly from the federal government, schools also must provide "matching" SEOG funds. The college determines which students receive SEOG money. Seven percent of college freshman received SEOGs in 1991, and the average award in 1993 was $730.

The third type of federal aid is a federal Perkins Loan, which provides up to $3,000 a year and is need-based for undergraduate or graduate students. This program used to be called the National Direct Student Loan Program (NDSL). In 1991, 7 percent of college students received federal Perkins Loans, with an average in 1993 of $1,261.

The fourth program is the Stafford Loan, formerly called the Guaranteed Student Loan Program (GSL). For many years prior to the 1993–94 academic year, federal Stafford Loans were based only on need. Now there are two "versions"—need-based (subsidized) and non-need-based (unsubsidized). In 1993, the average award was $2,959. In the 1993–94 school year, first-year students could receive up to $2,625, with second-year students receiving up to $3,500 and other students receiving up to $5,500. You have heard of another program called the Supplemental Loan for Students (SLS), which provided non-need-based loans totaling up to $20,000. Unfortunately, as of July 1, 1994, this program has been eliminated. I know of families who had counted on the SLS program as a loan source, and their education funding strategies had to be changed now that the program is no longer available. This is a good example of why you cannot count on any single financial aid program to pay your child's future college costs; chances are it may have very different rules (or be eliminated altogether) by the time you need it. The fifth type of federal aid available is the PLUS (Parent Loan for Undergraduate Students), which is available only to parents of undergraduates and provides funds up to the cost of attendance minus aid received each year.

Federal Aid Programs for Education

Name	Maximum Annual Amount*	Need Based?	Requires Repayment?
Pell Grant	$2,300	Yes	No
Supplemental Educational Opportunity Grant (SEOG)	$4,000	Yes	No
Perkins Loan	$3,000	Yes	Yes
Stafford Loan†	$2,625 (1st yr) $3,500 (2nd yr) $5,500 (other yrs)	Yes or No	Yes
PLUS	Total Education Cost Less Amount of Financial Aid Received	No	Yes
Work-Study Program	At Least Hourly Minimum Wage	Yes	No

* Amounts are for 1993–94 school year and are for undergraduate students.

† If you are at least a half-time student and demonstrate financial need, the government will pay interest while you are in school. For unsubsidized loans that are not need-based, you pay interest while in school.

From *The Money Diet*, by Ginger Applegarth.

Each of these loan programs has different repayment provisions; with most student loans (except PLUS), interest is paid by the government while the child is in school, and payments do not begin until a certain period of time after the child graduates. The interest rates are usually lower than those of regular unsecured loans. In addition to these federal grant and loan programs, there is the federal Work-Study Program in which 11 percent of college freshmen participated in 1991. These work-study jobs pay at least minimum wage, and often the jobs are related to the student's area of interest.

These federal programs are available regardless of the student's planned course of study, but other federal programs are tied to specific areas of interest. Most notably, a number of grants and loans are available if your child is planning to enter the medical profession. These include Health Education Assistance Loans (HEAL) for graduate students, Nursing Student Loans, Health Profession Student Loans (HPSL), and others.

■ State-level aid

The second source of financial aid available is through your child's state of residence. In 1991, 13 percent of college freshman took advantage of state aid programs. These are usually based on need and generally provide funds to attend in-state colleges and universities. Taking into consideration the fact that a sizable number of students may want to go to school out of state, some states now have reciprocal arrangements whereby state student-aid money can be used for an out-of-state school.

■ College-specific aid

The third source of financial aid you should investigate is aid that is specifically granted by the college or university your child wants to attend, paid for out of the college's endowment or other sources of revenue. In 1991, 22 percent of college freshman received grants from their colleges, and an additional 5 percent had college-funded loans.

■ Special programs

In addition to federal, state, and college financial aid programs, there are a variety of other private and group sources you may want to consider. These include special scholarships for veterans, children of union employees, merit-based scholarships, scholarship competitions, etc. Obviously, it is smart to apply for every program you can in the hopes that one source or school will give you a particularly outstanding deal.

Figuring out how much you will have to pay for your child's college education is confusing; your high school guidance counselor or university office of student financial aid can help by providing worksheets that estimate how much money you will be expected to contribute toward your child's college education. Some college admission offices may be able to help you. More precise figures will be available to you after you file the FAFSA; shortly after filing it, you will receive a Student Aid Report (SAR) that will list your Expected Family Contribution. This will enable you to reasonably determine your chances for getting federal financial aid.

COLLEGE FUNDING STRATEGIES

Some basic college funding strategies can help you come up with the amount of money you will have to provide yourself. Obviously, it is important to start saving early so that your investment dollars can grow as much as possible until they are needed. It is also important to invest *well* to maximize your return. Often, parents also try to take advantage of the following different strategies to maximize every investment dollar. And remember, you should approach college funding *as a family*; you should not have to shoulder the entire financial burden yourself.

INCOME-SHIFTING STRATEGIES

One of the most commonly used income tax strategies is to shift income from your higher tax bracket to your child's lower tax bracket.

You can do this with unearned (investment) or earned (job) income, and the rules differ depending both on the type of income and your child's age. The advantage is that this income may be taxed at a lower rate; nevertheless, the disadvantages may outweigh any advantage. First, when the time comes to apply for financial aid, 35 percent of your child's assets are assessed for college costs, but if you leave the money in your name, only 6 percent will be assessed. Second, once you take assets out of your name and put them in your child's name, you will ultimately lose control over those funds because your child can decide to use that money however he wants the day he legally becomes an adult. (This varies among states from age eighteen to twenty-one.) All those funds you scraped together for college may instead end up being "invested" in a new sports car or used to finance an extended period of unemployment. In most cases, I believe that these disadvantages far outweigh any small tax advantage you might receive unless you are extremely wealthy (in which case you would probably not qualify for most need-based aid anyway).

But if you are someone for whom income-shifting makes sense, remember these specific income-shifting strategies. First, you can shift *earned* income to your children by having them work in your family business so that they are earning a lower-taxed salary instead of having you earn that salary, which would be taxed at a higher rate, and then giving your children money for college. This can be especially valuable if your income and/or assets make you "too wealthy" by federal standards for financial aid because it won't matter that your child has substantial assets in his name. Second, you can shift *unearned* (primarily investment) income to your children by actually giving them ownership of assets. Each parent can give up to $10,000 a year to each child without incurring gift taxes (so you and your spouse can jointly give $20,000 to each child). Usually, this money is given to your children under either the Unified Gifts to Minors Act (UGMA) or the Unified Transfer to Minors Act (UTMA) and is placed in a custodial account. The UGMA is more restrictive than the UTMA; as we discussed before, these assets automatically become your child's when she reaches majority, and the kind of assets that can be shifted are very limited. With the UTMA, a wider array of assets can be transferred, including a business interest. Whoever is named custodian of the account is deemed to own it for estate tax purposes; this means the assets are taxed if the custodian dies before your child reaches majority age. All of these income-shifting strategies work between grandparents and grandchildren as well, but the older the custodian is, the more likely this last rule will become a problem. I have seen situations where grandparents made themselves custodians of accounts worth tens of thousands of dollars, all earmarked for their grandchildren. If they had died before the grandchildren became adults, these accounts would have shrunk by 40 percent or 50 percent or more due to federal and state estate taxes. (Yes, the IRS does get you when you die—more about planning for that later!)

How much income can be shifted to your child? You can, of course, shift as much income as you want, but depending on the age of your child that income may be taxed in two different ways. If your child is under the age of fourteen, there is no tax on the first $600 of his or her unearned income. The next $600 will be taxed at 15 percent, and after that your child's income will be taxed at *your* top tax rate (probably 28 percent or more). This is commonly referred to as the "kiddie tax." If your child is aged fourteen or over, his income will be taxed at 15 percent up to $17,850 of taxable income (earned or unearned). These amounts may change as tax laws are revised. The bottom line is that in most cases there is not much of a benefit to shifting investment income to a child under age fourteen. It is imperative that you know the tax consequences of shifting income to your child *before* you do so.

If you are shifting earned income (by paying your child to work for you), he can earn up to $3,000, pay no tax on that amount, and still be claimed as a dependent on your return. But, as I explained before, the problem is that on financial aid forms parents' assets are assessed at a 6 percent rate, but children's assets are assessed at a 35 percent rate. This often wipes out the advantage of shifting income into a child's lower tax bracket. I usually do not recommend that parents shift assets to their children unless the parents have no chance of obtaining financial aid.

What happens if you (or other relatives) have already put money in UGMA accounts for your child? Unfortunately, there is not much you can do but try to use these assets up first when college costs start.

As your children grow older, I also recommend that you start to tell them that you have set aside money for them that should be used only for college. This information serves two purposes. First, many children worry about whether or not the family will be able to afford college, and this will relieve some of those worries. Second, you want your child to get used to the idea that she has this sum of money in her name, and that it is to be used solely for education. After all, if you had suddenly discovered when you turned eighteen that you had $20,000 and you could use it however you wanted, wouldn't you have been the *least* bit tempted to take the money and run?

I have some clients who had already put substantial funds in UGMA accounts for their two children before they came to see me about their finances. Elizabeth and Michael had also asked their parents to contribute money to the children's accounts at birthdays and holidays in lieu of expensive gifts. (The grandparents, of course, also gave modest presents so their grandchildren would not feel completely deprived. After all, most children could care less about college at four, ten, or even older.) Instead of adding new gifts to the existing UGMA accounts, to which the children would have access at age eighteen, on my advice Elizabeth and Michael agreed to set up new accounts in their own names with the titles "Elizabeth—Robby's Education" and "Michael—Nathan's Education" (the titles were just so they could keep track of what money had been given for each child; the accounts are solely in the parents' names). These new accounts will always be in their control, and if financial aid rules stay the same, only 6 percent will be assessed for education instead of 35 percent if this family were to qualify for financial aid.

A more complicated way to shift assets to your child would be in a "minor's trust," or a 2503(c) trust; this is more complicated because you have to have a legal document drawn up, appoint a trustee, and file annual tax returns. In this case, the parent is usually the trustee and controls the money until age twenty-one. At that point, the child has a "window of opportunity" of thirty to sixty days during which he can demand that all the assets of the trust be distributed to him. If he does not take advantage of this window of opportunity, the trust continues until some age specified in the trust document when assets are distributed to the child (usually age twenty-five or so).

INVESTMENT STRATEGIES FOR EDUCATION

Coming up with an investment strategy for education is very similar in most respects to coming up with an investment strategy for any other goal. As we talked about in chapter 8, "Developing a Winning Investment Strategy," the longer you have before your child needs college money, the more risk you can afford to take and the greater the return you can hope to achieve. There are some specific educational investment strategies you may want to consider, however. The first is Series EE bonds, which are bought in the parent's name and specifically redeemed to pay for tuition. If you bought these bonds after 1990 and you cash them in to pay college tuition, the interest may be tax-free. In 1994, the interest was completely exempt from federal and state tax if a couple's adjusted gross income was $61,850 or less. The interest was partially deductible up to $91,850 adjusted gross income. After that, you lost the tax-free interest provision.

Another college-funding strategy that stockbrokers and financial planners often recommend is the purchase of zero coupon bonds because they often pay significantly higher interest than Series EE bonds. These are bought on a "deeply discounted basis," such as at 50 percent of the face amount. They do not pay interest along the way, but you can cash them at their maturity date for the face value. If it is a taxable zero coupon bond, you will pay taxes every year even though you do not get any interest in your pocket to do so. But if it is a non-taxable zero coupon bond (such as a municipal bond from your state), the interest is not taxable. Some zero coupon bonds have exotic names like CATS, STRIPS, TIGRs and LIONs, but the basic investment principle is the same.

Another investment option you may want to consider is a guaranteed tuition plan. Under these plans, which have recently been created by a number of states, you can pay years in advance for college tuition for any school in your state. One problem is that if your child does not choose to go to one of the colleges included in the program, you are charged a "penalty" and so may not get all the earnings on the money that you paid (although you always get your original investment back).

Another investment option for education is a special savings plan set up by a number of banks. The most popular is the CollegeSure CD, which is a CD that pays a floating rate of interest pegged to the cost increases of the 500 colleges that make up the Independent College 500 Index. You can find out about this by calling the College Savings Bank at 1-800-888-2723. Because you do not pay tax on the earnings until you actually take money out, annuities and other insurance products are additional investment options to consider (they have the additional advantage of being "invisible" investments when your Expected Family Contribution is calculated). An increase in the value of your annuities or an increase in your life insurance cash value is free from taxes until you take the money out. Permanent life insurance is often marketed as a way to save for college. But you should never buy permanent life insurance solely as an education-funding investment, because you are paying some hefty fees for insurance coverage, administrative costs, and probably commissions as well along the way.

PRIVATE SOURCES OF FINANCIAL AID

If you find that you need to borrow money to pay for college, it is smart to consider a home equity line or loan because the interest will probably be tax-deductible. Or you may be able to borrow from your retirement plans, so check the provisions carefully. Often you can borrow from the retirement plan on a tax-favored basis and essentially pay yourself back over time. Remember, however, always to make all possible tax-deductible contributions to your retirement plans before you set aside any money for college. You get a better rate of return on these contributions because you are not paying taxes along the way, and these retirement accounts are not considered available for federal (and sometimes other) college funding.

SOURCES OF FINANCIAL AID THROUGH THE ARMED SERVICES

These days, "the military way" can be a great opportunity to combine valuable job experience with guaranteed paid tuition for your child (or even you). A variety of programs are available that can even be tailored to your child's particular career interest and provide funding for college and beyond. Your local high school or college guidance office will have information on the various programs available; another source is a nearby recruiting office. With such a tight job market for twenty-somethings these days, experience in the specialized military jobs that teach skills needed for the civilian market can give your child a competitive edge.

FINANCIAL AID STRATEGIES

Let's suppose that your child is ready to go off to college, and you want to devise a financial aid strategy. If you have the ability to shift some of your income from one year to the next, try to minimize your income the year *before* your child starts college because that is usually the first year that is considered in determining awards. Also check your withholding to make sure you are not going to get a large tax refund, and avoid taking distributions from any pension plans. Anything that increases your income in one year may reduce your child's financial aid the next.

Your child should apply to a number of schools where he or she has a good chance of acceptance, and make sure that he or she applies to at least two schools that are very likely to offer acceptances, so that you can compare the aid packages—and perhaps bargain for a better deal. Public *and* private schools should be considered; a private college with a strong endowment may offer a larger financial aid package that leaves you with the same net cost as an equivalent public school. Be sure to complete every item on the financial aid forms and apply early.

Ideally, when the acceptance letters come pouring in, you can use the financial aid offers to bargain. About 10 percent of all college students contest their financial aid awards, and a significant proportion of those who do receive some kind of increase. This is not the time to be belligerent with the financial aid officer, but explain politely that another college has offered a much better financial package and ask if this particular college will match or exceed it. The more a college wants your child to enroll, the better the chances of success you will have with this strategy.

As we discussed earlier, another financial aid strategy is to use your children's assets to pay for college first because more of them are counted as usable for educational expenses. When your Expected Family Contribution is computed, some advisers recommend that you use your children's assets for expenses such as computers and transportation to and from school so that they are used up fairly early in the college program.

Planning for your child's college education is one of the most nerve-racking times of your financial life. The amounts you need to save are staggering, the financial aid process is sometimes bewilderingly complicated, and on top of that your child's educational future is at stake. No one ever wants to be in the position of denying a child's dream for a college education because of a lack of money, so it is smart to start saving as soon as possible. And if you do not have children of your own but are close to a relative's or friend's children, remember that non-parents are helping more and more with education costs. We all have a certain degree of responsibility to other family members, and who knows when we may need to rely on this future generation for our own financial stability sometime in the future? The goal is to provide a decent college education for your children at the same time you ensure that you will have a comfortable retirement. By taking advantage of all the financial aid sources available and being smart about the way you use them, you can maximize the chance that these competing goals can be reached.

CHAPTER ELEVEN

Buying and Selling
Your Home

ONE OF THE MOST satisfying moments in life is when you achieve a goal you have dreamed of and worked toward for years. It's like getting on the scale after months or even years of careful dieting and having the arrow stop at the weight you never thought you would be able to reach. The best part of any financial planner's job is when clients let us share in savoring their financial victories after we have spent so much time working with them to achieve their dreams.

About a year ago, my secretary answered what she initially thought was a breathless obscene phone call. It turned out to be a client breathless with excitement calling to share some thrilling news. Pam had just come back from the lawyer's office and was now the proud owner of a condominium. Many people would have looked at the reasonable price and shrugged this off as insignificant. But to Pam, it was the fulfillment of a dream of a lifetime.

To put this in perspective, let me backtrack a bit and explain exactly why buying a condominium was a watershed event in Pam's life. She was single, in her fifties, and had always wanted a place to call her own. So she had scrimped for years to save the down payment, until escalating real estate prices during the boom of the eighties seemed to put her dream out of reach forever. But miraculously, additional funds came her way, and the purchase was possible. When Pam combined her savings with her windfall, it was enough to buy a condo and decorate it exactly the way she had always hoped to. This also reinforces my earlier advice: Even if you do not think you can meet a goal, you should start saving for it—because you never know what can happen.

When Pam called and I picked up the telephone, I asked, "How do you feel now that your dream has come true?" Pam answered, "Ecstatic—and terrified!" That just about sums up what buying a house is like for most of us.

The ecstatic part makes sense. But why *terrified*? In two words, mortgage payments! Pam finally saw those monthly payments in black and white on the closing papers, looked at the tens of thousands of dollars of interest she would be paying, and saw how much she had already paid for up-front costs (points, taxes, etc.). This was enough to make her come down with a serious case of "buyer's remorse." (Keep this in mind if it happens to you before or after a house purchase; it is perfectly normal.)

Anyone who has recently bought or sold a house (I am using the term *house* generically to apply to any house, condominium, cooperative, multi-family unit, or other dwelling) or has even looked at house prices in the last ten years, knows that for most people buying a home represents the largest single investment they will ever make. If you look at the **Simplified Net Worth Statement** (page 22) from chapter 2, you may find that the value of your home is greater than the value of all your other assets combined. If you have bought and sold a few houses in your life and you add up the total value of all those houses, you may find this amounts to hundreds of thousands of dollars. Buying and selling houses is part of American life, and we often make these huge financial decisions on very short notice and without much independent advice. For my part, I am constantly amazed that so many people buy and sell houses worth hundreds of thousands of dollars yet do not consider themselves capable of making a decision about a $2,000 mutual fund purchase.

What role does real estate play in developing your Money Diet plan? First, owning a home is a goal of many Americans. Second, if you look at the impact that owning a house can have on your net worth (by looking at the net worth worksheets in chapter 2) or your annual expenses and savings (by looking at **Spending and Saving** in chapter 3), you see that home ownership affects your finances every day. In *The Money Diet*, I want to make sure that you maximize your chances of meeting all your goals. So in the development of your own Money Diet plan, it's important to figure out "how much" house you can buy without canceling out retirement, education, or new car. The ultimate plan is to buy smart when purchasing a house so you will have as much money as possible left over for your other goals. Even if you already own a home, I recommend reading this chapter. After all, the average American moves every six years, and if you are like most people you are occasionally tempted by "for sale" signs when you drive by. In fact, if you have already bought a house (or several), you can see how well your methods stack up—and you may be pleasantly surprised. Some of my recommendations may sound simplistic to you, but you would be amazed how easy it is to overpay in purchase price, closing costs, or interest charges or to just plain choose the wrong house to start with. When something as emotional as deciding on your future home is at stake, it is all too tempting to throw caution to the winds and end up with a purchase you love right now but may live to regret for many years to come. And if you are selling a home, this chapter will give you tips on doing so as well as a glimpse into the strategy of the opposing camp—potential buyers!

For many of us, the importance of housing runs in our genes. Our ancestors may have measured their family status by the amount of land they owned. The greatest shame was losing one's family estate. Unfortunately, many people got a taste of this in the last five years of the 1980s, when over 2 million houses were foreclosed on by mortgage lenders. A friend of mine went through this experience when he lost his job, and he said it was "the most horrible, worst public humiliation imaginable." Nick's only consolations were that he had lots of company, and that the conditions that caused this to happen weren't all under his control. Even now, if you look in the real estate pages of your Sunday paper, you are likely to see page after page of house auctions for owners whose dreams turned into nightmares.

Many of these sad real estate stories stem from old advice that people have considered sacred: first, to buy as much house as you can possibly afford because a house is such a good investment; and second, to offer the lowest down payment possible to maximize tax-deductible interest. What's wrong with the old advice? First, real estate's growth in value in the 1990s is not expected to match the growth of the 1980s, when median prices (and average mortgage payments) almost doubled. Second, many people don't end up being able to use the equity in their homes to meet other financial goals because to get their hands on their home equity they have to borrow against their homes or sell them altogether. Third, people often made very large down payments by using money from bank accounts and other liquid assets—money that would otherwise be available in an emergency and that produced income to boot. So what's my advice?

PART I:
BUYING A HOUSE

To buy . . .

I'll admit that houses are a wonderful thing—I have owned five myself, and I'm planning to live in my current one until they take me out feet first. It is great for the psyche to know that you own the place you live in (or at least you will when you pay off the mortgage), and it is a stabilizing force for children and other family members. You know that almost every dollar you spend to keep your home up will increase your comfort or pleasure and maybe even go back into your pocket in the form of increased property value. Historically, owning a house has been a good investment, as values have grown faster than inflation. And even though you may not anticipate selling your current home, you *do* have the option of selling it and moving to a smaller place or renting it if you need to free up cash. Finally, one of the last great federal (and usually state) tax deductions available to the American homeowner is mortgage interest and real estate taxes.

Even so, the IRS *does not* consider your personal residence an investment. This means that you cannot write off any losses you incur. (Of course, with typical IRS logic, at some point you *still* have to pay taxes on any gain!)

Recently, I counseled a client trying to decide whether to buy or rent. Frederick was newly divorced and could afford to buy, and I advised him to buy. Why? Frederick's children spent part of each week with him, and he wanted as much stability as possible for them. His tax bracket was high, and Frederick was very interested in using his spare time on home improvement projects, as he had always done in the past. For him buying made sense.

. . . Or not to buy?

The way money experts expect the real estate market to shape up through the 1990s, whether it is smart to buy just to "get into the market" as conventional wisdom mandated in the sixties, seventies, and eighties may depend on where you live. Sometimes it may be smarter to rent instead. Renting may be the preferred housing choice when you don't expect to live in a place for more than a few years. If you are in a low tax bracket (15 percent), the tax benefits of owning a house would not mean much of a tax savings for you. It may be that your part of the country has a glut of apartments available or that rent control is in effect, making rents a bargain. You may not be ready to make a commitment to home ownership yet; singles are marrying later (or not at all) and the average age of first-time homebuyers went up from 28.4 in 1985 to 31 in 1992. You may not have been able to scrape together a big enough down payment, or your income may be too low, or your credit history may be spotty (although I have some solutions to these problems later in the chapter). And finally, you may just not want the hassle and/or responsibility of home ownership, although a condominium (or cooperative in certain areas) may be an attractive alternative for you.

If you own a house and you are looking to buy a new one, *before* you get your heart set on buying, compare the costs of expanding your current home to meet your needs with the additional closing costs, moving expenses, broker's fees, redecorating and other costs you would incur by moving to a new home. I know from personal experience how easy it is to fall in love with a house and realize the *true* cost of buying it only when it is too late to back out. Years ago, when I was new to the Boston area, I fell in love with a Victorian house loaded with charm (which masked a load of problems). Most of the problems were discovered during the professional home inspection done prior to signing the purchase and sales agreement. But by then, I had already mentally picked out bedrooms for the kids and visualized how wonderful the Christmas tree would look in the bay window. I should have known better; after all, I had already bought and sold two properties at a profit. But I made the fatal mistake of believing it was the last house in the world for me—I absolutely *had* to own it. Thousands of dollars later, it did become the "last house" for me in a way—I vowed it would be the last house I would ever sink so much money into!

STEP 1: WHAT SIZE MORTGAGE AND DOWN PAYMENT?

The first step in buying a house is to figure how large a mortgage and down payment you can afford. Unfortunately, many people first decide where they want to live. My recommendation is to start by figuring out how much you can afford because doing so may make you downscale your dreams at once. Otherwise, you may get your hopes up and then be disappointed when you find you cannot afford to move to the town or neighborhood of your choice. (This seems to happen with my clients in Manhattan all the time, where a co-op apartment can cost $100,000 more than an identical apartment two blocks away.) In dieting terms, this is like deciding you want to weigh 130 pounds by the time your cousin gets married in two months—but you weigh 170 now. Even if you starve yourself in the meantime, you will not meet your goal. Why get your hopes up for nothing? It's better to make a realistic plan and lose *some* weight.

When buying a house (a purchase that is so large and such an emotional one) the worst thing would be to end up feeling you'd settled for less than you'd hoped for. You may find you can afford more than you thought you could, and you may then want to buy a bigger house or opt for a better location. But if it turns out that you can be happy with less house than you can actually afford, by all means do so; you can use the extra cash in your pocket every month, and you will not feel so house-poor. Do not plan to buy a house unless you'll be there at least five years because it probably will turn out to be a bad investment. By the time you pay the closing and moving costs and expose yourself to a potential drop in value, it could prove to be a very expensive mistake. After all, depending on your particular mortgage, it takes an average of four years to recoup your closing costs (including points) alone. The old days of buying a home and selling it a year later for a 20 percent profit are gone, at least for the time being.

■ Qualifying for a mortgage

Your local bank or mortgage company can usually "prequalify" you; this means that you give them all your financial information and they give you a letter showing how big a mortgage you can likely afford. This service is usually free and is a very useful negotiating tool when it comes time to make your bid (more about that later). In terms of affordability, most lenders use two ratios when determining how much money to lend. The general rule of thumb is that your total housing costs (mortgage payments and real estate taxes, homeowners insurance, and private mortgage insurance, if applicable) cannot be more than 28 percent of your combined gross monthly income from all sources. For "monthly income" you can include alimony and child support, but remember that you will be asked to show proof of the last few months' payments.

In addition to the 28 percent ratio, there is another ratio to worry about. Add your installment debt payments, student loans, and any other legal obligations such as alimony and child support to your proposed housing costs. This total cannot be more than 33 to 36 percent of your total income, depending on how large a down payment and mortgage plan you have. Banks will sometimes allow some percentage-point flexibility in the ratios if you have other things working for you (good credit or borrowing less than 90 percent of the

What Size Mortgage Payment Can You Afford?

Figuring Ratio One: Your Mortgage Alone

A. Total Monthly Income Before Taxes (Are You Over Your Head In Debt? p. 83, line B):	A.
Multiply by 0.28	× 0.28
B. Equals: Preliminary Maximum Mortgage Payment with Ratio One	B. =
C. Less: Estimated Monthly Real Estate Taxes/Homeowners Insurance Premiums*	C. −
D. Equals Your Maximum Monthly Mortgage Payment with Ratio One	D. =

Figuring Ratio Two: Your Mortgage Plus Other Fixed Monthly Payments

E. Your Current Non-Mortgage Monthly Debt Payments† (Your Current Debt Load, p. 75, line B)	E.
F. Plus: Your Current Monthly Legal Obligations (Where Does Your Money Go?, p. 59, Alimony and Child Support)	F. +
G. Equals: Total Current Monthly Fixed Payments	G. =
A. Total Monthly Income Before Taxes (see line A above)	A.
Multiply by 0.36	× 0.36
H. Equals: Preliminary Maximum Mortgage Payment with Ratio Two	H. =
G. Less: Total Current Monthly Fixed Payments (see line G above)	G. −
C. Less: Estimated Monthly Real Estate Taxes/Homeowners Insurance Premiums* (see line C above)	C. −
I. Equals: Your Maximum Mortgage Payment with Ratio Two	I. =

continued on next page

From *The Money Diet* by Ginger Applegarth.

What Size Mortgage Payment Can You Afford? (cont.)

Which Mortgage Amount Will You Qualify For?

D. Your Maximum Mortgage Payment with Ratio One (see line D above)	D.
I. Your Maximum Mortgage Payment with Ratio Two (see line I above)	I.
J. Maximum Monthly Payment You Will Qualify For (select the lower of line D and line I)	J.

* Your lender or broker can estimate this for you.

† Do not include mortgage payments or debt payments that will end in the next 10 months. If you currently own a home, this assumes you will pay off any existing mortgages by selling it. If you plan to keep your current home and buy a new one, add your current mortgage, real estate taxes, and homeowners insurance to line G.

Note: These ratios are generally used by mortgage lenders, but your lender may modify them based on your individual financial situation and its own lending procedures.

From *The Money Diet*, by Ginger Applegarth.

house value, for example). These rules are a little more strict than when I first started buying houses in 1975, largely because the real estate industry has learned from the foreclosures in the late 1980s that a tighter rein was needed. **What Size Mortgage Payment Can You Afford?** (above) helps you determine the mortgage you would likely qualify for. Percentage rules vary, so check with a local lender to find out what rules would apply to you. This worksheet walks you through the two ratios we just talked about so you can see how they apply to your own financial situation. At first it might seem intimidating, but the chart is easier than it looks, and you want to avoid the nightmare of house-hunting with a higher mortgage limit in mind than you might qualify for.

Start by writing down your total monthly income before taxes on line A of **What Size Mortgage Payment Can You Afford?** Multiply that amount by 0.28; the answer, on line B, is your Preliminary Maximum Monthly Mortgage Payment with Ratio One. Then subtract

Estimated Monthly Real Estate Taxes and Homeowners Insurance (your lender or broker can estimate this for you) on line C. Your answer, on line D, is the Maximum Monthly Mortgage Payment with Ratio One for which you would likely qualify.

Now it gets a little more complicated, because we have to take into account your other monthly debt payments, alimony/child support payments, and any other fixed payments to come up with Ratio Two. First, write down your Current Non-Mortgage Monthly Debt Payments on line E. You can find that information on line B of **Your Current Debt Load.** Do not include debts that will be repaid within the next ten months or your current mortgage payment if you will be selling this property when you buy your new house. Then, on line F, include your current monthly legal obligations, such as alimony and child support payments (which you wrote down in **Where Does Your Money Go?**). The total of E and F is G, your Total Current Monthly Fixed Payments.

To find out Ratio Two, multiply your Total Monthly Income Before Taxes (from line A) by 0.36 and write your answer on line H. Then subtract your total monthly fixed payments (from line G) and the estimated taxes and homeowners insurance premiums (from line C). The total, on line I, tells you the maximum mortgage you would qualify for under Ratio Two.

Now take a look at the figures you wrote down for Ratio One (line D) and Ratio Two (line I). Which monthly mortgage payment will you qualify for? The answer is the lower of the two amounts.

You may be wondering why lenders go to all the trouble of calculating out two different ratios. The reason is that so many of us are loaded down with credit card debt, student loans, and car payments when we go to apply for a mortgage. Let's say your household income is $3,200 a month and real estate taxes and house insurance will run $200 a month. If the lender just looked at these factors to figure out the amount to lend to you, you would qualify for a mortgage that has an $840 monthly payment. But what if you already have debts and other fixed payments such as child support that eat up $800 of your monthly income? If the lender didn't take those into consideration, you would both get in a financial jam rather quickly because every month you would have to shell out over half of your income (without even counting your income taxes!) before you would have even a penny to buy food and other basic necessities. You would end up defaulting on the mortgage, and the lender would get saddled with a house to sell.

The payment amount you just came up with is not cast in stone; these are guidelines that lenders use. Some lenders are stricter than others and a lot can depend on your own set of financial circumstances. One client with a good credit history but a new business and 10 percent down payment faced much stricter mortgage qualification rules than another who had 30 percent in cash to put down and had been in the same job for ten years.

Now that you know the maximum monthly mortgage payment for which you would qualify, it's time to figure out the size of the mortgage that produces this payment. At the top of **Total Monthly Mortgage Payment** (page 194) you will see how much the monthly payment (which includes principal and interest but not real estate taxes) would be for a $1,000 mortgage for thirty years at a variety of different interest rates. (You may decide to take a mortgage with a shorter term than thirty years, but your payments would be higher; here we are just figuring out the maximum mortgage you can afford.)

On line A, write the total monthly payment amount from **What Size Mortgage Payment Can You Afford?**, line J. Then, pick the interest rate nearest to the current rate in your area for a thirty-year mortgage. On line B, write down the monthly payment per thousand for that interest rate. Divide B by A, and your answer is C, your maximum mortgage amount (in thousands). Before you panic, keep in mind that many lenders can be somewhat flexible on the ratios.

Seeing how Ratio Two (which includes all your monthly obligations) works underscores the importance of reducing your credit card, auto, and other consumer debt before you get too far with your house search. I am often asked, "Should I pay off my consumer debt with some of my down payment money?" I recommend asking the lenders how much your monthly payments will go down for each $500 you pay off. For example, paying off $500 on an 18 percent credit card might reduce your monthly payment by $15. Then pay down *just enough* of your consumer debt to make sure you can qualify for the mortgage you want based on the ratios we discussed. Why

Total Monthly Mortgage Payment

Payments per $1,000 on a 30-year Fixed-Rate Mortgage
(includes principal and interest; does not include insurance or taxes)

Interest Rate	6%	6.5%	7%	7.5%	8%	8.5%	9%	9.5%	10%	10.5%	11%	11.5%	12%	12.5%	13%	13.5%
Total Monthly Payment	$6.00	6.33	6.65	7.00	7.34	7.70	8.05	8.42	8.78	9.15	9.52	9.91	10.29	10.68	11.06	11.46

EXAMPLE for $150,000 Mortgage at 10%

$$\underline{1317} \div \underline{8.78} = \underline{150}$$

Maximum Monthly Payment Amount ÷ Monthly Payment (per thousand) = Your Maximum Mortgage Amount (in thousands)

A.

$$\underline{\hspace{2cm}} \div \underline{\hspace{2cm}} = C.$$

Maximum Monthly Payment Amount
(What Size Mortgage Payment Can You Afford?, p. 190, line J) ÷ **Monthly Payment** (per thousand) (See chart above) = **Your Maximum Mortgage Amount** (in thousands)

just enough? You want to make sure you have enough cash on hand for closing costs, moving expenses, etc. The worst case is that the bank or mortgage company will approve your mortgage contingent on your paying off the debt, and at that time you can use up your cash if you have to. Also, if you wait until you can actually pay off *all* your consumer debt, house prices and/or mortgage rates may go up. Ironically, being conservative and signing up for faster amortization loans (such as a fifteen-year mortgage instead of a thirty-year mortgage) may work *against* you because the shorter the time period, the higher your monthly payment will be and the more difficulty you will have meeting these ratios. I counsel clients to ask their lenders to calculate how much they will be able to borrow under different scenarios (thirty-year versus fifteen, fixed versus variable).

■ Deciding on a down payment

The second part of the affordability question is figuring out how much money you have for a down payment (or want to use if you are in such a fortunate financial situation). If you do not have a 20 percent down payment, the standard amount, you might be able to go as low as 5 percent—or even 0 percent if you are a veteran! Your down payment requirements depend on which mortgage program you are hoping to use. With a regular mortgage from a bank or mortgage company, the standard down payment is at least 20 percent of the purchase price of the house. If you go below 20 percent, you have to pay private mortgage insurance (PMI), to cover the mortgage if you default. These are up-front and ongoing insurance costs; the lower the down payment percentage, the higher the premiums. The biggest premium jump is between a 10 percent and 5 percent down payment. But there is only a small advantage to putting down 15 percent instead of 10 percent. Premiums get higher as your down payment gets lower and when you use an adjustable rate mortgage. Private mortgage insurance is *not* tax-deductible, and it can be expensive, so put 20 percent down if you can. Generally, you have to put at least 5 percent of the purchase price down.

The other two loan programs for mortgages that might be available to you are through the government. These programs are run by the Federal Housing Administration (FHA) and Department of Veterans Affairs (VA). Especially if you are a first-time home buyer, you may want to look into them because the down payment requirements are lower than requirements for conventional (non-VA or FHA) loans. With FHA loans, you might even be able to put down less than 5 percent, but you have to pay a mortgage insurance premium. The problem with FHA loans (in addition to having to meet the ratios discussed earlier) is that they can be used only to buy homes whose values are under certain amounts that vary by area of the country. For many first-time homebuyers the least expensive homes in their areas may be tens of thousands of dollars over the limit. If you qualify for an FHA loan, you may even be able to finance some of the closing costs with FHA loans, but the rules can get complicated, so ask your broker for help in deciphering them. VA loans are great because you do not have to make any down payment and usually the loans can be assumed (taken over by the person who buys your house) when you sell. To qualify for a VA loan you have to be a veteran or currently in the military; being in the reserves does not count. Unfortunately, sellers generally do not like to deal with buyers who are using FHA or VA loans because the process takes longer, and there are more rules and more paperwork. Also, with a VA loan the lender cannot charge the home buyer more than one point. (Points are additional up-front interest charges added by the lender that you have to pay if you want a lower interest rate or want to put down a small down payment. One point equals 1 percent of the mortgage; one point on a $100,000 mortgage would be $1,000.) So with a VA loan the seller may have to pick up any extra points and closing costs. We'll return to points later in this chapter. The only good news about the one-point-per-buyer limit is that the IRS has finally ruled that for all loans, seller-paid points are deductible for the buyers.

If you can qualify under these government programs or you are willing to pay private mortgage insurance, you will be able to make a smaller down payment. This means that some of the money you have been able to save for a down payment can be used for moving expenses, closing costs, etc. Many people, however, just do not have money for a down payment at all or cannot afford the mortgage payments that a 5 percent (or smaller) down payment requires. Luckily, there are a variety of ways to come up with a down payment. A family member may be willing to give you money for a down payment, although to qualify for a mortgage you usually have to prove that you have come up with at least 5 percent of the purchase price yourself. If you have the down payment but cannot afford the monthly payments, perhaps a parent or other relative will co-sign with you. Her finances will then be taken into account when the bank evaluates your loan application. Although finding a cosigner is a win-win situation for the homebuyer, the cosigner must realize up front that her assets will be on the line and that late payments or defaults will go on her credit record as well. During the period of soaring real estate prices in the eighties, several of my clients offered to cosign just to get their kids in the real estate market before houses would become completely unaffordable for young adults just starting out, and one of those children has had to struggle to make payments on time to avoid blemishes on his parents' credit record.

If you are short in the down payment department, another option is to find a seller who is desperate to unload a house. To give you the down payment you need, the seller may be willing to "take back" a second mortgage (in other words, lend you the money himself) to supplement your part of the down payment so you can qualify with the bank or mortgage company.

Remember, the Money Diet is all about balancing what you have with what you need. The more you put down on a house, the less cash you will have for other goals. Whenever you tie up money in a house, you are taking it away from income-producing liquid investments and putting it into a non-liquid asset. Your house is not only non-income-producing, but you have to spend some of your income every month on mortgage payments! I usually recommend that clients make the lowest down payment they feel comfortable with, as long as they can avoid having to buy private mortgage insurance. Also consider whether you are interested in and skillful at investing the money you would have if you put down less money than you are able to, as well as the changing tax laws (e.g., the limit on home interest deductibility). Remember that even if you use a low down payment, you always have the option of making extra payments earmarked to reduce your loan balance, although these extra payments may not reduce your required regular monthly payment. Clients often ask about paying down their mortgages. Edward asked whether he should use his $15,000 bonus to do so. When I reminded him that two of his daughters would enter college in the next four years, he decided maybe he'd better hold on to that money after all!

When you're deciding on a down payment amount, your psychological comfort level is also important. I recently went through this with a couple who were purchasing a very expensive home and had enough money on hand to make a 50 percent down payment. Financially, the best advice for Stuart and Jennifer would probably have been to put down 20 percent, take a mortgage for 80 percent of the house's value, and invest the rest of their money elsewhere because they are in a very high tax bracket, have few other tax deductions, and are facing large education bills. As an added incentive, mortgage interest rates were at a twenty-year low. Psychologically, however, Stuart in particular did not want to make the large mortgage payment required every month if he borrowed that 80 percent. The compromise? More down (40 percent), less borrowed (60 percent). This illustrates a crucial element of financial planning. Financial advice that looks good on paper may not be right for you because every situation is unique. If you have no compelling financial need to take an action that you know will add a lot of stress to your life, *it is just not worth it.* Of course most financial decisions add some temporary stress to your life because they involve changing the way you are doing things. But if you are contemplating a financial decision that will add long-term stress to your life, and you will be all right financially if you do not take action, *don't.*

STEP 2: WHERE TO LIVE?

Once you know how much you can afford, half the battle is over. Why? In my experience, homebuyers hate this "number crunching"; it is confusing, difficult, and the answer you get may be unpleasant. The rest of the homebuying process is much more fun because the dreaming can begin.

Now you can figure out where you want to live. If you have lived in an area for a long time and want to stay there, this is obviously much easier than starting someplace new. I often recommend that clients moving to a new city rent for a few months to give themselves time to scope out various neighborhoods. Of course, a good realtor can offer invaluable help as well. You may think you want the excitement of living in the heart of the city until you rent there for a few months and find the noise and crime rate are more than you can bear. Or you may long for the peace and quiet of the suburbs, but soon find you resent being isolated and feel as if you are in the middle of nowhere. You have to consider many factors when choosing a neighborhood, but the most important one is to buy in the best location you can afford *even* if it means less house. This is the best way to protect your house investment.

The general rule of thumb is not to buy the best house in the neighborhood. Be wary of a situation where a house or even a whole neighborhood has been fixed up so that it is substantially nicer than all the others surrounding it. Less expensive homes surrounding a gorgeous house will usually bring the value of the house down. The same house surrounded by even fancier showcase homes will have a higher value. In terms of getting the best value, you are better off being in the average house on the block surrounded by nice houses than in the showcase house. A good idea is to look for borderline neighborhoods where you see home improvement projects going on and young professionals moving in. Chances are that home prices in these areas will surge and you may get the last "deal" in the neighborhood. The first house I bought, in Atlanta, was in just such a neighborhood. Now I hear this is a trendy section of town and houses have quadrupled in value in the last fifteen years. (In fact, hearing this makes me wish I had held on to that house, but as *The Money Diet* says, it doesn't do any good to dwell on past mistakes.)

What other factors should you consider when house hunting? Proximity to work is a big one, since commuting costs, lost time, and added stress can make you regret buying even the nicest house. Commuting two hours each way to work makes any quality of life during the week virtually impossible. Schools are another big issue, even if you do not have children and do not plan to have any. Why? Because when you sell, potential buyers may be concerned about schools. A good way to evaluate schools is to go to the local library and find out the results of the latest school surveys (usually printed in a local newspaper or magazine and also available in state publications). Check the school district's expenditures per pupil, standardized test scores, and the percentage of students who go on to college. If none of the public schools seem acceptable, your only alternative if you have children is to buy in a neighborhood and plan to send your children to private schools (and then do not forget to add tuition to your monthly budget).

With so many cities cutting back on their services, you should consider how much you may have to pay out of pocket for garbage pickup and other services. Sometimes these charges are rolled into your property taxes; in other cases, you pay for them separately. If you would have to pay $1,000 a year in town A for garbage pickup, dump fees, and whatnot (the norm in my town), you can buy a house in town B that is at least $10,000 more expensive (if these services are provided) and end up with about the same housing costs (and the additional mortgage interest is tax-deductible as well).

You will find that it is easier to obtain financing in some areas than in others. Buying in less stable areas may require a higher down payment, and some towns even offer low-cost financing through special programs (call your state housing agency). This requirement for higher down payments often applies to condos and co-ops, because co-op boards can force all new buyers to pay large down payments and banks may require higher down payments for condominiums in urban areas or in developments with a substantial number of vacant units. A friend of mine recently got a real bargain in Manhattan because the co-op board insisted on a 33 percent down payment, and he was the only bidder in months who had the money on hand to meet this requirement.

It is always important to find out whether houses have held their value. Brokers are not always the most reliable sources for this information because they may be operating on hearsay, and they want you to buy in their area. Check in your local library for old surveys published in the newspaper that report the increase (or decrease) in average sales prices of houses. Your state or local real estate board would also be likely to have this information. Remember, do not focus just on what has happened over the last two or three years, but on trends over the last ten or twenty years as well.

STEP 3: WHAT HOUSE FEATURES ARE IMPORTANT?

In addition to location and house values, think about what kind and style of house is best for you. These days many people wonder whether to buy a house or a condo, especially if they own second homes (see chapter 12, "Paying for Big-Ticket Items," for a discussion of second homes). When I was growing up, it seemed as if everyone lived in one-family houses. Now there are condos, co-ops, cluster houses, detached houses—and all are valid choices. Many builders are now accommodating different lifestyles and building new homes with unfinished spaces for extra rooms, distinct areas that can be made into separate in-law apartments or office suites, or even wall units with pull-down beds.

One big decision is how many bedrooms to buy. If possible, buy a house with an extra bedroom because it can be turned into an office, guest room, or bedroom for a new member of the family. Brokers have told me that the primary reason apart from relocation most people move or add onto their homes is the need for an extra bedroom.

You may be attracted to a certain type of house from the outside, but on the inside each one has advantages and drawbacks. For example, a living room with a loft ceiling looks wonderful, but you lose the space above it for a bedroom or bathroom. Does your family like to be spread out or close together? Do you want distance between yourself and your kids' stereos? Think about what will work best for your needs. And don't be put off just because you find a house's exterior or interior unattractive; use your imagination and think of what a coat of paint, window boxes, and better lighting can do.

One of the big traps that homebuyers fall into is falling in love with the little things about a house (remember my Victorian money pit?). They love the kitchen cabinets, the fireplace, or the wood paneling and realize too late that they spent too much or bought the wrong house. These buyers probably could have had any of these details installed in other, more suitable houses but thought the cost of doing so would be too high. If you fall in love with a house even though it has a major drawback such as price, layout, or repair problems, try to figure out exactly what it is that has captured your fancy. Then ask your broker and a local contractor (your realtor can suggest someone) how much it would cost to add those features to a house. A knowledgeable local building-supply salesperson can also be helpful here if you make it clear up front that you are only looking for ballpark numbers.

After you've considered your ideal price, location, type of home, and style, make a list categorizing features into "absolute must," "like to have," "prefer not to have," "absolutely not." **House Features** (page 203) gives you space to make this list. Try to keep the entries in the "absolute" columns to a minimum. The less flexibility you allow yourself, the harder it will be to find a house that's acceptable and to bargain on price. Realtors tell me that first-time homebuyers often insist on a fireplace and hardwood floors. Keep in mind that many "Absolute Musts" can be added to houses and many "Absolutely Nots" can be removed from them.

STEP 4: USE A BROKER OR GO IT ALONE?

Now it is time to decide whether to use a broker or to try to buy on your own. If you are a first-time buyer, I generally recommend you use a broker. If you are an experienced homebuyer, you may want to try purchasing on your own if you find a house that is for sale by the owner. Choosing a broker can be daunting because of the sheer numbers of brokers in most areas today. Real estate brokers are commissioned salespeople who handle the transactions of buying and selling homes. Normally the seller pays for the broker's commission out of his or her sales price, so even if a broker is showing you around, remember that he or she is *working for the seller!* For this reason, when you are in the process of buying a house you should *never* tell your broker how high you can go because your broker is *required* to tell the seller. I found this out the hard way a number of years ago when,

House Features

Absolute Must	Like to Have	Prefer Not	Absolutely Not

Examples: Fireplace, 3 bedrooms, 2 bathrooms, updated kitchen, hardwood floors, ample closet space, X town, Y neighborhood, quiet street, air conditioning, fenced yard, one story, pool, deck, patio, wall-to-wall carpeting, modern design, corner lot, attic, basement, expandable space, etc.

From *The Money Diet*, by Ginger Applegarth.

after negotiating back and forth for two weeks, the seller "miraculously" (or so I thought at the time!) gave a final offer that was exactly what I had told my broker was my limit. In fact, "buyers'
brokers" are becoming more prevalent because they represent the
buyer's interest in the real estate negotiation transaction. You can find
the names of buyers' brokers in your area by looking in the Yellow
Pages or calling your local realtors' association.

Owners usually sell their houses with brokers who participate in
Multiple Listing Service. When a house is listed in MLS, any other
broker can show it, but the listing broker coordinates the showing, handles the negotiation, etc. In some areas of the country, video
MLS-type services have sprung up that allow you to "tour" hundreds of homes while sitting in the video company's office. Also check
your local TV listings; TV home-tour shows can often be found on
weekends.

The total sales commission is usually the same whether two brokers are involved (the buyer's and the seller's) or if only the seller's
broker is involved. When a person puts his house on the market, he
usually lists it with one broker who has the option to sell it alone or
to sell it to the customer of another broker. They then split the commissions. If you buy straight from the selling broker, that broker gets
it all. The commission on buying and selling houses is usually between 5 and 7 percent; sometimes this is negotiable, so it never hurts
to bring it up. The commission is usually split equally between the
two brokers' offices, and each broker gets a portion of that. When
choosing a broker, ask your friends to find out who has had good experiences with their brokers. Also look through the real estate listing
in the Sunday paper; if you see an individual broker's name listed in
many ads, you probably have a good salesperson on your hands. Brokers tell me, however, that you should check out what the broker's
normal price range is; if you want to buy a $100,000 house and the
broker usually handles seven-figure properties, you may not get much
attention.

Training for brokers involves a state licensing course, supple-
mented in many cases by some basic training provided by the broker's
firm. Pick someone with several years of experience, who has a good
sales record. It is also important to pick someone you do not feel is

manipulating you or pressuring you. You are making a very emotional decision involving tens of thousands of dollars; you need to work with someone who will help you think through the issues and crunch the numbers, and then leave you alone to make up your own mind. (Chapter 16, "Choosing Your Financial Advisers," deals with this in more detail.) Find out the kind of clients your potential broker deals with. And by all means tell a broker you are serious about buying a house and give him or her a time frame in which you plan to buy. Brokers are inundated with phone calls from "Sunday shoppers," and you are more likely to get the attention your deserve if you show that you are serious. I recommend choosing a broker and sticking with that person. I do not think it is fair to see houses with several different brokers in a small town or neighborhood, although you should feel free to go to open houses on your own. You can wind up in the middle of a messy battle if two brokers show you the same house and you end up wanting to buy it. Your broker can also help you get a prequalification letter from a lender and help you figure out how much you can afford.

STEP 5: HOW TO NEGOTIATE THE PURCHASE PRICE?

Once you have found the house you want, how do you negotiate? General advice (such as "Do not ever offer the full asking price") is almost impossible to give. Every situation is different, and when you are negotiating you must consider how active the market is, how long the house has been on the market, and how fairly it is priced. For example, if the house has been on the market only one day, the seller has two offers, it's exactly what you are looking for, and the house is a good value, maybe you *should* offer the asking price (or even a small premium if need be). I know of a recent house sale where every bid received on the first day (and there were four of them) was *above* the asking price! This kind of scenario begs the question of whether the house was priced too low to start with.

To help you determine a house's value to you, make a list of the positives and negatives, checking this house's characteristics against the **House Features** worksheet you already filled out. Definitely look at the house at least twice, once in the daytime and once at night. Imagine what the house would be like in different seasons as well (such as what the views will be when there are no leaves on the trees). Think about how long you could possibly live in the house and if it can be expanded if needed. An experienced broker can be helpful. True, the broker works for the seller, but she also wants the sale *now* so she can get on to other prospective customers. You can be sure that the broker will be pressuring the seller to take advantage of an offer in hand instead of waiting for some unknown buyer to come along.

One rule that *does* hold is that your first offer should never be the last offer you're prepared to make unless you are in danger of losing to another bidder. After all, you have little to lose if you start with a low offer because you can always bring the price up if necessary. In fact, most first-time buyers I know think that they overpaid for their houses and that they did not negotiate as well as they could have. When you make the offer, it usually should expire soon—sometimes within twenty-four or forty-eight hours. Otherwise the seller has no incentive to say yes and can wait for other buyers to top your offer. Before you make your offer, it is always helpful to determine how anxious the seller will be to reach an agreement, so find out how long the property has been on the market, what if any other offers have been rejected, and whether the seller has already purchased another house. The worst situation you can face as a buyer is one where the seller has no incentive to bargain.

When making an offer, a good rule of thumb is to start at 10 percent below the asking price and come up as the seller counteroffers. I am convinced that my most recent real estate purchase was successful because I started by offering 20 percent less than the asking price on a house that had already been on the market for several months. I then persistently inched my way up by countering and countering and countering. But *to use this strategy you must be prepared to lose the house.* And if you still find yourself at an impasse with the seller, ask the brokers if they will reduce their commissions so the seller will end up with more money in hand.

Be sure you make clear in writing that your offer is good only if the house passes inspection. Usually you choose the house inspector and this is done at your expense. Your broker may recommend inspectors; make sure whichever inspector you choose belongs to the ASHI (American Society of Home Inspectors). The Yellow Pages also has listings under Home Inspectors. Follow the inspector around the house and take copious notes; you should also insist on a written report. A radon inspection may be initiated (the testing unit must be exposed to air and then the unit is mailed in later). Depending on what problems are found, you may decide to back out of the deal altogether, insist that certain problems be fixed by the owners before the closing, try to negotiate that the cost of repairs will be deducted from the house price or split with the owners, or accept the fact that you will have to pay them yourself. Be realistic in any of these strategies; no house is problem-free, and the older the house, the more problems you can expect. In certain parts of the country you will also want to bring in a termite inspector and/or lead paint inspector, depending on state laws.

STEP 6: HOW TO APPLY FOR THE MORTGAGE?

Once your offer has been accepted, it is time to look at financing. With fluctuations in the interest rates and the proliferation of mortgage plans, it's no wonder people get so confused about which mortgage is right for them. I recommend when you shop for a mortgage that you consider applying through at least two or maybe even three different sources. These might include a bank and a mortgage company. You usually have to pay an application fee for each source, but each lender handles unusual situations differently, so these extra costs may be worth it if

- you are purchasing an older home or a home that needs a lot of work, or
- you have an unusual credit situation, or
- you are planning to make a low down payment.

Another option in many areas of the country is to use a mortgage broker. A mortgage broker shops a variety of sources for you, and in many cases the broker's fee ends up being paid by the lender as an incentive to send business the lender's way. You may have to pay a fee up front, but you may recoup this cost in the form of lower interest rates if the mortgage broker negotiated a lower interest rate or lower closing costs because the broker places a large volume of mortgages with that lender. More and more, I recommend that clients in large cities use mortgage brokers because there may be dozens of lenders and it is difficult for the buyer to know which have the best deals.

Once you have applied for a mortgage, you usually have a short period of time to decide whether you want a fixed or a variable mortgage. With a fixed-rate mortgage, the interest rate stays the same for the life of the loan; with a variable-rate mortgage, the rate is adjusted periodically (usually every one, three, or five years) according to some standard or "benchmark" such as the rate on new U.S. Treasury bills at those times. Here is where the mortgage lender is key. Rates can vary greatly; they can even vary a lot from one day to the next with the same mortgage lender. What are the risks you take? With a fixed-rate mortgage, you take the risk that the rates will drop and you would have been better off with a variable rate. With a variable-rate mortgage, you take the risk that the rates will go up and you have not guaranteed yourself a lower rate.

If you do decide to go with a variable-rate mortgage, be sure to check on how long the rate is guaranteed, or "locked in," what the rate is based on, and what the maximum lifetime rate is. I usually recommend that inexperienced homebuyers avoid one-year "come-on" variable-rate mortgages: This type of mortgage is an enticement to get you to buy a house; then when the rate automatically jumps 2 or 3 percent, it is often quite painful for the new homeowner. If the only way you can qualify for a mortgage is by taking a low one-year rate, how will you be able to afford your payments when your rate goes up in twelve months (as it almost always will, because the one-year rate is artificially low)? I usually recommend a three- to five-year variable mortgage if you are going to use the variable rate. In general, if you plan to stay in a house fewer than five years or if you plan to refinance in fewer than five years, a variable rate makes sense unless you expect interest rates to skyrocket. In most other cases, a fixed rate is a better bet. With the three- or five-year variable rate, you will have three or five years to get used to the house, and you will probably have some idea how long you want to stay there. Also, by locking in the monthly payments for three to five years, you will have no sudden surprises. The problem is that with such a short period of ownership, if you do in fact own the house for only three or five years, you run the risk of your house decreasing in value or increasing in value so little that you cannot recoup closing and moving costs, etc.

Before you choose a three- to five-year variable mortgage, find out what the interest rate ceiling (the top rate possible over the life of the loan) is for a one-year variable. If the one-year ceiling is much lower and you plan to stay put, choosing the one-year rate may in fact make sense. Faced with interest rates that were so low they would almost certainly go up substantially, one client took a one-year adjustable rate because the maximum interest rate on this loan was a full 2 percent lower than the ceiling on a three-year adjustable rate.

Once you've thought about the type of mortgage you need, it's time to figure out points, those extra charges you pay the lender up front to reduce your interest rate or to compensate for a low down payment. How many should you choose? For example, you might pay 2 points up front to give you a ½ percent lower interest rate throughout the life of the loan. The big issue here is how long you plan to stay in the house or whether you think rates may drop and that you may then refinance at some point. The trade-off is paying points up front so that you lock in a lower interest rate for the long run. You want to find out, by comparing different mortgages, when you are better off paying points up front to get a lower interest rate. Every mortgage company or bank you approach should run a "break-even analysis" that will show you how long you would have to stay in the house if you choose a 1-point or a 2-point option with a lower interest rate to be better off than if you had chosen no points with the higher rate.

For instance, when I bought my current house, I had a choice of paying 1 point up front and getting a ¼ percent lower interest rate than if I did not pay any points at all. By paying 1 point up front I increased my costs initially, but in my case, because I plan to stay in the house for a long time and because interest rates were already very low (meaning this mortgage would probably be in place for many more than four years), I chose to pay the point. I knew I would gradually recoup this money because the lower interest rate made my monthly payments lower. The mortgage lender ran a "break-even analysis" showing that after four years I would be better off with this option.

Tax advantages are a major reason for buying a house. Mortgage interest on loans up to $1 million is usually deductible on your first or second home. Real estate taxes are also deductible, points are deductible, and some closing costs are deductible.

■ A word about refinancing

If you refinance, it's important to remember that the points you pay have to be amortized—or written off—equally over the time period of the loan, so you won't get all the tax benefit right away. And if you refinance, all the mortgage interest may not be deductible. This is because mortgage interest on home equity loans is deductible only for the first $100,000 of such loans ($50,000 if married filing separately).

You may have the idea in the back of your mind even when you are getting your mortgage that you will refinance it relatively quickly if interest rates go down, or if you expect your financial situation to improve so you can qualify for a larger loan and get some of your down payment back in cash, or if you expect to make extensive renovations and want a new mortgage to provide those funds. In this case you should pay as little as possible in points and closing costs to get this current mortgage so you minimize your out-of-pocket costs.

These home-buying steps may sound complicated, but they help break down the decisions you will be making along the way. By thinking ahead you will reduce your stress (because you won't feel so overwhelmed and you will have a "plan of action"), and you will minimize the chances of making a wrong decision along the way. Let's look at how one couple got through the process, from figuring out how much they could afford to choosing the right mortgage.

Many homebuyers face Beth and Charles's financial situation. Their combined income was about $42,000, and although they had only about $2,000 in the bank, they had just sold their condo and would be receiving a check for $28,000 once the mortgage was paid off. Beth and Charles had student loan payments of $200 a month. They weren't sure whether they wanted to sink all their money into a new house.

Beth and Charles got a "prequalification letter" from the bank for a $107,000 mortgage (Step 1), but they decided to borrow no more than $100,000 just to be safe. With a 20 percent down payment of $24,000 (from the condo sale) on a $120,000 home, they could take a $96,000 mortgage and be well within their affordability limit. This left $6,000 for closing costs, moving expenses, and an emergency reserve.

Step 2, where to live, was easy for Charles and Beth. They both worked in the same suburban area and wanted to live close to their offices. So they did some research and decided to limit their search to two nearby towns with good school systems. They identified a couple of neighborhoods in both towns that had homes in their price range.

Figuring out which house features were important was a bit harder. Beth favored contemporary-style homes, while Charles liked traditional architecture. They agreed to focus on single-family homes with three bedrooms and two bathrooms on quiet streets (Step 3). The only Absolutely Not on the list was an outdated kitchen. They had both realized (after much discussion) that architectural style was not as important as features that would have an impact on their day-to-day living.

After asking around at work, Beth and Charles interviewed two brokers who had been recommended and chose the one they felt most comfortable with (Step 4). This broker had sold many houses in both towns and spent several weeks showing them every house in their price range.

Finally, Beth and Charles found the house of their dreams (although they were determined not to let their excitement get in the way of a good negotiation!). After three days of bargaining, the owners agreed to sell for $118,000, which was $2,000 less than Beth and Charles's top price of $120,000 (Step 5).

Because they had already been prequalified by a bank and theirs was a straightforward application, Beth and Charles decided to apply to only the bank that had prequalified them after determining that the interest rates were competitive (Step 6). They chose a thirty-year fixed-rate mortgage with 1 point, were approved, and moved in eight weeks later.

Beth and Charles took their time, proceeded step by step, and treated their home purchase as a business decision. In the end, they got the house they wanted at a price that would not make them panic every month when the mortgage payment was due. All their hard work will pay off for years to come.

PART 2:
SELLING A HOUSE

STEP 1: HOW TO SET A PRICE?

What if the shoe is on the other foot, and you are getting ready to sell a house? The first thing I always tell clients is not to allow themselves to become too proud or too stubborn to take a realistic look at their homes. You should never begin the process of selling a house with a fixed number in your head of what you think it is worth or decide in advance how much you are going to negotiate and how many repairs you are and are not willing to make. Even with a broker's help or an appraiser's assessment, you never know what the true market value for your house is going to be until the day you accept the buyer's offer. My number one tip is: *Do not let your emotions get in the way of making the sale!* Remember, your primary goal is to make the sale (unless you do not have to sell and plan to do so only if you get the right price). If you are selling so you can buy another property, keep in mind that "bridge" loans (short-term loans for buying the new property before you get your equity out of the old one) are expensive and much harder to get than they used to be, so you have an incentive to sell.

How do you value a house? This is a hard job for an owner because a house has so much emotion tied up in it—so much blood, sweat, and tears—and holds so many memories. It is also hard because if you bought your house in the last ten years, you may find that its value may in fact be *less* that it was when you purchased it. If so, you are going to have to take a loss (which the IRS kindly says you cannot deduct). One way to assess your home's value is to hire an appraiser; another is to ask a couple of brokers at what price they would list it and at what price it would likely sell. The appraisers may be somewhat more reliable than brokers, but always get two opinions before you fix on a price. You cannot just determine a price by figuring out how much you paid for it and adding all the costs of your improvements; you may love what you have changed about the house, but those changes may not have increased the home's value. *Remodeling* magazine conducts an annual survey to determine how much of the cost of certain home improvements is recouped at resale time. In 1993, the survey reported that a major kitchen remodeling job recouped 93 percent of the cost; an additional bath, 92 percent; a bath remodeling job, 85 percent; a family-room addition, 86 percent; a sun space addition, 71 percent; a siding replacement, 67 percent; a master-suite addition, 85 percent; a window replacement, 71 percent; an outdoor deck, 77 percent; converting an attic to a bedroom, 84 percent. Certain home improvements such as a swimming pool and new landscaping may well increase your enjoyment of your home, but they won't necessarily increase its value (and sometimes a pool can *decrease* value because new owners do not want the hassle or may even want to have it removed altogether at a substantial cost).

If you decide to list your house with a broker, do not automatically use the broker who agrees to list it for the highest amount. Conversely, do not feel absolutely locked in by what the broker says if you have good, rational reasons to think that your home is worth more (such as recent house sales on your street). After all, most of us have heard stories of sellers who insisted that their homes be put on the market for a good deal more than any of the brokers recommended and then sold within one week at that price. If you put your home on the market for a high price, be sure that you are willing to drop down if the price appears to be out of line. *Always* look at comparable properties first to see what your competition is. And make sure the house does not "get stale" by being on the market too long just because the price is too high.

STEP 2: USE A BROKER OR GO IT ALONE?

When sellers start talking to different brokers and find out the amount of commission payable on a sale, they often think of selling it themselves. Before you do this, ask yourself these questions:

1. Do I have the expertise and stomach to advertise, negotiate, and go through the closing process myself (and have I lined up an attorney to assist me)? Do I have enough emotional detachment from my house to deal with prospective buyers who may criticize it and find fault with some of the very features I love the most?

2. Do I have the amount of time to devote to phone calls, showings, etc.? (If you travel a lot, selling it yourself may not be a good idea.)

3. Can I get as high a price on my own, negotiating on my own behalf, as I would if I used a broker and paid the commission? (You essentially need to end up at with at least 95 percent of the price you would likely get if you used a broker in order to break even.)

4. Do I know how to show the house to its best advantage?

If you feel that you can do better on your own, by all means try, but set yourself a deadline by which you will turn it over to a broker if you have not sold it. Even if you do advertise it on your own, brokers may call you. If you do not want any brokers to contact you, be sure to put "no brokers" in your real estate ads. A broker may call you and ask if he can show your property at your asking price plus his 5 or 6 percent commission. Then you have to weigh whether the potential buyer would have already seen it in the paper himself. I would recommend you do *not* let a broker list your property in the paper with his name on it if you are also advertising it yourself, because buyers get upset when they find out they are paying thousands of dollars more just because they responded to the wrong ad!

Having watched clients buy and sell houses without a broker, I can testify to the nerve-racking experience of going it alone. But in most cases it seems that clients end up with more dollars in their pocket for their efforts (of course, you never know for sure because you don't know what price your house would have commanded if it had been handled by a broker). In my personal experience of twice buying and selling on my own, I found it difficult trying to negotiate directly with the seller without the broker acting as a go-between; hence, negotiating was not fun *at all*. As a seller, I found it no picnic dealing with a first-time buyer who approached every tiny detail of the process suspecting that I was taking advantage of him. Think about the trade-off of aggravation and extra dollars, but whatever your decision, make sure you go into it with your eyes open.

Negotiating commissions is a topic that comes up frequently now that market prices are so high. These days, 5 or 6 percent of those high prices can mean that tens of thousands of dollars of your sales price goes to pay commissions. Do your homework before you put your house on the market, and find out whether commissions are being negotiated in your town. (If not, consider starting a trend!) Also, when you interview brokers ask them whether they will accept a lower commission in exchange for getting your business. It is better to get this resolved up front rather than in the middle of the sales process. But if you find yourself at an impasse in a particular negotiation and your bottom-line price is more than the buyer is willing to offer, you can always ask the broker at that point to reduce his commission. He may agree if it means getting the sale.

STEP 3: HOW TO PREPARE A HOUSE FOR SHOWING?

When it comes to fixing up the house before putting it up for sale, the best thing you can do is wash the windows, clean out junk, and clean those bathrooms! You want to make sure the property shows well so you don't have to apologize for what's wrong with it. Some people even rent furniture to improve a home's appearance. Other than that, what's worth and not worth fixing up varies from house to house. Repainting may make sense, but rewallpapering generally does not because it is a much greater investment and whoever buys your house may not like your choice. If you do repaint or rewallpaper, choose neutral tones. Minor repairs such as replacing panes of glass are also very important. Line up a regular cleaning service or allow yourself adequate time to clean every week when the house is on the market. And set down some ground rules so that every member of the family is doing his or her fair share to keep the house picked up. There is nothing worse than having to worry about a major cleanup every time a prospective buyer wants to view the house.

Every once in a while I have clients whose neighbors present problems when they are trying to sell their properties. These neighbors are typically people who have untidy yards, play loud music, park cars on the street, and so forth. I advise asking the neighbors to help out by keeping the noise down, keeping their yards clean, and so on. Sometimes a client has had words with the neighbors in the past on these same issues (and there is not a great deal of neighborly warmth in their relationship!). In that case, I tell my client to point out to the neighbor that the sooner my client's house sells, the sooner he will move away and the neighbors will not have to deal with him anymore. *This has never failed to work.* It also helps to point out to your neighbors that the higher the selling price of your house, the greater the market value of theirs, so your sale can become a great neighborly effort.

STEP 4: HOW TO NEGOTIATE THE SALE?

Negotiating the sale as a seller is very much like negotiating on the buyer's side but obviously from a different perspective. Again, here is where personal experience with real estate, a good attorney, or a good real estate agent can help. If you are doing it on your own and using a lawyer, make sure your lawyer is "on call" so she can pressure buyers, make sure financing is being arranged in a timely fashion, and so on. Finally, again, do not be proud! Too many times sales fall through because the owner is unwilling to make minor repairs or come down $500 on a $300,000 house. In one instance, a $1,500 request for a necessary roof repair was declined, and the house sat empty for a year (with twelve more months of mortgage payments due) until another buyer was found. Selling a house should be based purely on economics. You must put your emotions aside and treat your house like any other investment.

STEP 5: HOW TO TREAT YOUR GAIN (OR LOSS) CORRECTLY FOR TAXES?

When you sell your house you will, we hope, end up with a profit to put into another house or to invest for your other goals. Ironically, even though the IRS will tax you on your profit (it is treated as capital gain), if you lose money you cannot claim a deduction. In fact, if you "walk away" from a house, you may have to pay taxes even though you didn't get a penny out of the deal! Every time you buy and sell a house and make a profit, you have to either pay tax on the profit or use that profit to reduce the cost basis of your new house. The IRS has the final say over which method you use. If you buy a new house within twenty-four months before or after you sell your old house for at least the selling price of the old one, you can roll over your gain into the new house. Otherwise, your profit gets taxed at capital gains rates now, which can be rather painful—currently 28 percent of the gain! You should always be careful to time your purchases and sales so you can shelter this gain. If you are over fifty-five, you do get a one-time exclusion of $150,000 for your house profits when you sell and do not buy again or when you "buy down." This acknowledges the special circumstances of older people who are selling houses and moving to less expensive homes or becoming renters. Keep in mind that if you are over fifty-five and you are selling because you are getting married, you should sell your house first before you get married. This way, you can claim your one-time exclusion (and so can your spouse-to-be if he or she is also selling before the marriage). Otherwise, you lose your exclusion altogether if you marry someone who has already used his or hers. Still confused? Everybody is, and because there are so many factors involved, you should get advice about your individual situation before you act. You can call your local IRS office for help, but keep in mind that you have no legal recourse if the advice you get is wrong (which is about 10 percent of the time, as recent studies have shown). I recommend you talk things over with your tax adviser if you are seriously considering using your one-time exclusion.

After twenty-five years in her house, Margaret decided it was finally time to sell and move to a smaller place with less upkeep required. It was a tough decision—she and Ed had started their married lives together in that house, and Margaret knew how much Ed would have loved to tend the garden and make repairs if he were still alive. But the children were long grown and gone, and it was easier for her to hop on a plane to visit them than make them pack up their growing families and buy plane tickets for everyone to make the trip to see her. Last year, Margaret had turned fifty-five, and her tax preparer told her she could now sell and avoid paying taxes on $150,000 of her profit by claiming her one-time exclusion. Ever since, she had been keeping an eye on house sales in town to get an idea of how much hers was worth.

Even though the decision to sell was hard, an even tougher one had to be made—and quickly. Two of Margaret's friends were real estate brokers with many years of experience, so she had a tough time deciding which one to list her house with. (She knew that she was too attached to the house and too inexperienced to try and sell it on her own.) To help with her decision (and hopefully diminish any hard feelings on the part of the one who was not selected), Margaret asked each broker to tour the house, provide a written summary of its good and bad points, and include the price at which it should be listed and the price at which it might sell. She also asked how many houses each broker had sold during the previous two years and what the average house sales price had been. Margaret told each friend that her two children would be helping her select the broker, so her own vote was only worth one-third (as her children said, this way they could take the blame for the decision!), and that it would be totally a business decision, based on the facts—not based on friendship. As she explained, the friendship part had already come into play when she narrowed her list to just two brokers among the many she knew in the community.

Margaret was surprised when she sat down with her sons to look at the two proposals. It turned out that Jackie, the closer friend of the two brokers, had sold fewer houses (eleven), seemed to be more active in the condo market, and had a low average sales price ($96,000) compared to average prices in the area—a very different scenario than Jackie had presented when asked how her real estate business was going. It was clear that the buyers Jackie usually worked with probably would not be able to afford even the lowest price at which Margaret thought her house might sell ($160,000), and Jackie did not offer an explanation of how she planned to attract buyers. She also failed to point out some of the best features of Margaret's house.

Sue had a higher average house price ($190,000) and suggested a listing price of $165,000 for Margaret's house, with a probable sale in the high $150s. Margaret was concerned that Sue's customers were out of her house's price range. However, Sue provided an excellent written explanation of how she would "position" the house as the perfect alternative for any buyers who wanted a more expensive house. The house had a third-floor walk-up attic with lovely views of the nearby mountains, and someone could buy the house for less and build a master bedroom suite or children's playroom in the attic. Margaret decided to list the house for $165,000 (step 1) and chose Sue as her broker with an agreed-upon commission of 5 percent (Step 2).

From that point on, the remaining steps were easy. Margaret was a meticulous housekeeper, so the only thing she had to do to prepare the house for showing (Step 3) was to go through Ed's closet and workroom—a task she had put off but that was made easier now that there was a good reason for doing it. Within three weeks, Sue had found a family with two small children who were willing to pay $155,000 for the house. These buyers had a prequalification letter for a $140,000 mortgage, and had $40,000 in savings and gifts from family members for the down payment and conversion of the attic to a playroom. Two days of spirited negotiating brought their offer up to $160,000, and at that point Margaret decided to accept (Step 4). Holding out for perhaps a few thousand dollars more in an uncertain real estate market did not seem worth it.

Margaret was fortunate because she and Ed had paid $10,000 for the house twenty-five years ago and put in about $40,000 of capital improvements over the years in the form of a garage, house addition, and new kitchen. Her meticulous records, sales receipts, and canceled checks documented everything. Margaret's gain was $110,000; she was able to use her one-time exclusion for the sale of her personal residence, so her entire profit was tax-free. Her gain was properly reported on that year's tax return, so Margaret treated it properly for tax purposes (Step 5).

If you think about how much time, energy, and money you will invest in a home, you can see how your decisions here can make or break your Money Diet. The right decision can give you the ability to keep up comfortably with your mortgage payments and required maintenance, while at the same time leaving enough money in your pocket to save for goals. The wrong decision, however, can drain your pocketbook and peace of mind so that other financial goals become unattainable. You may find yourself in the dilemma of having to choose between your home and adequate retirement income, for example. All too often homebuyers discover *after* they have moved in that their decision was a mistake, but by then it is too late. If you follow these Money Diet steps, you will minimize your chances of finding yourself in the same position.

CHAPTER TWELVE

Paying for
Big-Ticket Items

EVERY ONCE in a while I get a call from a client or friend who is suffering from "post-vacation buys." No, "buys" is not a typo for "blues." My friend or client has gone away on vacation, has found the house or condominium of her dreams, and is thinking about buying it. I also get the occasional call from a client suffering from auto fever—that heady feeling that grips you when you walk into a dealership set on buying a station wagon but the luxury car or tiny red convertible seems to have your name written all over it. This happens to all of us. It's nothing to be ashamed of, but in order to stay on the Money Diet you need to be prepared for such temptations because you are looking at potential big-time goal-busters. They can do to your Money Diet what a daily 600-calorie hot fudge sundae would do to your food diet—except with the Money Diet, it takes only *one* decision on a *single* day to wreck your goals.

Based on my experience with clients and friends as well as my own occasionally poor resistance, I have found that one can suddenly become caught up in these big-ticket items as goals, but once you take a long hard look at your financial situation you may realize that succumbing to temptation may make it impossible for you to meet your *other*, more important goals of retirement, education, etc. And, of course, you probably will have to buy certain big-ticket items such as autos from time to time throughout your life, whether you like it or not.

The problem with big-ticket items is that in most cases to purchase them or put money down on them you must use liquid assets from the total you have earmarked for other goals. This means that you not only lose the income and growth on what you shell out now but may also reduce your annual savings because for some big-ticket items you will be facing additional mortgage or car payments, taxes, maintenance fees, or other costs for some time.

You may rush to disagree, pointing out that real estate prices in the vicinity of your dream vacation house have been going up, or that the make of your car has been holding its value very well, or that stamps or expensive jewelry have been increasing in value over the years. While this may certainly be true, *in your case you may not be dealing with a true investment.* (In other words, you may very well have not bought your big-ticket item primarily because it would grow in value and/or pay you income *until you sell it.*) The problem is that if you do not plan to sell the big-ticket item during your lifetime or at least sell something else in its place (such as your primary residence to end up with only the vacation home), you end up with a *reverse* investment (one that takes money away from other investments). After all, you can't pay for your retirement with a Hummel or a beach cottage.

Let me hasten to say that some things are worth it. The vacation home may be important enough to you—it becomes a gathering place for your children and grandchildren when you grow older—that you are willing to accept a lower monthly retirement income in order to buy it. The expensive car (and expensive insurance and maintenance) may be worth it to you because you are in a business where displays of wealth are crucial to getting new customers and maintaining the ones you have. And you may find the hobby of collecting coins, figurines, stamps, or china plates relaxing and fun. The key is to balance reality and dreams; be sure you see these big-ticket items for what they are, rather than thinking of them as good investments. *If you do not plan to sell these non-income-producing big-ticket items during your lifetime, they are not good investments except as part of your children's inheritance.* And the first premise of the Money Diet is that you have to take care of your own basic needs first before you start worrying about what you are leaving the kids.

Whenever you are tempted by a purchase or are faced with having to make one, take the time to give yourself the Money Diet Five-Question Test. This has prevented me from wasting a lot of money over the years, and clients have found it useful as well. The questions to ask before committing your hard-earned money are:

1. Do I need this—is it critical to my physical or psychological well-being? If not, why am I doing this? As we discussed before, you may see this beach cottage as the glue that will hold your family together as the kids grow up, move away, and perhaps have children of their own.

2. What is the before-tax cost of doing this? That beach cottage may have a $60,000 price tag, but the real cost may be much higher when you consider how long you had to work and how much in taxes you had to pay to get that $60,000. The real cost could be as much as $100,000 of your income.

3. What is the impact on my ability to meet my more important goals such as retirement, education, etc? Let's say you use your hard-earned cash to buy the $60,000 beach cottage. In five years, your first child starts college, or you plan to retire, or some other goal materializes. If you had invested that $60,000 and gotten a 7 percent annual return after taxes, your nest egg would be worth almost $85,000. Your total "opportunity cost" (purchase price, expenses, and lost income) would be even more than $85,000 because of the real estate taxes, maintenance, cost of furnishings, etc. The decision to buy the beach cottage may have a negative impact on *all* of your goals. Refer to the bottom-line facts about your financial situation that you learned with the Willpower Worksheets you have completed. Use those facts to help you make the right decision.

4. Is it still worth it to me to make this purchase? Even though you do not absolutely need the cottage and are appalled when you see how much it will actually cost you and know that you are putting other goals in jeopardy, you may just decide to buy it anyway. (Let's face it, that kind of thinking is human nature!) If you do, make sure you understand *why* it is still worth it to you. In fact, write the rea-

sons down and file them away so that if a few years from now you regret your decision, you'll be able to remember exactly why you made it at the time.

5. Is there a less expensive alternative? For example, when you stop to think about it you may realize you will use the beach cottage only a few weeks a year and it would be cheaper (and less of a hassle too) to rent a place for your summer vacations.

If, after answering these five questions, you still want to take the plunge and buy your big-ticket item, it's time to stop daydreaming about how wonderful life will be when it's yours. Until you actually own it, your focus must be on how to purchase the right house, car, or whatever at the right price. After all, if you pay too much for something that's not right for you, your happy daydreams may turn into ongoing nightmares when you realize you just made a big mistake. We're talking about a major case of buyer's remorse.

BUYING A VACATION HOME

Most of us have dreamed of a place on the beach, or in the mountains, or even in the city. This dream becomes more pronounced when we are on a wonderful vacation and we have left the real world behind. That is one reason why we often throw caution to the wind and overspend while on vacation. But if you get back from vacation, run the numbers, do the Five Question Test, and still want to buy, what should you look for in a second home?

Here are some basic questions to ask when you are buying a second home:

1. Is the asking price fair, or am I caught up in the urge to buy?
2. Will I be able to handle the maintenance expenses, and who will handle the maintenance?

3. If the house I want is part of a development, how financially strong is the developer? How organized is the condominium association?

4. Can I control the development around my vacation home? For example, if you want a rural setting, make sure that the area surrounding you will stay pristine. Some friends of mine recently purchased a home in the country. They realized that part of the property's allure was the fact that no other houses could be seen. The cottage came with enough land to keep future development out of view on three sides, but to protect their home's value (and preserve its unique character), they were able to purchase enough land on the fourth side to keep civilization at bay.

5. Can I rent the property and get income when I am not there?

6. Will this vacation home be suitable for my potential guests and all the activities I want to do there (such as visits from active grandchildren, sedentary friends, skiing, etc.)?

7. Will I enjoy being around my neighbors?

Time-shares are often a good way for people to get into the vacation home market without paying a lot up front. It is important to know, however, that time-shares as investments rank at the bottom of the real estate market when it comes to resale values. There is often virtually no market for time-shares that are put up for resale after having been purchased from the developer (this is called the "secondary market"). In other words, if you buy your time-share from the developer and then want to sell it yourself, you may have trouble. Recent surveys of time-share owner satisfaction and resale value are troubling. If you do decide to invest in a time-share, try to buy from a current owner instead of the developer because you can often get resale properties for less than half the developer's price. Also, make sure that you plan to stay in the time-share for the long run, and accept the fact that most banks will not lend money for a time-share because this type of real estate has very little resale value. Over the last decade I have seen several clients sell their time-shares at fractions of their original purchase prices—if they were lucky enough to find buyers at all.

Once you have decided to go ahead with buying your second

home, you can use the tips in chapter 11, "Buying and Selling Your Home," to negotiate and obtain financing. Be aware, however, that it is often more difficult to get financing on second homes than on first homes. Also, you may have to make a much larger down payment, and the mortgage rate may be higher.

As the experience of my clients Helen and Al shows, the time-consuming process of actually buying a vacation home is a far cry from the thrill of the initial idea. After an especially relaxing holiday, they returned from Florida wanting to preserve that feeling and escape from winter weather several months of the year. There was just one problem: Although two of their three children were out of college, their youngest, Ronnie, still had two years to go. Helen and Al wanted me to tell them whether they were out of their minds to even be contemplating such a move.

When we met to discuss their prospective purchase, we first addressed the "big picture" questions that apply to any big-ticket item and then moved on to those directly pertaining to vacation homes. First, while Helen and Al didn't really need a condo or cottage in Florida right away, they had already decided to sell their large house when Al retired and move someplace smaller in the South. Second, we calculated the before-tax cost of buying in the price range they considered acceptable ($60,000 to $70,000), which came to just over $100,000. This number by itself would have been alarming, but since their house was valued at over $200,000, it didn't seem so bad. Helen and Al had always lived frugally except for vacations, and Al had been contributing to his 401(k) since the first year he was eligible in order to get his employer's matching contributions. Because of their frugal living, they actually had most of Ronnie's tuition already socked away.

We determined that as long as they stuck to a price of under $70,000 and followed through on their commitment to sell their current house when Al retired, Helen and Al could actually buy the vacation home *and* have enough money to retire comfortably. The only less expensive alternative would be a time-share purchase, but that option would eliminate their ability to sell their big house because they needed somewhere to live full-time. Helen and Al were naturally delighted when we went through the numbers together, and they made plans to return to Florida within a few weeks and look at properties, after they had researched and picked a town and a broker. Then, after they narrowed their search down to three properties, it was time to deal with the specific second-home questions.

Once Helen and Al started looking around, they decided to consider a small single-family house as well as two condos in different developments—one in a high-rise building and the other in a small, duplex-type community. They felt that enough time (and hours of research!) had passed to keep them from being overwhelmed by the urge to buy, allowing them to evaluate prices with level heads. With the small house, Helen and Al would obviously control and handle all maintenance, while with the high-rise they would have no maintenance; the duplex condo ("condex") offered a combination of general duplex exterior maintenance by the association and specific yard maintenance by each owner. Based on these differences, they then ruled out the high-rise condo because Al liked to "do things his way" and enjoyed making home repairs, while Helen wanted to have a garden. Controlling development around the property was a non-issue in their case, because both the condex and cottage were in the middle of what were already highly developed areas.

In terms of rental income, Helen and Al would have to handle all the arrangements themselves if they bought the cottage, whereas with the condex the developers would do so for absent owners (for a fee of 10 percent of the rent). Because Al planned to retire in a few years, this was really a short-term issue, so they discounted its importance in their decision-making process.

As Helen and Al thought more and more about this purchase, they realized their decision would be based on how their new home would accommodate their children, future grandchildren, and friends. Helen and Al love to entertain, so they anticipated a steady stream of visitors, and they figured with three children of their own, grandchildren were bound to be in their future. The thought of family reunions with everybody cooped up inside or on a small deck (along with constant worries about noise going through walls and disturbing their neighbors) was too much to deal with. They chose the single-family cottage and got it at a good price because it was a classic "fixer-upper." As Helen now says, buying that cottage also bought Al his retirement hobby!

BUYING A CAR

While buying a second home may not be in your future, buying a car probably is. That's because the most common big-ticket item for most people—a necessity for most of us—is an automobile. At first glance, buying or leasing a car may not seem as though it would have a major impact on your financial future. But if you add up all the cars you will buy over your lifetime, the total expenditure can be staggering. This fact was recently brought home to me when I purchased a Jeep—far from a "luxury" car—and spent more than half of what I spent on the first house I purchased in 1975. The average price of a new car has risen 70 percent in the last ten years, and no one can predict whether that steep increase in prices will continue. But with the average price of a new car now hovering at almost $20,000, it is easy to top $100,000 if you add up the price of all the cars you will likely buy over your lifetime. Many people will spend more out of pocket on cars than they will on homes over their lifetime, especially if they live in one or two houses but buy a number of cars. After all, buying a new car every five years from the time you are twenty-five on (a conservative assumption given our culture's passion for new automobiles) means you are likely to own twelve cars. And while your mortgage payment is relatively low, your car payment may be half or more of your house payment—and none of the interest is deductible unless you use your car for business.

Most of us need automobiles, so successfully buying one is a skill most of us must have. Why do we spend so much on automobiles? We spend too much on the extras! Automobiles are a depreciating asset. The minute you drive a new car off the lot its value has gone down as much as 20 percent, according to conservative estimates (some run as high as 30 percent). Buying a car is like buying stock that ends up worthless and costs even more money along the way. This is why I see red every time I spot a car ad that heralds a particular model as an "investment." Though some cars may in fact hold their value fairly well, few increase in value. Of course, a car is more useful in your everyday life: You can't drive a stock certificate! But mile for mile, the cost of those "extras" can be staggering: $600 for a stereo system, $800 for a sunroof, $1,500 more for leather seats, and so on.

We don't buy houses that will go down in value, so why do we buy cars that will? We have been conditioned to believe that's just the way it is; cars wear out, and our culture puts a high value on expensive cars. Does the $40,000 luxury car really have $20,000 worth of gadgets over the $20,000 car? Part of the extra cost you pay is for image and prestige. For a relatively small investment, we can feel rich driving around in a fancy new car we have just bought for "only $x a month." If we lease for a short period of time we can get an even *more* expensive car than if we bought a car and took out a loan. It is virtually impossible for a middle-income family to buy one of the most expensive houses on the market. By leasing, however, or by purchasing a car with loan terms of several years, that same family can drive around in an automobile that makes them feel rich beyond their means. This feeling is a real selling point for cars. And of course, no one ever called a house sexy!

Unfortunately, it is all too easy to fall into the automobile trap—you can have instant gratification every time you open the door, but those car or lease payments that allow you to feel rich now may contribute to the fact that you do not have enough money to retire on later. The smart approach is to be prepared *before* you walk into the dealership so that you do not become mesmerized by "new car mania."

You should know, incidentally, that this process may not be fun. Greeting you at the dealership will be a whole host of salespeople whose mission is to convince you that *of course* you deserve to drive around like royalty, and *of course* you can afford that car that is just a "teeny-weeny" bit more (words actually said to me by a salesperson the last time I bought a car).

The best way to resist the pressures of these salespeople when buying or leasing a car is to have a plan of attack. You can map out your mode of operation in this important part of developing your Money Diet in the same way you might map out how you are going to handle your food diet *before* you go out of town to your cousin's wedding over a weekend jam-packed with parties morning, noon, and night.

There are usually three distinct steps in the process of getting a new car. Step 1 is what to do *before* you set foot in the dealership, and it includes the crucial decisions of how much you can afford, whether to buy or lease, and what car models to choose. Step 2 is what to do from the time you set foot in the dealership to signing on the dotted line for your car. This includes negotiating a price (or using a fixed-price dealer instead) and financing your purchase (if you are buying) or deciding on the leasing period (if you are leasing). Step 3, if applicable, is trading in your car—a negotiation you should always handle *after* you've nailed down a price on your new car.

STEP 1: BEFORE YOU WALK INTO THE DEALERSHIP

- Figure out how much you can afford.

So what is the first thing to do when you are considering buying a new or used car or leasing a car? You have to figure out how much you can afford. You should know this before you go shopping because as you walk in the door of a car dealership one of the first things a salesperson may ask you is how much you can afford to pay per month for a new car. (The best answer is "I haven't decided.") The reason you don't want to reveal this information is that it can become very confusing for you to compare different cars with the same monthly payment. One car may cost $5,000 more than the other but have the same monthly payment because the loan is repaid over several more years.

Start by completing **How Much Can You Afford to Borrow for a Car?** (page 232). When one of my clients did this he found he would probably qualify for a car payment up to $450 a month. This was beyond his comfort level, so he made a decision to stick to $400 or less. The catch? The car dealer may show you a more expensive car that has a very long loan or may quote you a figure that is for a lease.

Just as with a vacation home, the issue in determining how much you can afford to pay for a car is not just how much you can afford to pay out of your current income and assets but how your car purchase will affect your other goals. I have a method for figuring out these trade-offs in chapter 15, "Putting It All Together," but the key is to keep in mind that every dollar you spend on your car is *at least* one dollar less for retirement, education, etc. (because you lose both the dollar and any investment return you could have earned on it as well).

A quick-and-dirty way to figure out how much you can afford is to look at what you wrote in **Simplified Net Worth Statement** (page 22) and **Spending and Saving** (page 28). Your options: First, to pay all cash; second, to make a down payment (this can come from your assets, or the sale or trade-in of your current car) and take an auto loan for the balance; or third, to lease (you can also trade in and apply the proceeds to your lease). Very often, people lease or take auto loans as a way to get their hands on a more expensive car. But instead of stretching for the most expensive car you can afford, why not aim for the least expensive car you can stand to drive? **How Much Can You Afford to Borrow for a Car?** can help.

Many advisers recommend paying all cash for a new car; in theory, this advice is great. But now that you have looked at some of your other goals (retirement, education, buying a home), you may have concluded you can't afford to use up your money on hand (if you are fortunate enough to have that much stashed away!). In fact, only 6 percent of new car owners pay all cash. If you are one of the lucky few who can, make sure you have enough money left over for emergencies, and compare the interest rate you are currently getting on your money with the rate you would have to pay on a car loan. Keep in mind that you can always take out a loan now and pay it off more quickly than it calls for. (This is usually a good idea anyway.)

For many people who do not have enough cash or trade-in value to buy a car outright, an auto loan or leasing is the only option. In **Spending and Saving,** line I, you found out how much you are currently saving, and in the chapters on some of your other goals, such as retirement, you may have already decided to use those savings to meet these goals. (And we haven't even talked about buying more insurance yet!) For an auto loan, my recommended maximum "total monthly debt payments to before-tax income" percentage is 38 percent if you have a mortgage or 15 percent if you don't. So, if your current monthly income is $3,000, all your monthly payments (see **Your**

How Much Can You Afford to Borrow for a Car?

A. Maximum Safe Debt Load (Are You Over Your Head in Debt?, p. 83, line C)	A.
B. Less: Total Current Monthly Debt Payments* (Are You Over Your Head in Debt?, p. 83, line D)	B. −
C. Equals: Maximum Car Payment	C. =

* Do not include auto loan payments on any car you plan to sell or trade in for the new car.

From *The Money Diet*, by Ginger Applegarth.

Current Debt Load, page 75, line C) plus the payment on your new car cannot total more than $1,140 if you have a mortgage (38 percent of $3,000) or $450 if you don't (15 percent of $3,000). On line A of **How Much Can You Afford to Borrow for a Car?,** write your maximum safe debt load amount from **Are You Over Your Head in Debt?,** line C. This is the absolute maximum amount for all your current monthly obligations, including car loans or lease payments. Write the total of all your monthly payments on line B; take this from line D of **Are You Over Your Head in Debt?** Subtract line B from line A; your answer on line C is the maximum amount your monthly auto loan or lease payment should be. But, as you can imagine, having such a large amount of money automatically disappear each month to make loan and other fixed payments can make for frugal living, so if you can get by with a less expensive car requiring a lower monthly payment, that strategy makes sense.

■ Decide whether to buy or lease.

Now that you know how much you can afford for your monthly payment, the big decision is whether to buy or lease. I'm not focusing on buying outright because few people these days pay all cash for a new car. Sixty-six percent of car buyers finance their purchase; 28 percent end up leasing. Part of the reason leasing has become so popular is that car prices have increased dramatically in the last ten years. The auto industry has been heavily promoting leasing as well. The most important rule of thumb in making the buy-or-lease decision is to buy a car if you plan to keep it for four or five years or more because it will usually be less expensive than leasing over the long run. If you need the car for three or fewer years, you should lease. And if you are in the "twilight zone" of between three and four years, your decision depends on your particular situation.

Of course, one advantage of buying is that you have a car that is worth something at the end of the loan, whereas you get nothing at the end of the lease (except the right or obligation to buy the car). A disadvantage to buying is you usually have a higher down payment and a higher monthly payment than if you lease the same car. If you lease, however, there are other charges you need to take into account, which we will talk about shortly. Confused? By filling out **Should You Buy or Lease a Car?** (page 234) you can compare the math of buying versus leasing, assuming you take out a loan if you buy. This worksheet gives you the bottom-line cost of paying all cash, taking out a loan, or leasing.

The first thing to do is estimate how many years you expect to keep the car and multiply the number by 12 to come up with the number of months you will own the car. Write your answer on line A. If you are considering paying all cash, add the estimated price of the car, sales tax, and the amount of interest you would have earned if you hadn't "invested" it in a car. The total is your cost to buy. Find out the estimated future value of the car (you can get this number by asking the salesperson what the lease buyout price would be if you leased the car now and wanted to buy it when the lease ended x months [line A] later. Lease buyouts are covered in more detail later in this chapter). Write your answer, which is the Net Cost if You Pay All Cash, on line B. Determining the cost if you take a loan is similar to the previous calculation, except you add your down payment, the sales tax, total monthly payments, and forgone interest on the down payment. Subtract the future estimated resale value (again, your salesperson can provide this number). The result, Net Cost if You Borrow, goes on line C. Finally, the cost if you lease is the sum of the down payment, security deposit, total monthly payments, and sales tax (if not already included in the monthly payment); the total on line D is Net Cost if You Lease.

Should You Buy or Lease a Car?

A. How Long Will You Keep the Car?

Number of Years	
Times 12	$\times$ 12
Equals: Number of Months	**A. =**

B. Cost if You Pay All Cash

Price of Car	
Plus: Sales Tax*	+
Plus: Interest Lost on Your Money (Price of car x 0.06† x number of years)	+
Equals: Cost to Buy	=
Less: Future Value of Car‡	−
Equals: Net Cost if You Pay All Cash	**B. =**

C. Cost if You Take a Loan

Your Down Payment	
Plus: Sales Tax*	+
Plus: Total Monthly Payments (Monthly payment x no. of months, line A)	+
Plus: Interest Lost on Down Payment (Down payment x 0.06† x number of years)	+
Equals: Cost to Buy	=
Less: Future Value of Car‡	−
Equals: Net Cost if You Borrow	**C. =**

D. Cost if You Lease

Your Down Payment	
Plus: Security Deposit	+
Plus: Total Monthly Payments (Monthly payment x no. of months, line A)	+
Plus: Sales Tax*	+
Equals: Total Cost if You Lease	**D. =**

E. Compare B, C, and D. Which is the lowest?

* The sales tax is usually included in your monthly lease payment, so you don't have to pay it up front (unlike when you buy a car).

† This assumes your money can earn 6% after taxes if you invest it instead of spending it on a car. You may change 6% to another, more accurate figure, if you like.

‡ "Future Value" is the estimated value of the car at the end of the time period you specified on line A. Your salesperson can give you this figure, based on the price you would have to pay at the end of the lease period.

From *The Money Diet*, by Ginger Applegarth.

By comparing B, C, and D you can determine which course of action makes sense for you. Remember the client who qualified for a payment of $450 a month but decided to limit himself to $400 a month or less? He decided he would buy or lease a car with a price tag of $18,000 or less. When he ran the numbers on **Should You Buy or Lease a Car?** he determined that since he planned to keep his car for five years, it made sense to buy instead of lease. And since he didn't have the money to pay all cash, he decided to put $3,000 down (from the sale or trade-in of his old car) and finance the balance with a loan.

In addition to financial factors, you should consider lifestyle factors when deciding to buy or lease. If you are driving much more than 12,000 to 15,000 miles a year, consider buying to avoid a per-mile surcharge of 10¢ to 15¢ that usually comes with a lease.

When are the times you *should* lease?

- when you do not have the money for a down payment
- when you want to drive a more expensive auto than your money can buy (although I don't advise this)
- if you need the car for only a couple of years

I do not, however, recommend that you lease just so you can have a new car every two years or so. To me and many other advisers I know, doing so seems too much like paying and paying and paying the minimum payment on credit cards without ever paying off the balances. The fact is, if you plan to consistently lease cars every few years over your lifetime, you will probably spend much more than if you buy the same cars and keep each for four or more years. That's because every time you get a new vehicle (whether you buy or lease), your investment immediately loses value due to depreciation, and you have to pay sales tax to boot. So the longer you hold each car, the fewer cars you have to lose money on.

■ Do your homework first.

Now that you know how much you can afford and whether to buy or lease, it's time to do some non-financial homework. Look at your lifestyle before you set foot in the dealership! It is a good idea to think about several things, such as:

- what you usually use your car for
- how many people usually ride with you
- how often you take long trips
- if you need lots of space for sports equipment, trash cans, hobby equipment, etc.
- what style of car you like
- what part of the country you live in

Also think about how long you will need this car because if you are planning to keep a car for up to ten years, it is obviously more important to buy one that has an impeccable repair record than one with fancy extras.

Next, do your research about must-have features of specific models before you set foot in the showroom, where you may feel rushed or forget key questions. There are a number of excellent auto books available, including *The Car Book* by Jack Gillis (a consumer advocate and contributing correspondent for the *Today* show), and books by *Consumer Reports* and *Consumer Guide* books. It is a good idea to look through these books to see which cars appeal to you and to check their safety and repair records. If you find a car that looks promising, these books will tell you if it has a "twin" (identical car, with a different make and name, like Dodge Caravan and Plymouth Voyager). A "twin" car may be less popular and therefore it may be easier for you to negotiate down the price. The resale values of these cars may vary substantially as well over time. The goal is to end up with a list of three or four cars that meet your criteria. If you narrow your search down to just one car, you may end up paying more than if you keep several cars in mind. Make sure that the cars you are considering are not on the car insurance high-theft list for your state (or if they are, be prepared to invest in an approved car alarm so that your insurance premiums will be reasonable). Finally, check out the reputations of dealerships near you. Ask your friends what dealerships they have had good experiences with, and call the Better Business Bureau to see if any complaints have been filed against them.

You do not have to have your car serviced where you bought it (there are a number of approved service centers that qualify to keep your car in warranty if you use them), but many people report they get much better service if they do so. Some dealerships give preferential treatment to their own new car customers by always giving those customers appointments right away but making others wait several weeks. I know, because I recently experienced this.

STEP 2:
FROM THE SHOWROOM DOOR
TO THE DOTTED LINE

■ Negotiating if you plan to buy

Let's assume you have decided to buy a car. How do you negotiate? First, do not rely on newspaper ads—some of these promise real deals until you read the fine print and find out that thousands of dollars are required as a down payment, or that what looks like a monthly payment to buy is actually a lease payment, or that the loan is for as long as six or seven years. Negotiate on the basis of the *total cost* of the car (the amount you would have to pay if you were going to write out a check for the whole thing), not the monthly payment, because that is the only way you can compare one car with another. *Consumer Reports* has a pricing service that will give you the dealer cost and retail price for most cars and their option packages, as well as a list of all current factory-to-dealer incentives and dealer-to-customer incentives such as rebates. You can also use your research as a negotiating tactic. I have a client who visited car dealerships with her *Consumer Reports* printouts in hand. Jean was having trouble getting the salespeople to take her seriously (if you are a woman and you have ever bought a car, you know *exactly* what I mean). Those highly visible printouts made the salespeople realize she knew exactly what she was doing. As she said, "No one called me 'honey' or 'little lady' after that!"

When you are greeted at the door, the salesperson may ask you how large a monthly payment you can afford and whether or not you plan to trade in your old car. As mentioned before, the best answer to both questions is "I have not decided." Most experts agree that it is smarter to negotiate your trade-in and negotiate your purchase in two separate transactions because otherwise it can become very confusing to tell if you are getting a good deal. What may look like a good trade-in value may be offset by your being charged a higher price for the new car. Remember, salespeople do not call this negotiating process "the grind" for nothing! In a traditional dealership where negotiating is expected, the salesperson will offer you a price, then you counter with a lower price; if it is too low, then she may go back to the sales manager and return with yet another price. At this point you probably feel overwhelmed (sometimes these few steps can go on for two or more hours); the salesperson's goal is to wear you down and keep you from going to other dealers. You may still consider this price too high and counter again, which just continues the process. If you continue to bargain hard, the sales manager may come out to talk to you in person (I have even had the owner of the dealership come out). In fact, you may find yourself literally surrounded by people trying to sell you the car, and this can be very intimidating. A strategy that has worked for me and others is to let the salesperson know you are going to leave and go visit other dealers (and then follow through unless you get the price you want). After all, you can always come back!

Remember to write down each price that is offered and counteroffered, and note what features it includes as well. Show this price you have written down to the salesperson and ask her to verify that this is the price she quoted (and the right conditions). I have found that so many numbers are thrown around, it can get very confusing. Also, I have had offers "corrected" when I went back to buy the same car. Remember, the first discount off the list price is usually not the last discount! And you cannot always trust what you hear over the phone. For example, when I bought my Jeep I was trying to negotiate by telephone because my leg was in a cast. After I told one of the salespeople I was coming in to talk to him, he called me back to say he had misquoted and the price was actually $800 more than he had said in the previous phone call. Needless to say, I never set foot (or cast!) in that dealership.

If you have gotten your best offer in writing and you feel that there is still negotiating room, you are now armed to go to other dealers and negotiate as well. Again, tell the salesperson you plan to negotiate with other dealers; this makes you a potential sale walking out the door and puts added pressure on the dealership (the "bird in the hand is worth two in the bush" idea). Do not feel pressured to buy that day. Even if the car you want is not on the lot (or you are warned that the car you want may be gone by the time you come back from car shopping elsewhere), the dealer can usually swap one of his cars for the exact car you want from another dealership.

What is the right price? It is hard to say, because it depends on the area of the country you live in, how popular the car is there, and how available it is there. Just keep in mind that you almost always have negotiating room between the retail price and the dealer invoice price (the wholesale price that the dealer pays). Again, this is where the *Consumer Reports* car-pricing service can be so helpful, because you know exactly how much room there is between the dealer invoice and the asking price. I usually start bargaining at $200 over the invoice price plus destination charges, and then inch up in increments as small as $100. Granted, this approach can require a strong stomach, and many people are not willing to bargain that hard. Don't be too hard on yourself if, try as you might, you can't bargain the price down to be near the dealer invoice price after using every one of these techniques. Car buying is a process of supply and demand, and if the car you want is very popular (so there is great demand) or in short supply, you will have to settle for the best price among a few different dealers. I remember when Honda Accords were so popular that a friend had to pay *above* retail price to get one! But don't cave in if the first dealer you visit won't budge much on price; chances are there's another dealer who will.

■ Using a fixed-price dealership

One way to avoid the bargaining process altogether is to go to a fixed-price dealership that may advertise "below invoice pricing" or "1 percent over invoice" or that handles car models sold only on a fixed-price basis (such as Saturns). If you do not have the stomach for negotiating or you know you are a pushover, by all means go that route. This does not mean, however, that you should walk into the first fixed-price dealership you see and buy. Prices can actually vary widely among fixed-price dealers. If you are willing to try negotiating, I recommend you shop at fixed-price dealers as well as at traditional dealers where you can bargain. You may actually get a better price at a traditional dealer, although the process of buying the car may not be much fun. Remember, car buying is a process of supply and demand—the dealer has the car you want but knows you can go elsewhere in the area and purchase it—hence my argument for flexibility about car model, color, and options. You, however, are in the stronger position because you have the cash (or can get the car loan or qualify for the lease), you are sitting in the dealership, and you are willing to make a deal *today* if the price is right. Don't fall for the old trick that "prices are about to go up." Ask to see the price increase notice in writing, and when you go to another dealership selling the same kind of car, see if they produce a similar letter. Several years ago this happened to me—two dealers showed me identical notices of a price increase, but one of the letters showed an obviously altered price increase date that was the following week, *not* three months hence, as on the original notice date of the price increase! Remember, however, if you are stuck on one car and one color, you've got less negotiating room.

Car salespeople I have spoken with have always told me they much more enjoy selling a car to an informed car buyer who knows how to negotiate than to someone who comes in and starts throwing prices around without knowing the facts and then becomes suspicious and belligerent when his below-cost offer is rejected. In fact, there are many excellent salespeople who will treat you fairly, be direct and honest with you, and refrain from pressuring you to buy. If you find such a person, try to buy from him if at all possible—and even if you don't, be sure to compliment him on his professional demeanor and tell the sales manager of your satisfaction as well. All too often, salespeople are judged only on the basis of how many cars they sell, and this sole criterion serves to reward aggressive sales tactics.

If the salesperson tries to negotiate with you based on monthly payment, be firm about sticking to the price of the car as if you were going to pay all cash today. Remember that two cars with vastly different price tags can have identical monthly payments; but one could have a loan lasting up to seven years! And because you are negotiating based on the *total cost of the car* instead of monthly payments, be sure to look at all the charges on the sticker. Sometimes charges show up that the car manufacturer never intended to be there; they are added on to the invoice at the dealership and they represent pure dealer profit. Look for such charges as "import tariffs," "MVA" ("market value adjustments"), "CVF" ("currency valuation fees"). My personal favorite is "ADP" ("added dealer profit") because it's the one charge that states its purpose clearly! Other sources of profit for dealers are extra warranties, rustproofing, and expensive security systems. Most cars are already rustproofed, have fewer parts that can rust, and have long rustproofing warranties, and it is usually not worth it to pay extra for longer-term warranties of any kind. On my previous two car purchases, I paid about $500 each for 70,000-mile warranties against major repairs, and in both cases less than $100 of work was covered under warranty (out of thousands of dollars of repairs). It was an expensive lesson (and it took *two* cars for me to learn), but I was smarter this time around and passed up the opportunity to buy an extended warranty.

■ Financing your purchase

Since two-thirds of all cars are financed, for most people it is not a question of deciding *whether* to finance a car purchase but *how*. One important thing to know about most dealer financing is that the better your credit, the lower the interest rate. Also, the larger the down payment you can make, the lower the rate. (At this point in negotiating, you do not have to reveal where your down payment will come from—savings, selling your old car, or trading it in.) Before you sign on for dealer financing, check with your bank or credit union to find out what the required down payment and the interest rate would be through those sources. Dealer versus bank financing can vary according to where you live; often the bank interest rate is slightly lower, but the down payment required is higher. It is usually easier and faster to get credit at a dealer than a bank. If your car qualifies for dealer financing at a very low rate, look into it (but keep in mind that those loans normally run for a short duration of two or three years). Be sure to get a firm interest rate quote from the dealer, not just a statement declaring that "depending on your credit report, the rate will be between x percent and x percent." The last time I purchased a car, the salesperson and the credit manager at the dealership both said the rate could vary "between about 6 percent and 8 percent." I insisted on a firm quote, and I was glad I did—I later found out that the highest rate could have been as high as 9 percent, a full percentage point higher than the local bank's maximum rate. And remember, whenever you are financing a car, it is important to pay the loan off as quickly as possible and to finance it for as short a term as possible. Interest on the loan is not tax-deductible under current tax law unless you are using the car for business purposes.

Wherever you obtain financing, be sure to tell them you do not want credit life and disability insurance. These coverages are often included automatically, and you have to specifically ask for them to be excluded. Having adequate life and disability insurance is important to the Money Diet (see chapter 13, "Protecting Your Future with Insurance") but the monthly premiums for the amount of insurance coverage that you get through automobile and other consumer loans make credit insurance a very expensive option. If you don't have enough life and disability insurance already, you probably need more coverage from other, better sources.

■ Trading in your old car

Once you finalize the negotiations on your new car purchase or lease, it is time to bring up trading in your car. In 1993, 35 percent of people who bought or leased new cars traded in their old ones. Buying and trading in may seem linked in your mind, but as far as the dealer is concerned, they are two separate transactions because someone else will buy your used car and that person has nothing to do with your new car! The dealer may try to link these transactions but it just gets too confusing to keep track of. It shouldn't matter to the dealer *where* your down payment comes from.

The first thing to do is to call your bank's commercial loan department and get the "retail" and "wholesale" values (including options) for your used car. There are standard publications such as *The Official Used Car Guide* that are used by banks, dealers, and others to value used cars for sale. Generally speaking, the retail value is the price at which a car would be listed at a dealership, and the wholesale value is the value of the car when it is traded in. But it's important to know both values because the dealer may be willing to give you above wholesale or retail may be so much higher that you may decide to try and sell it on your own. Do not forget to take all your car's options into account; options include CD or cassette players, air conditioning, trailer-tow equipment, leather seats, tinted windows—in other words, all the options you paid extra for when you originally purchased the car. If you decide to sell the car yourself, you will usually be able to get somewhere between the retail and the wholesale values.

Many people decide to trade in simply because they do not want the bother of selling the car themselves or do not want to pay the cost of advertising it. And, of course, many people need to sell their old car and buy their new one at the same time because the proceeds from the old one will be the down payment for the new one. Another thing to take into consideration is that in some states there are "lemon laws" that make the seller fully responsible if the buyer has major mechanical problems within the first thirty days or so after purchasing a used car. Dealers will usually waive the lemon law if you trade in, so they take full responsibility. The bottom line is that you will likely end up with more dollars in your pocket if you sell on your own, but it does require some work and inconvenience. The key is to do your homework to learn your used car's "official" retail and wholesale (trade-in) values, get your dealer's best trade-in offer in writing, and decide whether it's worth it.

After doing his homework, Clark decided he needed a car that would seat at least four people because he is an avid golf player and drives three golf partners to the course. He also needs storage space for four sets of golf clubs. Clark rarely drives on long trips and he lives in the city, so he wants a car that is small enough to maneuver into parallel parking spaces. He usually buys cars and "runs them into the ground," so he researched repair records. Clark narrowed his choices down to two basic cars (one of which has a lesser-known "twin"). Once he decided how much he could afford, he researched various models and dealerships and was ready to start shopping around.

Because he enjoys matching wits with salespeople and considers himself a good negotiator, Clark went to a traditional dealership where bargaining is the rule. He then narrowed the field to two cars and started negotiating on his first choice, with the "fall-back" plan of switching to the second-choice car if he couldn't reach agreement on his first choice. After two hours at one dealership and several offers and counteroffers, Clark and the salesperson were still $400 apart in their prices. He decided to try another dealer, where he negotiated a price that was $200 less than the first dealer's. Clark was much more impressed by dealer number one's service record (he had called the Better Business Bureau to check on complaints filed, and talked to friends), so he went back to the first dealer and asked the salesperson to meet dealer number two's offer. When faced with the prospect of losing the sale altogether, the salesperson at dealer number one agreed. Clark got the car he wanted from the dealer he wanted, and he was satisfied that the price was as low as it possibly could be.

Clark checked his current car's retail and wholesale prices, and the difference was about $700. He figured if he sold his car on his own instead of trading in he might get half the difference—$350 extra in his sales price. Clark traveled a great deal for work, and the only times he could count on being in town were on the weekends. He did not consider the possible $350 "profit" worth the hassle of using up his weekends, advertising in the newspaper, and trying to negotiate with buyers. Therefore, Clark decided to trade in his car, and because he had already nailed down the details of his new car purchase, he could figure out exactly how much the dealer was actually offering.

After comparing the local bank's rates with his credit union's and the dealer's, Clark opted to go for dealer financing because the car manufacturer was offering below-market interest rate loans for up to thirty-six months. He saved 3 percentage points on the interest rate, which allowed him to stick to his $400-a-month car payment budget even though the term of the loan was two years less than he had figured (three years versus five). Why? So much more of every monthly payment could go to paying down the loan balance because so much less interest was due.

LEASING A CAR

Let's assume that when you completed **Should You Buy or Lease a Car?** (page 234) the numbers showed clearly that you should lease. Leasing makes sense when you plan to keep the car for less than four years, you don't have enough for a down payment, you couldn't afford the monthly payments for this model if you bought it, or you want a new car every couple of years. Thankfully, the leasing process is less confusing than buying because there is less commitment on your part—you merely agree to "rent" for a period of time. When you lease from a leasing company or dealership, usually they buy the car and then lease it to you; you have to return it or buy it at the end of the leasing period. The monthly payment is lower than it would be if you were buying the car and making payments for the same time period, but the downside is that you do not build up equity in the car. When you turn it in, you have to lease or buy all over again. Furthermore, leasing incurs expenses in addition to the monthly lease payment. You usually have to pay a down payment (and in some instances, a security deposit), as well as sales tax on the full price of the car. (The real kicker about the sales tax is that if you actually buy the car later on, you have to pay sales tax again, as though you bought the car twice.) So if you are leasing cars every few years, you are paying sales tax on a new car every time.

You may be wondering how companies determine what to charge when they lease you a car. The cost of leasing is usually determined by looking at the current market value of the car you are going to lease and then estimating what its value will be when you turn it in (based on used car prices). Remember, in **Should You Buy or Lease a Car?** I recommended you ask your salesperson for the estimated future value at the end of the leasing period. This future value is also called "residual value." One concern I have about estimating this "residual value" in some future year is that the popularity of leasing is increasing dramatically, and the market is going to be flooded with used cars from people who have turned cars back in at the end of the leasing period. This means your leased car may be worth a lot less than the leasing company anticipated when it estimated your car's resale value at the end of your lease. Why? If the market is flooded, prices will have to drop in order to beat the competition.

■ Negotiating your lease

Although leasing is simpler than buying, you still need to watch out for some things. Make sure your contract states in writing that your security deposit is refundable. Check to make sure you have a closed-end lease instead of an open-end one (the words *closed-end* or *open-end* will be in the contract.) Why? Open-end leases give *you* the responsibility of coming up with the difference if the car is worth less at the end of the lease than was originally estimated. And you always want a closed-end lease so you are not locked into buying the car at the end of the lease period. Avoid leases with low annual mileage caps (under 12,000 miles or so) because if you go over the mileage cap stated in the contract you will have to pay a per-mile surcharge (often up to $.15). Or you can try to negotiate up that mileage cap; some leasing companies are more flexible than others on this point.

Just as with buying cars, watch out for built-in disability and life insurance premiums because the premiums are very expensive for the amount of coverage provided. If you need disability and life insurance, you probably need it for a lot more important things than covering your auto lease payments, but make sure you have enough life and disability insurance to meet all your needs. Avoid contracts with an early termination penalty, or you may be charged a whopping penalty if you decide to get rid of the car before the end of the leasing period. Make sure your contract includes "gap insurance" so you do not have to pay the cost of the car if it is wrecked or stolen. Finally, if there is a chance you will move, make sure that you can return the car in any one of many different cities when it comes time to do so. A few years ago, a friend of mine had to drive over 1,000 miles to turn in a leased car and then buy a one-way ticket back home. Most important of all, make sure you are dealing with a reputable dealership or leasing company because of the "excessive wear" clause. The leasing company gets to decide how much wear and tear you have caused to the car, and whether that wear is "normal" or "excessive." Read the definition of excessive wear carefully before you sign! An unscrupulous company can charge you thousands of dollars for what it calls excessive wear and tear when in fact the car is in normal condition.

BUYING OR LEASING: THE BOTTOM LINE

Finally, the bottom line with buying or leasing a car is to try to get what you need and avoid the fancy options. Remember that you are buying or renting a depreciating asset and that every dollar you put into a car is a dollar that you cannot use for education, retirement, buying a home, or any of your other major goals. My advice is to buy or lease the least expensive car you can bear to drive and put those extra dollars you save toward other goals. Buy a car if you can and drive it as long as possible even if you have to make major repairs; in the long run, that is usually the cheapest way to provide transportation for you and your family. When your old car is finally on its last legs, you can go through the process all over again. This way, you minimize the number of times in your life that you have to waste your money on 10 percent depreciation overnight.

BUYING OTHER BIG-TICKET ITEMS

Of course, there are other big-ticket items people like to purchase besides second homes and cars. One big-ticket item I think every person needs, regardless of individual financial situation, is a "dream of a lifetime" vacation. To keep those happy memories, though, it is smart to save the money in advance so that you are not still paying for your dream vacation for years after you return. Many years ago I met a remarkable family who had saved for several years so they could take a year off and travel around the world on a boat. They bought no new clothes, rarely went out for entertainment, and literally ate tomato soup for a year so they could take this trip. In fact, one of the children told me before they set off that he would never be able to stand the sight of tomato soup again! They had worked hard for this vacation as a family, and they had earned it, and their sacrifices made the trip all the more enjoyable. Another family who took the same vacation but made all the sacrifice *after* they returned probably would find the memories of their trip less satisfying. Why? Their most recent memories would be of sacrifice, not of enjoyment, and it would be hard to resist wondering if the "dream of a lifetime" vacation was worth it after all.

Expensive jewelry, collectibles such as stamps, coins, or plates, and other items are often purchased because they are considered "good investments" (and, of course, this is how they are marketed!). They may be good investments for someone else, but remember that they are not an investment for you if you never plan to sell them. My recommendation for clients who want to start building collections is to pick a hobby where they can make an initial, relatively small investment and then build their collection by buying and selling pieces with little or no additional cash required.

The hardest thing about big-ticket items is that we all would like to have these things but we all cannot afford them and meet lifetime goals at the same time. Remember that the key to the Money Diet is balancing your short-term needs and wants with your long-term goals. Before you spend a penny on a big-ticket item, you must figure out whether what you are considering is a short-term want or long-term goal. Remember to give yourself the Five Question Test at the beginning of this chapter. The Money Diet approach may not give you much instant gratification, but the fact is, if you buy a big-ticket item and you cannot afford it, somewhere inside, *you already know this and your pleasure is already diminished.* You may be surprised at the enormous relief and sense of accomplishment you feel when you tell yourself "no" (a hundred times more satisfying than saying "no" to a hot fudge sundae!). You will have taken a major step toward getting control of your financial situation, and each step you take makes the next one a little easier. The quickest way to sabotage your future goals is to succumb to an unnecessary or unnecessarily expensive big-ticket item, so resisting these temptations is among the most valuable lessons you can learn in sticking to your Money Diet.

CHAPTER THIRTEEN

Protecting Your Future
with Insurance

IF YOU ARE like most people, you are probably tempted to skip this chapter altogether because the focus is on everything bad that can happen. But my advice is: Don't. I will let a few true-life examples bring home to you why you should not.

A young couple just starting out, with no children and at the beginning of two careers, sits down to talk with an insurance agent. They want to get their insurance right from the start, and the wife knows she needs disability insurance. They diligently review the disability insurance proposal, and she puts it in her "to do" file at work. It sits there for a year. In the meantime, she becomes pregnant and develops complications during the pregnancy that turn out to be a congenital back disorder. She ends up being virtually bedridden for five years, and almost every day during those five years she thinks of the $800 tax-free income they could have had every month if she had not kept moving the disability application to the back of her "to do" file.

A couple comes home from vacation and opens the door of their condominium. "Opens" is perhaps an inappropriate word, because when they turn the knob the door falls flat, just like in the cartoons. It turns out that thieves have ransacked their condominium and propped the door back up so that it would look perfectly normal until someone tried to open it. The couple dutifully fills out the insurance forms, listing each piece of family jewelry that was stolen. It turns out that because the jewelry pieces were not individually listed on the policy, there is only a $500 settlement for *all* the jewelry instead of a $500 settlement for each piece as they had thought.

A working mother, hurrying home to relieve the baby-sitter, stops at a stop sign near her house. She glances in her rearview mirror, only to see a car hurtling toward her in which a driver appears to be putting on eye makeup. The driver of the other car pulls her hand away from her face, but not soon enough to avoid crashing into the car ahead. This working mother, whose family depends on her income, suffers a broken collarbone, whiplash, and severe back strain that makes it impossible for her to go to the office for over three months. The driver at fault has the minimum insurance required by the state, not nearly enough to cover all the single parent's expenses and lost income. The working mother's underinsured motorist coverage, which kicks in when the other driver's insurance reaches its limit, is not enough either.

You probably recognize the first scenario from my preface, but who are these other idiots? Well, they are all the same person, and that person is me. For a long time, I suffered from the "cobbler" syndrome, as in the phrase "The cobbler's children have no shoes." I was so busy advising others that I never took the time to plan for myself. So even if you are considered an expert on financial matters, you can make the very human mistake of not wanting to think about such unpleasant possibilities as becoming disabled, being burglarized, or getting involved in an auto accident. Don't assume "It won't happen to me." Those can be the saddest words of all. So once you have determined that you need insurance, *do something about it.*

In chapter 1, "How the Money Diet Works," I described insurance as the invisible circle surrounding and protecting your income and your assets. Just as exercise, vitamins, stress reduction, and cutting down on fat protect your physical health, insurance protects your financial health. It is all too easy to sail through this step in the book—**Developing Your Money Diet Plan**—by focusing only on its positive parts. But all your work on those positive parts can be wiped out in a split second. That's why, these days, virtually everyone needs *some* form of insurance. Insurance can replace your income if you die or become disabled so your assets do not get used up by living expenses. Insurance can also protect you against damage to or loss of your home, automobile, or other assets. Finally (and critically important), you need to be protected against lawsuits in this increasingly litigious society. If you think about how much you would worry if insurance had never been invented (because then there would be no way to guard against these losses unless you were very rich), insurance is one of the best stress-reduction methods around.

Even some of our founding fathers were interested in protecting aspects of our lives other than our liberty. Benjamin Franklin himself started the first American insurance company in 1752, some twenty-four years before he signed the Declaration of Independence. Insurance is a complicated set of products, and the buying process usually makes it even more complicated. But insurance is not a complete mystery, and you can look for certain basic principles and specific policy features. That is precisely what this chapter will help you do.

BASIC BUYING PRINCIPLES

There are certain basic principles to follow when you buy insurance. The first insurance principle is to protect against the largest losses first. We would all like to be insulated from every conceivable danger. But few of us can afford all the premiums for so much insurance. So you have to set priorities, first in the kind of insurance you buy and then in the amount of coverage you get in each policy. This is where trade-offs come in. Be sure to comparison-shop, but never buy a particular policy just because it is the cheapest. Insurance can be expensive, and just as in other aspects of life, cheaper isn't always better. The problem is you may not find this out until the time comes to collect.

An adequate insurance program is critical to the success of the Money Diet. Of course, insurance premiums increase your expenses and thereby reduce your annual savings, but, believe me, the sacrifice is worth it. With the right coverage, you are protecting yourself against a financial catastrophe that could, in a single moment, eliminate any chance of achieving your other financial goals.

LIFE INSURANCE

Let's look at life insurance first, because my clients dread dealing with it the most. Why? Life insurance obviously starts with a negative premise. Because most of us do not want to admit that we will die, and because insurance is often sold in an aggressive way, many people are drastically uninsured. In fact, in a recent survey, *40 percent* of those surveyed felt they needed more life insurance coverage. I am always amazed when a new client with a six-figure income comes to see me and thinks that $50,000 of life insurance is just fine. Often, she says she does not believe in insurance; my response to that is she may not believe in insurance but I bet her family would if she died and they found out after the fact that she didn't have enough. One of my clients insists on carrying a huge insurance policy on his life—even more than is needed. Justin still recalls how angry and upset he felt when he realized his father had never owned a cent of life insurance, even though his father had five children and a wife to support. Luckily, Justin never had to find this out the hard way, because his father is still alive. But he still cannot forgive his dad for being so pigheaded about the supposed evils of insurance that he would not even protect his family from the threat of bankruptcy.

Plain common sense tells us the odds of dying increase with age. If you are twenty-five years old now, your odds of dying within the next twenty years are 1 in 41. If you are forty-five, the odds are 1 in 6. On top of the emotional devastation your loved ones would face if you did die, they would be hit with expenses right and left. First, there are the death costs—funeral expenses, estate and inheritance taxes, administrative expenses, and any uninsured medical expenses incurred before your death. Second, there are ongoing living expenses for your family, which will now need to be paid for without your income. And third, there are your family's future goals such as education, retirement, and perhaps paying off the mortgage. But before you start worrying about where the money will come from to cover all of these expenses, the first thing to do is to find out exactly how much of a shortfall you have. I frequently get calls from people who want my advice about which insurance policy to buy. More often than not, they have not stopped to figure out exactly how much insurance they need in the first place—they have just picked a number out of the blue.

HOW MUCH (MORE) LIFE INSURANCE DO YOU NEED?

How much insurance you need obviously depends on your particular situation—primarily, on how many people depend on your income. These days, that can mean elderly parents and other relatives as well as children. You may have heard of different rules of thumb, such as "seven times your annual income," or "five times your expenses," and so on. I have never met a client whose insurance need could be accurately calculated on this basis. The problem is that every family has different needs and goals. The most accurate way to figure out how much insurance you need is called the Capital Needs Analysis. **How Much (More) Life Insurance Do You Need?** (page 255) is a simple capital needs analysis. If there are two adults in your household, complete two versions of this capital needs analysis—one for each of you. You may be shocked at how much insurance you need, but the goal is to buy as much of this amount as you can reasonably afford. Always make sure that you have enough insurance on all breadwinners and on a spouse with child care responsibilities before you take out insurance on your children.

The first part of **How Much (More) Life Insurance Do You Need?** lists all the one-time or lump-sum expenses associated with your death, but not ongoing living expenses. These include Funeral and Final Expenses, such as medical costs not paid for by insurance and Estate Taxes (which vary by state of residence and size of estate). A good rule of thumb is between $5,000 and $10,000 for funeral and final expenses combined. If you want your Mortgage and Other Debts paid off (see **Simplified Net Worth Statement**, page 22, lines I through L); list them on lines D and E here. My advice to clients is to be conservative and make sure your heirs have the money to pay off all debts; they can make the actual decision whether or not to do so when the time comes. If you have children and want a college

How Much (More) Life Insurance Do You Need?

Lump Sum Need	What You'll Need
A. Funeral	A.
B. Plus: Final Expenses (medical, etc.)	B. +
C. Plus: Estate Taxes*	C. +
D. Plus: Pay off Mortgage (optional) (Simplified Net Worth Statement, p. 22, line I)	D. +
E. Plus: Pay off Other Debts (optional) (Simplified Net Worth Statement, p. 22, lines J–L)	E. +
F. Plus: College Fund (Setting Your Financial Goals, p. 42, line D)	F. +
G. Plus: Special Need[†]	G. +
H. Total	H. =
Living Expense Need I. Your Current Living Expenses (Spending and Saving, p. 28, line H)	I.
Times 0.7[‡]	× 0.7
J. Equals: Family Living Expenses After Your Death	J. =
K. Less: Spouse's Take-Home Pay/Other Income	K. −
L. Less: Social Security Survivor's Benefit (Social Security Survivor's Benefits, p. 257) _____ × 12 = Annual Benefit	L. −
M. Equals: Additional Annual Living Expense Need	M. =
Times: No. of Years Needed	×
N. Total Living Expense Shortfall	N. =
O. Total Assets You Need (H+N)	O.
P. Current Insurance Death Benefits	P.
Q. Current Investment Assets (Your Current Investment Strategy, p. 126, line A)	Q.
R. Total Assets You Have (P+Q)	R. =
S. Your Additional Insurance Need (O–R)	S =

* Estate taxes vary by state of residence and size of estate.

† This can be any amount you want your family to have after your death.

‡ If you are your family's primary child care provider, someone would have to be hired in your place if you die. In this case, do not reduce your current living expenses amount.

From *The Money Diet*, by Ginger Applegarth.

fund, write on line F the amount you listed in **Setting Your Financial Goals,** page 42, line D). Finally, on line G, write down any amount you want for a special need: I have seen these range from a special bequest to a relative or friend, to an emergency fund to act as an extra cushion for your family, to something as unusual as a "remembrance" party, complete with a band, for friends to attend in the event of your death. The sum total of all these one-time expenses goes on line H.

The next number to nail down is the total amount needed to cover your family's living expenses, taking Social Security into consideration. **Spending and Saving** (page 28, line H), shows your current expenses; write that number on line I here. Because they would likely be reduced at your death, multiply that number by 0.7 and write the result, Family Living Expenses After Your Death, on line J. However, if a child care provider would have to be hired in your place to take care of your children, do not reduce your current living expenses amount. Depending on the cost of child care in your area, you may even want to *increase* living expenses. Add up the annual amount of your Spouse's Take-Home Pay, Other Income such as rental and investment income; write the total on line K. Then, in **Social Security Survivor's Benefits** (page 257), find the monthly benefit amount for the age, income, and family situation nearest yours. Multiply that number by 12 to get the annual benefit, and write your answer on line L. Subtract lines K and L from J; the answer (line M) is your Additional Annual Living Expense Need. Think about how long your family will need this additional income (some clients are worried about providing extra income until the kids leave home, and others want to take care of their spouses for life). Multiply your annual need (line M) by the number of years of annual income you want. Your answer, on line N, is your Total Living Expense Shortfall.

If your answer is a negative number, your family has enough income to live on; and you would only need insurance or other assets to cover the one-time expenses on line H. But if you are like most people, you will get a positive number, which means your family would need more money than they would have. The Total Assets You Need, line O, is line H plus line N. Then add up your existing Insurance Death Benefits (also perhaps listed as "face amount" on the policies)

Social Security Survivor's Benefits

Monthly Benefits

Age at Death	Your Family	Earnings the Year before Death				
		$20,000	$30,000	$40,000	$50,000	$59,000 or more
25	Spouse & 1 child[1]	1,118	1,504	1,684	1,875	1,951
	Spouse & 2 children[2]	1,398	1,759	1,970	2,191	2,279
	1 child only	559	753	843	938	975
	Spouse at age 60	533	716	804	894	930
35	Spouse & 1 child[1]	1,189	1,597	1,799	1,991	2,097
	Spouse & 2 children[2]	1,487	1,866	2,102	2,325	2,448
	1 child only	595	799	900	996	1,049
	Spouse at age 60	567	761	858	950	1,000
45	Spouse & 1 child[1]	1,189	1,597	1,795	1,946	2,007
	Spouse & 2 children[2]	1,487	1,866	2,096	2,273	2,342
	1 child only	595	799	898	973	1,004
	Spouse at age 60	567	761	856	928	957
55	Spouse & 1 child[1]	1,189	1,589	1,740	1,836	1,875
	Spouse & 2 children[2]	1,487	1,855	2,031	2,144	2,189
	1 child only	595	795	870	918	937
	Spouse at age 60	567	758	829	875	894

[1] Amounts shown also equal the benefits paid to 2 children if no parent survives or surviving parent has substantial earnings.

[2] Equals the maximum family benefit.

Note: These figures assume you die in 1995; your earnings over the years have remained steady; and, you have earned enough credits to qualify for Social Security. They are calculated in today's dollars.

To find the correct amount, select the age and family situation nearest yours and move right until you reach the column for the salary nearest yours.

Source: Social Security and author's estimates, based on previous years.

From *The Money Diet*, by Ginger Applegarth.

and write the total on line P. Then write the total of your investment Assets (**Your Current Investment Strategy,** page 126, line A) on line Q. Sometimes a retirement plan's death benefit will be higher than its current investment value. If so, use the death benefit amount. Add lines P and Q to get line R, Total Assets You Have. Your additional need (if any), on line S, is O minus R. If you get a negative number, that means you have more than enough insurance, but think twice before you drop any policies. Insurance gets more expensive as you age, and you may not be able to get new insurance due to poor health.

As you can see, the financial costs of dying and of supporting family after your death can be astronomical. Your assets can be sold to help pay these costs, but it is highly unlikely that you have enough on hand to pay for everything (I can count on one hand—with fingers left over—the number of new clients who could have done this without buying additional insurance). Social Security and group life insurance can help, but they are not usually enough. Where else can you get the money? For many people, an additional life insurance policy is the only solution.

WHAT KIND OF LIFE INSURANCE TO BUY?

In **How Much (More) Life Insurance Do You Need?** you figured out how much additional life insurance to buy. The next question is what type of insurance to buy. Here is where the life insurance debate often takes on a nearly religious fervor, partly because there are commissions at stake and insurance salespeople are trained in different schools of thought. There are two basic types of individual insurance policies— *term* (which has a death benefit but no value if you cash it in beforehand) and *permanent* (which has a death benefit or, if you cash the policy in before you die, a built-in savings account called cash surrender value). This distinction is very important; if **How Much (More) Life Insurance Do You Need?** showed a shortfall, probably the biggest (and most confusing) insurance decision you are facing is whether to buy term or permanent life insurance.

Some proponents of term life insurance believe that permanent insurance is a life insurance company deception. Permanent insurance advocates say term insurance is like throwing money down a hole. The important thing to keep in mind is that *there is no one correct answer that applies to every person* (this is one reason why the term-versus-permanent issue can become so emotional and confusing). As with anything else, some term insurance contracts are better than some permanent ones, and vice versa. What matters is the financial strength of the insurance company, how good the policy is, and your particular situation.

In general, commissions on permanent insurance are much larger than commissions on term insurance, unless you choose a "low-load" (no-commission) policy. I do not mean to imply that permanent insurance is therefore bad, but as a consumer you should be aware that such factors may influence the advice you are given.

With term insurance, the premium goes up periodically and becomes very expensive as you grow older. The advantage to term insurance is that for any given age, the premiums for a new policy are much less expensive than permanent insurance premiums because no cash value builds up for you to take if you live. When purchasing term insurance, you want a policy that you can automatically renew at least until age seventy and convert to a permanent insurance policy regardless of your health. Also look for a death benefit that at least stays the same throughout the life of the policy—so, for example, whether you die at age thirty or fifty, the policy would pay $100,000 to the person or persons you designate as beneficiary. This is because these days, even though children leave home and start taking on their own living expenses and education costs, a surviving spouse will probably need a lot of money in the bank to cover retirement costs.

The other major type of life insurance, permanent insurance, combines a savings account feature with a death benefit. Initially, the premium is higher than with term insurance because some of your money is going to the savings account, or "cash value." The reason permanent insurance can be attractive as an investment is because under current tax laws the investment portion of the policy is tax-deferred, so income taxes do not have to be paid unless the policy is cashed in during your lifetime. (If you die, all death benefits are usually income-tax-free regardless of whether the policy was term or permanent.) You can cancel at any time and get back your current cash surrender value. Keep in mind, however, that these values are usually very minimal in the early years, so the amount you would get back if you cash the policy in early on may be less than the total premiums you paid.

Different types of permanent policies have different savings vehicles, but they are all based on the concept that extra premiums paid in the early years go toward a savings or "cash value" account. That is why, no matter how old you are when you are shopping for insurance, the premiums will always be higher for a permanent policy than for a term policy.

The best-known type of permanent insurance (because it has been around for more than one hundred years) is whole life, ordinary life, or straight life—all different names for the same product. Whole life offers a guaranteed premium (the amount that you have to pay each year to keep the policy in force) and death benefit (the total paid at your death) as well as a guaranteed minimum cash value, which you can borrow against if necessary.

The insurance industry has also designed a number of more investment-oriented permanent policies. The first is called universal life. With universal life, the premiums are flexible, there is a minimum guaranteed death benefit and interest rate, and the insurance company decides which types of investments to make. Because you can sometimes skip payments once you build up enough cash value, you need to have the self-discipline to keep paying premiums as planned if you buy universal life insurance. The second kind of investment-oriented policy is variable life insurance. With variable life insurance, there are guaranteed fixed premiums and a guaranteed death benefit but *no* guaranteed cash value, so it is riskier than other types of life insurance. You do, however, get to pick the types of investments you want—usually money market, stock, bond, or real estate funds—so you might get a better investment return with variable life than whole life or universal life.

My recommendation is to focus on the amount of insurance you need—**How Much (More) Life Insurance Do You Need?**, line S—before deciding whether to buy term or permanent insurance. Your first priority is to buy as much of that insurance amount as you can. By now you should have a good idea of your income and expenses, as well as of what you would want insurance to pay for (education, family income, mortgage and/or other debt to pay off). If you can afford to buy the amount you need only as term insurance, do it and forget about permanent insurance. If you have extra room in your budget, however, and want to consider using permanent insurance as part of your investment portfolio, you have a bit more work to do. In that case, my recommendation is to cover short-term needs (those that will disappear within the next ten years) with term insurance and long-term needs (those that will still exist ten years from now) with permanent insurance.

For example, Patrick and Beth are both employed, so if one of them dies, the surviving spouse would need to supplement family income as well as college tuition only until the youngest child graduates from college in seven years. Term insurance makes sense to cover this short-term need (they estimate the cost to be $90,000). But their mortgage of $106,000 will not be not paid off for twenty-five years, so a permanent policy for $106,000 may be cheaper for this long-term need. (In fact, the mortgage balance will decline over time, but it does so very slowly, and Patrick and Beth consider the extra insurance a cushion against inflation if the policy pays off when the mortgage is lower.) An experienced insurance adviser or agent can help you determine the amount of term and/or permanent insurance you should have.

One type of insurance to avoid is travel insurance that you purchase in the airport or with a credit card whenever you charge a ticket. If you need insurance, you need it all the time—not just for the short time you are in the air. Also, avoid policies offered by mail that guarantee you insurance regardless of health. These policies are usually very expensive for the coverage you get, the death benefit is usually $5,000 or less, and if you die in the first few years, the policy usually pays only the sum of your premiums less a large "administrative charge."

DECIPHERING LIFE INSURANCE PROPOSALS

Deciphering life insurance proposals can be almost impossible. These proposals, also called "illustrations," often run ten or more pages and have a thousand or more numbers. The good news is that a term insurance proposal is fairly straightforward. It will tell you the premiums and amount of insurance for each year the policy will be in effect. The permanent illustrations, though, can be very confusing. If you cannot make sense of a permanent life insurance proposal, you are not alone. I have seen doctors, lawyers, and college professors almost rendered speechless with frustration when trying to figure them out.

The problem? Permanent proposals usually show you two "what-ifs" based on different interest rates—the guaranteed minimum rate (usually 5 percent or so), and the current rate (usually several points higher). So what the proposal may show you are *two* cash values, *two* premiums, and *two* death benefits for *each* year the policy will be in force! Keep in mind that the amount you will likely get each year is somewhere between these two numbers.

A competent and qualified insurance agent or adviser is a critical part of any insurance decision. Avoid any insurance agent who quotes his or her company's current rate of return on their overall investments and implies that your insurance policy's cash value will do the same. Those two figures are often only indirectly related to each other, and a company's rate of return does *not* take the company's expenses into account. Also, avoid any agent who gives you a proposal that assumes you will get a double-digit interest rate that looks too good to be true. Some companies promise very high interest rates to start (say 10 or 12 percent for the first year) and then make up their losses by paying below average rates (5 or 6 percent) thereafter. Even in today's low interest rate environment a proposal occasionally crosses my desk with an assumed interest rate of 12 percent for the next thirty years. When I see something that unrealistic, I tell the client to get rid of the proposal *and* the agent!

SOCIAL SECURITY

You probably noticed that **How Much (More) Life Insurance Do You Need?** included Social Security benefits available at your death. It may seem strange to call Social Security "insurance," but it is. Your "premiums" are the Social Security taxes you must pay out of your earned income, and your benefits are what you or your beneficiary get back upon disability, retirement, or death.

Social Security is designed to provide a basic level of income when a participant dies (through survivor's benefits), becomes completely and permanently disabled, and/or retires. Survivor and disability benefits go down the older you are when you make a claim, but retirement benefits go *up* the older you are when you start to receive them. Even if you do not have a job right now, you can get benefits if you worked long enough in the past to be a "paid-up" participant in the system.

Two types of Social Security death benefits are available, neither of which is adequate for most families. The first is a lump-sum death benefit of a whopping $255 to help pay funeral expenses. There are also survivor's benefits for your dependents (this can include your spouse, children, dependent parents over sixty, and even your former spouse). It is hard to figure out what your survivor's benefits would be if you died because they depend on a number of factors. You can get an estimate of your potential benefits from Social Security by calling 1-800-772-1213 and asking for the Request for Earnings and Benefit Estimate Statement. You should verify your earnings record and get estimates of your future benefits approximately every three years so you can catch any errors before you file for benefits. **Social Security Survivor's Benefits** (page 257) shows the benefits your family might be entitled to if your death occurs in 1995, assuming very conservative increases in benefits. An important point to keep in mind is that if you are married, your spouse may face a "black-out period" during which no benefits will be paid to him or her. This generally occurs after the youngest child turns sixteen (although your child will continue to receive benefits for a few more years) and continues until your spouse turns sixty. Without those Social Security benefits, your spouse may be facing poverty if you do not have enough life insurance.

GROUP INSURANCE POLICIES

Another source of funds in the event of your death is group insurance provided by your employer or by organizations to which you belong. Group insurance is great because you can get insurance inexpensively, often regardless of your health. The primary drawbacks to group insurance are that you may lose the coverage if you change jobs and the maximum amounts available are usually low.

Social Security Disability Benefits

Monthly Benefits

Your Age	Your Family	Earnings the Year before Disability				
		$20,000	$30,000	$40,000	$50,000	$59,000 or more
25	You	793	1,065	1,200	1,328	1,410
	You, your spouse & 1 child[1]	1,189	1,598	1,800	1,992	2,114
35	You	793	1,065	1,201	1,328	1,391
	You, your spouse & 1 child[1]	1,189	1,598	1,800	1,992	2,008
45	You	793	1,065	1,195	1,291	1,329
	You, your spouse & 1 child[1]	1,189	1,598	1,794	1,937	1,993
55	You	793	1,060	1,160	1,225	1,251
	You, your spouse & 1 child[1]	1,189	1,589	1,740	1,837	1,876

[1] Equals the maximum family benefit.

Note: These figures assume you become disabled in 1995; your earnings over the years have remained steady; and you have earned enough credits to qualify for Social Security. They are calculated in today's dollars.

To find the correct amount, select the age and family situation nearest yours and move right until you reach the column for the salary nearest yours.

Source: Social Security and author's estimates, based on previous years.

From The Money Diet, by Ginger Applegarth.

IF YOUR FAMILY HAS A CLAIM

If your family ever has to make a claim for your life insurance, you will not be there to guide them through the process. So you must tell them *today* where your insurance policies are kept (your desk or a safe at home is a good choice), even if you do not want to tell them the details of each policy. Do not keep the policies in your safe-deposit box because your family will not have access to them until the court permits them to, and they may need the insurance proceeds to live on in the meantime.

DISABILITY INSURANCE

If you need to work to maintain your lifestyle—and virtually everyone does except the independently wealthy—you need disability insurance. This kind of insurance provides an ongoing monthly income to you and your family if you are unable to work due to accident or illness—acting as a sort of insurance policy on your income. Ironically, people often worry about accidents when the chances are much greater that they will become disabled due to illness.

We tend to think of disability, like death, as something that always happens to someone else. But the odds of disability before a very old age are even greater than those of dying. Every year, 12 percent of the U.S. adult population suffers a long-term disability, and 1 out of every 5 workers will suffer a five-year or longer period of disability before age sixty-five. If you are thirty-five now, you have a 30 percent chance of experiencing a long-term disability (three months or longer) before you reach age sixty-five. The basic problem is that when you become disabled, your income stops *but your living expenses continue.* And as the bills mount up and you have no income with which to pay them, your family can face painful decisions. A recent study showed that 48 percent of all home mortgage foreclosures are due to long-term disability. You would not think of leaving your home uninsured, but your chances of becoming disabled are much higher than of having a fire in your house.

Many people assume that as long as they have contributed to Social Security for a few years, they are covered in the event of disability. Wrong! You may have a big problem getting the Social Security Administration to agree that you are totally and permanently disabled and unable to work at any job. Currently, approximately 80 percent of all claims for Social Security benefits are denied the first time around. In fact, insurance companies are so aware of the difficulty of qualifying that many offer options on their policies that will pay the equivalent of your Social Security benefit if you are not sufficiently "disabled" for Social Security purposes but you *are* considered disabled by the private insurance company! Even if you do qualify, benefits from Social Security are probably not enough to meet your individual family needs. Right now Social Security payments increase with inflation, but there is no guarantee of that for the future. **Social Security Disability Benefits** (page 264) shows the benefits you might be entitled to if you were to become disabled in 1995. If you are entitled to Social Security disability benefits, you would also be entitled to Medicare, which can help pay your medical expenses. The wisest approach is not to count on Social Security at all and to consider it a windfall if you do qualify. Another source of disability income is workers' compensation (a government-mandated program to which employers contribute, which pays very limited benefits only if your injury or illness is job related and only for a short period of time). It's smart not to count on workers' compensation either.

HOW MUCH DISABILITY INSURANCE DO YOU NEED?

You already figured out how much disability income you need in chapter 4, "What's Your Financial 'Goal Weight'?" You can calculate how much additional disability insurance you need by completing **How Much (More) Disability Insurance Do You Need?** (page 267). Be sure to include only those policies that provide coverage for five or more years because we are focusing on long-term disability here. Add up your total disability benefits from your group and individual policies (lines A through C), as well as Social Security (line D); write the answer on line E. On line F, write the monthly income required in the event of disability from line G of **Setting Your Financial Goals** (page 42). The Additional Disability Coverage Needed is line H, or line F minus line G.

It would be great if you could decide on and qualify for any amount of disability insurance monthly benefit you want, but insurance companies figured out long ago that you might choose a benefit that is more than you are currently making and so you would have no incentive to work. Most insurance companies will insure 40 to 70 percent of your income, depending on what you do for a living and how much you earn.

How Much (More) Disability Insurance Do You Need?

What You Have for Monthly Income*

A. Long-Term Employer Group Disability Policy	A.
B. Long-Term Association Group Disability Policy	B. +
C. Individual Policies	C. +
D. Social Security (Soc. Sec. Disability Benefits, p. 264)	D. +
E. Total Current Monthly Disability Benefits	E. =

What You Need

F. Monthly Income Required (Setting Your Financial Goals, p. 42, line G)	F.
G. Less: Current Monthly Disability Benefits (line E, above)	G. −
H. Additional Disability Coverage Needed	H. =

* Include only disability coverage that pays for 5 years or more.

From *The Money Diet*, by Ginger Applegarth.

GROUP COVERAGE

Disability insurance is like term life insurance because if you cancel your disability policy you have no cash value. Group disability insurance is usually provided through your employer or associations or groups to which you belong. In most cases, benefits are determined as a percentage of your salary. Sometimes your employer will pay some or all of your disability insurance premiums. See if you can have your disability insurance premiums deducted from your pay and then have your salary increased to make up for it. The reason is that if you pay your disability insurance premiums yourself, then all benefits paid out would be tax-free. For example, let's assume my firm pays my $25 monthly disability premiums for a policy with a $2,000 monthly benefit. If I receive benefits, each $2,000 is subject to income taxes. But if I pay the $25 myself, and then have my firm pay me a little higher salary to make up for that $25 out-of-pocket cost, my benefits of $2,000 a month are completely tax-free! The primary advantage of group disability is that you can often qualify without proof of insurability, but keep in mind that you may lose the coverage if you change jobs. Also, most group benefit payments are reduced by the amount of Social Security and workers' compensation you receive.

INDIVIDUAL COVERAGE

Individual disability insurance policies have several basic distinguishing features you should watch for. The first is the *definition of total disability*, which varies by occupation. If possible, you want to have an "own occupation" definition that will cover you as long as you cannot do your specific job, instead of an "any occupation" policy that covers you only if you cannot do any job that is in line with your skills and education. Also, make sure you purchase a policy that is guaranteed renewable and noncancelable; this way the company cannot cancel the contract or increase premiums even if it has had bad claims experience with other policyholders or it finds out that your health has declined.

BUYING ADVICE

My general recommendation for disability insurance is that you *buy as much as you can from whatever sources you can, with benefits paid to age sixty-five or life if possible*. Remember that at any given age your odds of becoming disabled are much greater than your odds of dying. Take advantage of any group insurance coverages and supplement those with as much personal disability insurance as you can buy. Keep in mind that although group coverage is usually less expensive, it has certain disadvantages when compared with individual policies: The premiums are not guaranteed, the contract can be canceled, and you may lose benefits if you leave the job or group. This means that you should probably hold on to any individual policies you already own even if your group benefits seem adequate by themselves.

The important thing is to make sure you have disability insurance in whatever form obtainable because accidents and illnesses happen to everyone, not just the independently wealthy. Check to make sure you are signed up for the maximum benefits available at work, and ask your insurance agent or financial adviser for help reviewing your choices and identifying good individual policies as well, if you qualify.

MEDICAL INSURANCE

Medical insurance protects you by paying for some or all of your actual medical expenses. It differs from life and disability insurance policies in two fundamental ways. First, the payments the medical policy makes are tied to your actual expenses, instead of paying some fixed amount, such as $10,000. Second, the insurance company will not guarantee your medical insurance premiums for the rest of your life.

Few people need to be convinced that medical insurance is a basic necessity in America. Just witness the public outcry for some kind of universal health care coverage for all Americans regardless of medical condition or income. The cost of the average hospital stay is currently more than $3,500. Our total health care costs in 1993 averaged $3,900 a person. Chances are that someone in your family will be hospitalized within the next three years. And medical insurance does not pay for everything: Americans now spend an average of more than $1,300 per capita annually for out-of-pocket medical expenses not covered by insurance.

Thirty-eight million Americans have no medical insurance, and these people are not only poor. Almost half of those 38 million people without medical insurance are middle- to upper-income people. Why don't they have insurance? Various reasons: They cannot participate in any employer's group insurance plan, they cannot afford the premiums, or they have poor medical histories and cannot get individual insurance. The need for medical insurance is especially acute for the elderly, which is the reason for government programs such as Medicare. Medicare is intended to cover short-term hospital and some outpatient benefits for disabled individuals and those over sixty-five, but its coverage is not adequate. The truth is, Medicare often pays less than 50 percent of health care costs for its recipients.

Most of the medical insurance policies available today are considered "major medical"—they cover a large variety of medical expenses. These policies usually have high lifetime benefit amounts (such as $500,000, $1 million, or even unlimited benefits). Most medical insurance available is group coverage, not individual. You may have heard the "alphabet soup" of medical insurance—HMO (health maintenance organization), PPO (preferred provider organization), and BCBS (Blue Cross/Blue Shield). These plans all have different provisions for who gets to choose the provider of your medical care and how that provider gets paid. With an indemnity plan, you can pick anyone as your medical provider. The disadvantages are that you may have high out-of-pocket costs due to deductibles and coinsurance, you may have to do the paperwork yourself, and you may have to pay up front and then wait to be reimbursed.

Health maintenance organizations, or HMOs, are straightforward in theory: The members pay a fixed monthly or annual fee in advance for all the medical services offered by the HMO and then perhaps nominal fees thereafter for office visits or prescription drugs. The advantages of HMOs are that you can project your medical expenses for budgeting purposes, you are protected in case of catastrophic illness, and there is no paperwork. The disadvantages are that you have to choose a doctor and hospital within the HMO organization, you may not always get to see the same doctor, and you may have to wait for days, weeks, or even months to see a specialist. HMOs vary greatly; some people I know swear by theirs, while others have sworn off HMOs altogether due to delays in getting appointments and other difficulties.

Another type of comprehensive medical insurance coverage, preferred provider organizations (PPOs), was specifically designed to combine the best features of indemnity plans and HMOs. As with an HMO, you pay one monthly or annual fee with a small office visit charge. You can, however, use a provider outside your network, although you will have to pay more. The primary disadvantage is that a PPO may be more expensive than an HMO, especially if you choose to use providers outside the network. These days, many states' Blue Cross/Blue Shield programs offer indemnity, HMO, and PPO plans.

Group medical insurance is probably the most important group benefit you can receive from your employer because individual policies are almost always more expensive and have more limited benefits. If you are self-employed, you may be able to join a group plan offered through professional associations or fraternal organizations. In fact, it is not uncommon for people to switch jobs or go to work simply to obtain medical insurance! You can usually join a group policy almost as soon as you are hired. Also, each year there is usually an "open enrollment" period (about a month) when you can switch from one insurance plan or another into the group plan without worrying about "preexisting conditions." Preexisting conditions are prior medical problems that the company may not cover for a specified period of time.

Congress has recognized how difficult it is to obtain medical insurance on an individual basis by enacting a law called COBRA (short for Consolidated Omnibus Budget Reconciliation Act). This law states that in most cases you have the option to continue your group policy for a certain period—usually eighteen months—after you leave a company, as long as you pay all the insurance premiums plus a small administrative fee. If you have not found another job with group insurance right away, or even if you have but the new insurance has restrictions on preexisting conditions, be sure to continue your COBRA coverage. This is the first thing I counsel clients to take care of when they tell me they are changing jobs.

LONG-TERM CARE

A note about long-term care is in order. In the past, when older Americans could no longer care for themselves, most moved in with family members. As we have already discussed, this trend has changed, and along with it has come a need for insurance to cover the additional expenses of long-term care by others. The big problem is that Medicare covers only skilled nursing care, not the custodial care of dressing, eating, and bathing that most older Americans need. For that reason, perhaps even before your children leave home (because the premiums increase the older you are when you apply), you may want to consider purchasing a long-term care policy for yourself. Make sure the policy *specifically states* that it covers Alzheimer's disease, that care can be provided in the hospital, in a nursing home, or at home, and that the policy covers "activities of daily living."

MEDIGAP

Medicare supplemental insurance, called MediGap, is designed to do exactly what its name suggests—pay for expenses not covered by Medicare. Because these policies have gotten so complicated, the government has now mandated that they all have the same sets of features from one company to another. The policies go from type A to type J, and the further up the alphabet you go the more comprehensive the policies. So, policy F from one company has the same features as policy F from another company. Before you choose among the options from A to J, look at the different features and think about whether you need prescription drug coverage, coverage when traveling overseas, and so on.

It goes without saying that you need medical insurance because without it your assets can disappear in a matter of days or weeks if a medical emergency occurs. If you can afford to buy only coverage against catastrophic bills, at least do that. With health care reform possibly on the horizon, the medical insurance marketplace is in a state of constant change, but one thing is for certain: Every member of your family needs it!

AUTOMOBILE INSURANCE

You probably have automobile insurance. An auto insurance policy is actually a package deal covering you against four kinds of losses: physical property you damage, lost wages, medical expenses, and liability for personal damages claimed by others, such as pain and suffering. This coverage is very worthwhile because an automobile accident that is even partially your fault can wipe out your assets. You could lose your home, your business, and in fact everything you own if you are not adequately insured.

You may have a false sense of security if you have the minimum amount of insurance required by your state law; these requirements are really only a fraction of what you need. Clients always ask me which people their insurance policy covers. Basically, you and anyone else named on your policy are covered when you are driving *any* private passenger car. For example, if your son is listed on your auto policy as a driver and he borrows a friend's car and wrecks it, your insurance policy will pay if the other company will not. Someone who is driving your car is covered as long as he or she has your "expressed or implied permission." This means that you actually gave the person permission to drive on this outing or else you have done so in the past and would have been likely to do so again if asked. Your passengers may be covered under your policy depending on which state you live in. And your policy also covers pedestrians injured in accidents that are your fault.

Several types of automobile insurance coverage are included in your policy. You can find out what coverage you have by looking on the declarations page, which is the first page of your policy. Three of the coverages have to do with personal injury, and the fourth has to do with property damage. *Bodily injury liability* covers anybody other than yourself for the injuries caused by you, even if you are only partly at fault. State minimum limits are typically "10/20"; this provides $10,000 of coverage per person, up to a maximum of $20,000 per accident. You should have *at least* 100/300 ($100,000 per person up to a maximum of $300,000 per accident).

The second personal injury coverage is *uninsured and under-*

insured motorist coverage. This is by far the most inadequate provision in most people's policies; you should have at least 100/300. This type of coverage protects you, your family, and your passengers when you are injured by a hit-and-run driver or when the other driver has inadequate insurance or none at all.

Property damage liability is the third type of coverage; it protects against damages to somebody else's property. I recommend you have at least 20/50 coverage. *Medical payments* cover medical expenses for your family (when they are riding in *any* car) and (depending on your home state) your passengers, usually for one year. *Collision* coverage is for damage to your car when you have collided with an object of any kind (it does not have to be another car). In fact, when I was growing up, a friend had his car replaced under this provision when he hit a herd of cows in the road. Somehow the cows were fine; his car was not. *Comprehensive* coverage pays for all other accidental damage to your car, it is your main protection against theft and vandalism. For both collision and comprehensive, take the highest deductible you feel comfortable with, and consider dropping them if your car is more than five years old because the value of your car may not be worth enough to worry about.

If you marry or move, if you are no longer using your car for business, if you install an anti-theft device, or if other drivers listed (especially teenagers!) should be taken off your policy, be sure to notify your company immediately. You may save a bundle on premiums. Passing a driver's education course or taking a refresher course if you are a senior citizen, driving safely, and paying premiums annually instead of monthly will help reduce your premiums.

HOMEOWNERS INSURANCE

If you own a house, condominium, or cooperative, it is probably the largest single investment you will ever make. And if something were to happen to that investment, your personal balance sheet might never recover. For that reason alone, it is important to have enough of the right kind of homeowners insurance. Even if you do not own a home, chances are you still need a policy for your personal property. But you would be amazed at the number of people who don't think they need homeowners insurance because they rent.

The homeowners policies available today are sophisticated packages that include fire, theft, and personal liability coverage. Most people need this coverage because they cannot afford any of these losses. And it is not just the loss of things that is the problem. Liability is a major concern as well. Lawsuits against homeowners are increasing in number, and the awards in those suits tend to be very high. Without insurance, you might have to sell your home and possessions to pay a claim. You also need insurance to protect what you *owe*; very few people would risk purchasing a home knowing that if it burned down, they would still be completely responsible for repaying the mortgage. Usually, the mortgage lender requires you to maintain insurance on your home at least equal to the amount of your debt. But this often lulls people into becoming underinsured, because the amount of their mortgage is typically much less than the replacement cost of their home.

Homeowners insurance includes property damage and loss of personal property, as well as liability coverage in case a lawsuit against you is successful. Keep in mind that there are maximum amounts you can collect on certain types of valuables such as jewelry, furs, silver, boats, and other kinds of personal property. So if you have five items of jewelry and each is worth $500, you would still get a check for only $1,000 if that is the jewelry limit of your policy. You need to have all your valuable personal and household property appraised and listed individually on your policy. Believe it or not, many people assume their pedigree dogs or cats are covered as personal property; they are not. Conversely, most people do not realize that their homeowners policy typically covers credit card charges if your cards are stolen and amounts are charged on them. (The credit card companies usually make you responsible for the first $50 of each card's unauthorized charges, and these can add up quickly.)

Liability insurance is the second type of coverage provided under homeowners policies. If your dog bites the mail carrier, or a neighbor slips on your wet kitchen floor, or your child hits a baseball and smashes someone else's window, you are liable and can be sued. This is especially important because it covers you and your family away from home as well. For example, if you lose control while skiing and run some unfortunate skier down, you are covered. If you accidentally hit someone with a stray tennis ball, or your children leave their bikes on the neighbor's sidewalk and a passerby trips, or your son hits a pedestrian while biking, you are covered. You need liability coverage of at least $300,000 to help protect you against the large lawsuits filed these days.

Every once in a while I run into someone who thinks that she can overinsure her home and then make out like a bandit if it happens to burn down. This is an idea a good agent will disabuse you of; you cannot get insurance for more than your home is worth. And "worth" is defined as the cost to rebuild your home, *not* its current market value. Most companies now work on the basis of *replacement cost,* which means they will pay based on how much it will actually cost to rebuild your home if it is damaged or destroyed. To have the total cost of replacement covered, you need to insure for at least 80 percent of the amount the company actually has to pay to totally rebuild your home. Even better, look for a policy that has *guaranteed replacement cost.* This means that if you insure your home for 100 percent of the value as determined by the insurance company, your home will be fully rebuilt no matter how much it costs.

Always ignore market value when you are deciding how much homeowners insurance to buy. Market value has *nothing* to do with it. Why? First of all, market value includes land, and insurance policies do not cover your land. Also, market value may be much higher (especially if you live in a prime location) than the cost to rebuild. Third, if you own an older home with a great deal of fine craftsmanship, the market value may actually be less than the replacement cost.

BUYING ADVICE

Here are some rules of thumb about buying homeowners insurance. Buy replacement cost coverage if you can and make the insurance company or agent tell you how much you should insure your house for. That way, *they* could be held liable if they misjudged its value. For deductibles, the old rule of thumb applies: Take the highest you feel comfortable with and apply the premium savings to additional coverage if you can. If you have antiques, jewelry, furs, etc., you need to have them appraised and listed individually on your policy. If you are operating a business at home or even occasionally using it for customer meetings, storage, or working with employees, your homeowners insurance may not cover this. You can often buy a policy endorsement (called "incidental office occupancy") to cover certain kinds of office uses in your home.

UMBRELLA LIABILITY POLICIES

Personal umbrella liability policies were developed in response to America's passion for suing. They provide overall protection against a variety of claims. The need is clear; the media regularly reports successful lawsuits of $2 million to $4 million as a result of automobile accidents, accidents at home, or libel or slander. Unfortunately, it seems to have become the rule rather than the exception to sue, and to sue for huge damages. The bottom line: If you have assets, you are at risk of losing them without adequate protection. It used to be that the liability coverages you could get in your homeowners and automobile policy were adequate. But now, although these coverages can be as much as $300,000 or $500,000, it is not enough. What happens if someone slips on your sidewalk, sues, and wins a $1 million judgment against you? You are personally responsible for coming up with whatever your homeowners insurance does not pay. And without insurance, you could end up losing everything that you own and declaring personal bankruptcy.

Personal umbrella liability policies are available in amounts of up to $10 million and more, but most are written in the range of $1 million to $2 million. The annual premiums are relatively low, usually under $200. They cover items that your auto and homeowners insurance policies cover but also insure against slander, libel, invasion of privacy, and the cost of defending yourself against groundless accusations. Keep in mind, however, that your personal umbrella liability policy will not automatically cover business or professional losses. You need a separate policy for that.

A final thought: If you own a business, chances are you need several different kinds of insurance to adequately protect against the kinds of losses to which you are exposed. These different kinds of insurance will protect your business and your family if you die, if you become disabled, or if you get sued. You also may need a separate automobile policy when you use your car for business or allow your employees to drive your car.

MAKING TRADE-OFFS

Chances are that after reading this chapter you have realized you are underinsured in two or more areas. But what do you do when you don't have enough cash to pay all these premiums? In chapter 15, "Putting It All Together," we deal with this universal financial planning problem. But in the meantime, keep in mind the buying principles explained at the beginning of this chapter.

First, protect against the largest losses. For example, when I reviewed insurance policies for my client Dan, a single father with one child, it became clear that he needed at least $200,000 of life insurance to support Emily until she turned twenty-one and to pay for her education. Plugging that insurance gap was top priority, but Dan did not have the money for a lot of extra premiums. The solution I proposed was to buy the life insurance and increase the deductibles on his auto and homeowners insurance. While Dan would have to pay an additional $500 or $750 out-of-pocket in deductibles if necessary, he gained $200,000 worth of protection for Emily if he died, which was more important.

Second, comparison-shop, but don't buy a particular policy just because it is the cheapest. Rita insisted on sticking with a homeowners policy that would pay only $500 total for her collection of antique dolls. I advised her to spend $150 more for a policy that covered each doll for its actual value (the total collection was worth thousands of dollars), but she considered it a waste of money. After all, what could ever happen to *all* of them? You guessed it: Something did—frozen water pipes that thawed and burst in her home while she was in Florida escaping the cold and snow. The basement was flooded, and everything was covered in water or mildew by the time she returned. As Rita now says, even more painful than losing the dolls is knowing she's at fault for losing this asset because she was so pennywise and pound-foolish about insurance.

SUMMING UP: CHOOSING AN INSURANCE COMPANY AND AGENT

Insurance is admittedly a complicated subject, but you need a basic understanding of it to deal effectively with insurance companies and agents. You can then better determine if an agent is competent and if an insurance company is providing good products because you will know what features to look for and what all the terms mean. No two insurance companies do business the same way, and you might be the one to suffer if you choose the wrong one.

The first step in evaluating an insurance company is to check with insurance-company rating services. There are five principal services; they all use letter grades just like in school, but each goes about it a little differently. Just like in school, A is better than B, and so on. With A. M. Best, the top rating is A++; Standard and Poor's top rating is AAA; Moody's is Aaa; Duff & Phelps is AAA, and Weiss is A+. If you are familiar with bond ratings, you will see that the Standard and Poor's and Moody's systems are identical to their bond ratings. For life insurance policies, I recommend you purchase insurance from companies that have one of the top two ratings from at least two of these rating services. With disability insurance, a company should have one of the top four ratings from two of the companies. With property casualty insurance, top ratings are not as critical because these policies are short-term contracts that are renewed every year and can easily be purchased from other companies if need be. I do recommend, however, that you buy auto, homeowners, and umbrella policies from companies that have A ratings or above from two of these services. Most major libraries carry these insurance reports, and they can give you a wealth of information about these companies. The easiest way to find out a company's rating is to ask your agent for it. If you encounter resistance, this may well be because the report does not look so good.

The second step in choosing an insurance company is to ask friends and coworkers which insurance companies and agents they have done business with and how satisfied they have been. Here, service is the key; I would be concerned about any reports of a company that is hard to deal with. Choosing the insurance agent or adviser is also critical. Chapter 16, "Choosing Your Financial Advisers," gives specific guidelines to follow.

Insurance is a necessary part of the Money Diet because it is the only way to make sure your family can still meet their goals if catastrophe strikes. The best retirement or investment strategy can be rendered useless in one split second if catastrophe strikes. Insurance is an invisible shield protecting your income and your assets so that the Money Diet can work for you. The premiums you pay are a small price for this peace of mind.

CHAPTER FOURTEEN

Planning for
the Unthinkable

TWO YEARS AGO I was accidentally run over by a relative as I was getting out of his car. It was a nightmarish situation I could not imagine was actually happening, and it occurred so quickly that I did not have time to think. I will never forget my terror as I hit the ground and bounced under the car, then almost by reflex rolled away to keep the tire from running over most of my body. Unfortunately, although I was able to shift myself almost completely out of the way, my right ankle was crushed by the tire. It was one of those classic scenarios you always hear about where you imagine your life "passing before your eyes." But did this happen to me? Did I have visions of my motherless children? I am embarrassed to say that the answer is no—the only thought that went through my mind was that I had never changed my will and moved my life insurance into my trust so that it would escape estate taxes when I died. In that split second, I knew that my failure to do so would have cost several hundred thousand dollars in administrative costs and taxes on my large insurance policy if I had not been able to get out of the way of that oncoming tire.

I tell you this to reassure you that if you have not planned for the unthinkable—your death—you are not alone. Sixty percent of adult Americans do not have a will (the legal document in which you state where you want your assets to go, and if you are a parent, who is to take care of your children). Many wills already in existence are out-of-date and do not accomplish what the people who drew them up would want today because so much time has passed since they were reviewed. Among that 60 percent of the population without wills are a lot of people who should have known better, especially attorneys. In fact, it is a running joke in the legal profession that attorneys are often the last to have wills. Remember the "cobbler" syndrome I mentioned in chapter 13 about insurance: "The cobbler's children have no shoes"?

Thus far in *The Money Diet* we have been focusing on how to accomplish your goals. But what will happen if you die tomorrow? Have you taken all the necessary steps to make sure that your assets will continue to work for your family and that your children are properly cared for? If you haven't, you have no control over whether the Money Diet will continue to work for your family after your death.

You may be thinking you are all set even if you do not have a will. It seems logical that your spouse would get all your assets or that your children would inherit them if you are a single parent. But every state has its own set of "intestacy" laws that automatically control the distribution of your property if you have no will. Unfortunately, these laws often do not make a lot of sense; I cannot imagine a body knowing less and caring less about your personal situation than your state legislature. If you are single and die, all your assets may go to your parents equally—even if one of your parents needs much more money than the other (or none at all) or you have a sibling with six children to raise. If you are married and have no children, do not assume that if you die everything will go to your spouse, because your parents may end up inheriting half your estate. And if you are married with children, you may be in the worst situation of all. Your spouse may share equally with your children—with your children's assets being controlled by the court until they reach adulthood. The problem with all these scenarios is that they are one-size-fits-all solutions to your unique personal situation.

If you do not have a will, your problems are much more serious than the wrong people getting your assets when you die. The whole estate settlement process can take much longer without a will and be more expensive because court-appointed administrators will have to be bonded and will have to do a lot of extra legwork to get your estate in order. If you have children, their guardian will be appointed by the court and may not be the person you would like, especially if there is a large sum of money involved. (Unfortunately, some relatives and friends are suddenly very interested in becoming guardians when the children in question have substantial assets available for their care.) Your loved ones will be in a position of making financial decisions without your guidance and without knowing exactly what it is you wanted done with your money. The result is that you may be leaving them a legacy of guilt in addition to your assets.

To make matters worse, unscrupulous salespeople may even convince your loved ones that you had given them instructions to do certain things (such as allow them to manage the estate money) or buy certain things (from Bibles to property) in the event of your death. Without a will you have probably kissed any potential estate tax savings good-bye, and whoever ends up taking on the settlement of your estate is taking on a huge headache. So, if you do not do anything else because of *The Money Diet*, call an attorney *today* and make an appointment to get a will. It may cost you as little as $100, and rarely more than a couple of thousand dollars for even a very complex will and trust arrangement. (A trust is considered a separate "person" by the IRS and the law; it is like an invisible person who can own and distribute your assets according to your instructions when you created it. I will discuss this in detail later.) This small investment in estate planning is your best insurance that things will happen the way *you* want them to when you are not around to give directions.

SAFEGUARD YOUR MEMORY AND YOUR FAMILY

Even if you do not care who gets your money, how much the lawyers get, or who will be responsible for your children after you are gone, you probably do care how your family remembers you. One of the saddest situations a financial adviser can face is dealing with a spouse's or other relative's pain and anger that you cared so little that you dumped the settlement of a messy estate on her with no guidance and no cash. This person's last memories of you may be so unpleasant that she forgets the happier times together. And keep in mind that your death may bring out the worst in those people you leave behind because money is involved. I cannot count how many estate settlement situations I have seen (especially if second marriages are involved) that started out on a perfectly amicable basis and ended up with families decimated and not speaking to each other for years because the will was nonexistent or out of date. For example, Jean's adult children have not spoken to her brother Ted's children in the last ten years, even though the cousins considered one another "best friends" growing up. Why? When their grandmother Avis (Jean and Ted's mother) died, it was discovered that her will was fifteen years old and written during a time when Ted was living in a commune and disdained the "corrupting power of money." Avis had been mad enough at Ted's behavior to take him at his word when he said he didn't want to inherit anything: she left him $1,000, with the rest of the estate going to Jean. Once Ted settled down, got married, had three children, and began working for a Fortune 500 company, Avis kept meaning to change her will so Jean and Ted would each get half her assets. She never did. Although Jean did give Ted some of the money she inherited from her mother, when Avis died she kept most of it for herself. So the cousins have taken on their parents' battle, and the way things are going the feud may extend down to future generations, just like the Hatfields and the McCoys. The saddest part of this story is that one of the things Avis had cherished most in life was the close friendship her children shared. Her inaction cost them that friendship and split her family apart.

What is the solution? Estate planning. Estate planning is, quite simply, planning for what happens after you die. Estate planning is not limited to wills; it can also involve trusts, powers of attorney, and other documents that will help accomplish what you want and, more important, what is right for your family.

HOW MUCH IS YOUR ESTATE WORTH?

The first step in estate planning is to add up all the assets that would be included in your estate at death. **How Much Are You Worth When You Die?** (page 286) shows what your estate would be worth if you died today. Start with the asset information you put together in **Detailed Net Worth Statement** (page 24). A few changes will make a big difference between your financial weight during life and at death. One is that instead of including the *cash value* (also called face value) of your life insurance, the *death benefit* amount should be used. It may well be that you have an insurance policy that will pay $100,000 if you die but has only $1,500 worth of cash value if you were to cancel the policy now. Now that we are planning for your death, we are talking about the $100,000 value. Your employer-sponsored retirement plans may also have death benefits that are higher than your current investment balances; here you will include those higher amounts.

When you completed the **Detailed Net Worth Statement**, you probably lumped your assets together with your spouse's if you are married. For purposes of estate planning, however, you need to separate your assets out according to who owns what. And who owns what depends on *how* your property is owned—whether you own it jointly or by yourself. For example, if your house is owned as *tenancy by the entirety* (which only spouses are allowed to elect) or as *joint tenancy with right of survivorship* (which any two people can elect), you and your spouse automatically inherit each other's interest and you each own 50 percent of the property value. With *tenancy in common,* however, you can decide in your will who gets your portion of this jointly owned real estate, and ownership does not have to be split 50–50. Your trust, if you have one, can also determine who gets your share if you put the property in the trust during your life. Your house deed, will, and various bank and investment accounts list exactly how you and your spouse own the property; after your names, it will say TBE, JTWROS, or TIC, or have the actual words spelled out.

The other complicated way you can own property is as *community property,* where you and your spouse each has an undivided half interest. This happens only if you have lived in any community property states (Arizona, California, Idaho, Louisiana, Nevada, New

How Much Are You Worth When You Die?

What you OWN

Checking	
Savings	+
Money Market Funds	+
A. Bank Accounts	**A. =**
Mutual Funds	
Stocks	+
Bonds	+
Life Insurance (death benefits)	+
Annuities (death benefits)	+
Investment Real Estate	+
B. Investments	**B. =**
Savings — 401(k) and 403(b)	
Company Plan	+
IRA	+
Keogh	+
C. Retirement Plans (Death Benefits)	**C. =**
D. House (Market Value)	**D. =**
Car #1	
Car #2	+
E. Cars	**E. =**
F. Personal Property	**F. =**
Loans Receivable	
Collectibles	+
Business Interest	+
Other	+
G. Other Assets	**G. =**
H. What you OWN (add lines A – G)	**H. =**

continued on next page

From *The Money Diet*, by Ginger Applegarth.

How Much Are You Worth When You Die? (cont.)

What you OWE

First Mortgage	
Home Equity Loan	+
I. Mortgage	**I. =**
VISA	
MasterCard	+
Other	+
Other	+
J. Credit Cards	**J. =**
K. Total Car Loans	**K. =**
Education	
Life Insurance (cash value)	+
Other	+
Other	+
Other	+
L. Other Debts	**L. =**
M. What you OWE (Add lines I–L)	**M.=**

Your NET WORTH at Death

H. What you OWN	**H.**
M. Less: What you OWE	**M.–**
N. Equals: Your NET WORTH at Death	**N. =**

Mexico, Texas, and Washington). Wisconsin has a similar law, called the uniform Marital Property Act (UMPA). Generally, property you acquired in a community property state during your marriage automatically belongs half to you and half to your spouse. When you complete **How Much Are You Worth When You Die?** you will see what the total of your estate value at death would be. Based on the **Detailed Net Worth Statement** and the changes just noted, add up your assets on lines A–G and write the total of What You Own on line H. Add up your debts on lines I–L and write the total of What You Owe on line M. Your Net Worth at Death, line N, equals line H minus line M.

SOME ESTATE PLANNING QUESTIONS

Once you know what your estate is likely to be at your death and what assets are included, it is time to ask yourself both some financial and some non-financial questions. On the financial side, you need to decide these issues:

- Whom you would like to get your assets
- How much you would like each beneficiary to receive
- Who should get your assets if the beneficiaries you designate die before you do
- What specific bequests you have—that is, whether you want certain pieces of property to go to certain relatives, or money to go to particular charities, and so on

On the non-financial side, the following questions need to be answered:

- Who the guardian of your children will be if you die before they become adults (Usually, the surviving spouse becomes guardian, but the situation gets more complicated if you are divorced or if you and your spouse die simultaneously.)
- Who the executor of your will will be (The executor is a person you may name in your will who will shepherd your assets through the estate settlement process.)
- Whom you want to name as trustee, if your will directs that any trusts be set up at your death
- Who is to have decision-making authority in your place in case you become incapable of making decisions during your lifetime due to physical or mental impairment (These duties range from arranging payment of checks to making decisions about medical treatment.)

The terms of your will govern the disposal of both your financial and your non-financial assets, but you can also express wishes in your will about how you would like to be buried, what kind of memorial service you would like, and any other last requests you would like carried out.

WHAT HAPPENS TO YOUR ESTATE WHEN YOU DIE

Let's look at how your property moves from your hands to someone else's after you die. There are four ways:

- First, your will covers your "probate property," or everything that is owned outright by you and not in a trust. This might include bank accounts in your name, your car, and the stock your father left you.
- Second, if you have set up a trust, the terms of the trust will dictate how the assets in the trust are to be distributed. For example, during your lifetime you may have set up a trust to hold some of your assets because you wanted someone else to completely manage them for you. When you die, the trust does what your trust document tells it to do.
- Third, you have named *beneficiaries* on your retirement plans and your life insurance polices; those funds go directly to those named and are not controlled by your will, although they *are* subject to estate taxes. (This is another good reason to periodically review your finances. I once counseled a client to run, not walk, to her company's employee benefits office immediately to change the beneficiary named on her company pension and 401(k) plans. Why? Lucy's ex-spouse was still named as beneficiary on several lucrative retirement plans, although the two had not spoken outside of a courtroom for years.)
- Fourth, any jointly owned property you have passes according to how the property is held (again, with tenancy by the entirety and joint tenancy with right of survivorship, it automatically passes to your surviving spouse). For example, Fran owns a

beach cottage with her brother as joint tenants with right of survivorship. Her half-ownership interest is included in her estate, but it automatically goes to her brother even if her will says it should go to her children.

ESTATE TAXES

One of the financial impacts of death is estate taxes. You do not get taxed when you enter this world, but you may well get taxed when you leave it. Depending on the size of your estate, you can get taxed on the value of the assets you give someone else at your death. These taxes differ from income taxes because income taxes are levied on your income; estate taxes are levied on your *assets*. It doesn't matter whether an asset is owned directly by you, or is in a trust that you control, or is a life insurance death benefit, or is in a retirement plan. If you own it, you may have to pay estate taxes on it. You can transfer a total of $600,000 to any persons you choose during life or at death without paying federal estate tax. With state taxes, the death taxes can start at much lower amounts and, depending on the state, are paid by you or by whoever inherits your money. If your estate's assets are over $600,000, your executor may be forced to pay taxes at rates between 37 percent and 55 percent on any amount in excess of $600,000, so you can see why smart estate planning is crucial if you own this much and you would rather that your family or friends get it instead of the IRS. If you are married and each of you owns up to $600,000 of assets in your own names, you can shelter up to $1.2 million of your joint assets without tax.

The one break you get if you are married is that the federal government has graciously said you can leave everything to your spouse and not have any taxes due until your spouse dies (called the unlimited marital deduction), so you essentially get your taxes deferred until then. Otherwise, any estate taxes you owe are due nine months after you die, in cash, unless you are able to make other arrangements. This means that if your executor does not have enough cash on hand in your estate, she may be forced to sell investments, real estate, or other property just to raise enough money to pay the estate taxes. And if the real estate or investment market is depressed, your estate may face a huge loss in value due to this forced sale. With all your hard-earned assets at stake, you can see why it can be profitable to pay attention to your estate planning *now*.

WILLS

Most people are familiar with the concept of wills even if they do not have one themselves. Your will is a document that says what you want to happen with your property as well as what you want your guardianship and executor arrangements to be. In most states, you have to be eighteen to make a will, but this means even children in college should have one. I always recommend that clients use attorneys for wills, because if any part of a will is invalid the entire document may come under question. For instance, you should definitely use an attorney if you plan to disinherit any of your immediate relatives (children, parents, siblings, etc.). The language should read that you are leaving them out "for reasons known to them."

All fifty states have laws that make it impossible to disinherit your spouse. At the very least, your spouse may be entitled to the amount he would have gotten anyway if you had died without a will. Let's say, for example, that Jerry decides to disinherit his spouse Janie and leave her nothing. He puts language in his own will to that effect. But, when Jerry dies Janie contests his will because under the state law she would be entitled to at least one-third ($100,000) of his $300,000 estate. No matter what Jerry said in his will, Janie gets at least $100,000.

Even if you are sure you have put everything you own in a trust (that invisible person who holds property for you for as long as you have specified in your trust document), you need a will just in case anything gets missed. You also want to name an executor. Wills are easy to change: You either attach an amendment (or "codicil") or draft a new will altogether. Be sure to sign only one copy of your will, and do not put it in your safe-deposit box (usually your attorney keeps the original in the law firm vault). Otherwise, there can be a delay because someone will have to petition the court for an order to open the safe-deposit box. Make sure that people in your family know you have a will and *tell them* where it is, along with any trust documents or powers of attorney.

The most common type of will is a simple will, in which you leave property directly to beneficiaries and you do not create any trusts. For example, a simple will might read, "I leave $10,000 to my brother, Tim, and the rest of my estate to my dear wife, Laura." With a "pour-over will," your will says that all your assets are to be dumped into a trust. In that case, a pour-over will might read, "I direct that all of my estate be given to my trust, the Nathan Jones trust."

TRUSTS

Trusts sound complicated, but their basic features are not difficult to understand. The law considers a trust simply to be a separate entity, like another person. There are two basic kinds of trusts. A *living trust* is one that you set up during your lifetime, and a *testamentary trust* is one that your will sets up when you die. There are two kinds of living trusts: With a *revocable trust* you can dissolve the trust and get all your money back at any time; with an *irrevocable trust* you have given property away forever once you give it to the trust.

You have probably seen advertisements for free seminars about living trusts (with great PR flair, they are also called "loving trusts"). This is a new marketing theme on an old idea, and obviously part of the purpose of the free seminars is for the presenters to get legal business if they are attorneys or insurance clients if they sell insurance. However, a sound legal technique is behind the hype. There are certain advantages to living trusts:

- They avoid probate, so administrative costs would be less and money could be made available to your beneficiaries immediately instead of waiting for months or sometimes even years while your estate is settled.
- What is in the trust is not a matter of public record, so you get some privacy about what you own (making your estate less vulnerable to unscrupulous strangers—*or* relatives or friends).
- Challenges to a will do not include whatever is in a living trust

unless the reason for the challenge is that you were incapacitated or unduly influenced so that when you did your estate planning you didn't really mean to do what you did. So if you anticipate anyone having problems with your will provisions, a living trust is one way to circumvent a legal challenge.

■ The trustee can also take over and manage your affairs if you become incapable of making financial or medical decisions.

The key to making a trust work for you is, however, actually *giving the trust the assets you meant to,* and doing so is very easy. You transfer assets simply by changing the name of the owner from your name to that of the trust. You can do this on bank and investment accounts, real estate deeds, life insurance policies, etc. In my case, when I fell under the wheel of that car I had a beautiful estate plan with a will and a trust all set up, but I had never actually gotten around to changing the ownership of the assets so that they were owned by the trust. If that tire had not missed my head, my trust would have been worthless because there would have been absolutely nothing in it.

Irrevocable trusts are most often used to hold insurance polices, and this is the type of trust I've been talking about when I discuss my own estate-planning foibles. The advantage is that the life insurance proceeds will not be included in your estate for tax purposes (unless the policy was transferred to the trust within three years of your death). The disadvantage is that once you put any asset—insurance policy, stock, or whatever—in the irrevocable trust, you lose the ability to change the beneficiary, take the asset out, or control the asset because *you don't own it anymore.*

DURABLE POWERS OF ATTORNEY AND LIVING WILLS

Two other legal documents are very important in the estate planning process. The first is a durable power of attorney, in which you designate someone else to act in your place if you become incapacitated and cannot make financial decisions. The second is a living will with a health care proxy in which you state exactly under which circumstances you want medical treatment and what kind of treatment it should be. The living will should contain a health care proxy, which means that you designate someone as the person to make medical decisions in your place if you become incapacitated. With advances in medical care and the prolonging of life with machines, this is the only way to control how long you are kept alive and under what circumstances you receive medication or surgery if there is no hope of recovery.

PERSONAL ISSUES

Just as important as the financial aspects of estate planning are the non-financial aspects. First, you need to decide who will be the executor of your estate. This person has a big job, because he will have to make sure that everything proceeds as it should throughout the estate settlement process. Some of the executor's duties:

- making sure that all the beneficiaries get a copy of your will;
- publishing death notices in the newspaper so that other potential beneficiaries and creditors will be notified;
- getting the attorney to file all the necessary papers with the court;
- gathering all the documents together concerning your assets and then distributing those assets.

As you can see, this can be a very time-consuming job; it is not something to assign to someone lightly. Always make sure that your will states that your executor can be paid for her services (there are standard fees that vary by region) if you think your estate settlement will infringe on her job or personal life. Most important, make sure that your executor is willing and able to do the job. The worst thing you can do to someone is to make him executor of your will without first asking him; far too often I have seen situations where the named executor feels too guilt-ridden to turn down the job when he discovers after his relative's or friend's death that he is executor, but isn't able do the job that the deceased was counting on him to do.

The second major non-financial decision is naming a guardian for your children, if you have children. More and more, I see families naming friends as guardians instead of other family members. This is becoming more common as people tend to move around and end up in different cities or parts of the country. In naming a guardian, do not worry about the feelings of your other family members who think it is their right to be named guardian! You need to choose a guardian who is best for your child or children. You will be dead, so do not worry about hurting someone else's feelings! And above all, if you name a couple as guardians, make sure your will says that they are both to be guardians only as long as they are living together. But also name the person who would become guardian in the event of divorce. If the couple divorces and you have named both parties as guardians, your children could find themselves in the middle of a complicated and nasty legal battle. Further, it is always crucial to make sure that your guardian is left with enough assets to raise your children as you would like to have raised them yourself. In chapter 13, "Protecting Your Future with Insurance," there is a chart that will allow you to figure out whether you are adequately covered on this point. More than any other provision of your will, your choice of guardian should be revisited every year or two because as children grow older and as their needs change, you may decide it makes sense to change your guardianship designation.

TAX-SAVING TECHNIQUES

No one wants to pay any more taxes than necessary, and there is something particularly galling about being taxed when you die. Still, taxes and administrative costs are a fact of life, and they do not exempt the wealthy or famous. There are a number of tried-and-true estate tax-reduction techniques. First, a bypass trust can save taxes if you are married and your gross estate is over $600,000. Let's say you are married and your estate is worth $1 million. You can leave everything to your spouse and pay no taxes at your death by claiming the Unlimited Marital Deduction. But whatever is left at your spouse's death is part of his taxable estate (unless he marries again and wills his money to his new spouse, which you probably don't want). You can save taxes *and* control the final destination of your assets by setting up a trust for any assets you own over $600,000. Your spouse gets the income and usually the principal as well, but at his death the trust proceeds pass to the beneficiary(ies) you named in the trust, and the trust is not taxed in his estate.

Other ways to reduce your estate are to make annual gifts to those named as beneficiaries in your will (or others). Each person can give $10,000 a year to another person without paying any gift tax, and the recipient of a gift is exempt from tax also. As we talked about, however, in chapter 9, "Planning for a Comfortable Retirement," before you give any money away you must make sure that your own basic retirement needs have been met. If you want to give away more than $10,000 in any one year to one person, of course you can do so. You still won't have to pay any gift taxes, but the value of your gift reduces the $600,000 that can be left tax-free at your death. So, if Francis wants to give $15,000 to his son Francis Jr. in 1995, he can give $10,000 totally tax-free (called the annual exclusion), and the other $5,000 will reduce the amount he can give away tax-free at death by $5,000—or from $600,000 to $595,000. You can always give away as much as you want to your spouse tax-free.

If you have a piece of property that will likely grow in value very rapidly and you know you do not need it during your lifetime, you may want to give that to a beneficiary so that all the increase in the property value occurs outside your estate. For example, Leon is a wealthy man, and he has $25,000 he doesn't need during life. He has $25,000 in mutual funds and a vacant lot worth $25,000. He figures the mutual funds won't grow much in value because they are bond funds, but the vacant lot should double its value in the next few years because the land around it is being developed. He gives away the vacant lot to his nephew. Five years later, Leon dies, and in the meantime the value of the vacant lot has skyrocketed to $50,000, but all that growth occurred outside his estate! If Leon had kept the vacant lot until he died and then left it to his nephew in his will, his estate would have had to pay taxes on *$50,000*, the lot's value at death. Unless those taxes are paid by some other asset in the estate, the lot would have to be sold (perhaps at a loss, depending on the real estate market at the time), and taxes of 35 to 55 percent would have to be paid, so instead of a $50,000 lot free and clear, Leon's nephew might end up with under $25,000—less than half the value of the asset.

As you may well imagine, there can be some real problems when you have non-liquid assets in your estate (assets not readily convertible to cash, such as real estate and business interests) because they may have to be sold in order to pay the estate taxes. The IRS may value them quite highly, but there may be no cash available to pay the taxes on these non-liquid assets (remember Leon's vacant lot?). This is where insurance can be useful, to avoid a situation where your executor has to sell assets just to pay estate taxes. There is a special kind of life insurance called survivorship life insurance, which is a policy on both spouses and pays a death benefit at the death of the second spouse. The primary purpose of purchasing survivorship life insurance is to pay the estate taxes that will be due nine months after death unless special arrangements are made. You may want to consider this when you are discussing your estate situation with your attorney. You should consider buying insurance if **How Much (More) Life Insurance Do You Need?** (page 255) shows there will not be enough cash to pay taxes and debts and to provide family income.

When you make gifts, you may want to give them directly to the recipient, or you may want to put them in trust if she is a minor. A common estate tax-savings technique is for grandparents to set up UGMA (Uniform Gifts to Minors Act) accounts for the grandchildren. This may be a good idea, but a grandparent should never be named custodian of the account because otherwise the value of the account is considered part of the grandparent's estate if she dies while the child is still a minor. Another alternative is the 2503(c) trust, which is usually used for larger gifts to minors. There are a few advantages to the 2503(c) trust, and these advantages primarily deal with control of the assets. With UGMA accounts, the child automatically gets the assets when he reaches adulthood (age eighteen in most states), but with 2503(c) trusts the assets can be held until age twenty-one. Second, with the 2503(c) trust, as long as the beneficiary does not elect to get the money within thirty to sixty days after she turns twenty-one, the value of the funds *has* to stay in the trust until the date the grandparent has stated they should be distributed (usually age twenty-five). Of course, giving assets to minors does not have to be limited to grandparents; this technique is commonly used by parents as well. As I have discussed in the preface and in the chapters on retirement and education planning, you should never give away any assets you may need for your own financial health. And keep in mind that when applying for financial aid a greater percentage of assets in a child's name is considered fair game than of assets in a parent's name, so you may qualify for less financial aid by giving money to your children. These gifts to minors are discussed in detail in chapter 10, "Planning for Your Children's Education."

SUMMING UP

Estate planning can be complicated, and I have covered a number of aspects of the process, but there are several basics that are worth repeating. First of all, make an appointment with an attorney *today* to draw up a will or review the one you already have if you have not done so recently or if your circumstances have changed. If you do not have a good attorney, your local bar association can provide you with the names of several, or you can ask friends for references. Do not use just *any* attorney—estate planning is a specialized field, and the attorney who handled your house closing may not be the best person to draft your will. If you decide to use pre-printed, fill-in-the-blank wills or software programs that generate will documents, *be sure that whatever you have produced is reviewed by a lawyer in your state before you sign it.*

Second, follow through with whatever asset ownership changes need to be made in order to make your estate plan the best it can be. It doesn't do any good for you to have a will that leaves everything you own to your children if your spouse owns all the assets! For example, Pete and Sally had very sophisticated will and trust documents, and they thought they were all set to pay as little tax as possible when they died. When I reviewed their finances, however, I discovered that $2 million was in Pete's name only; the *only asset in Sally's name* was a $2,000 checking account. If Sally had died, she and Pete would have missed their chance to get almost $600,000 out of their estates *tax-free* by having Sally leave that much to a trust instead of to Pete so that when he died he wouldn't own it. In fact, that's what her very fancy (and expensive) will and trust said *would* happen. But she had only $2,000, so only $2,000 would have been tax-free.

Even more common was Margaret and Joe's situation. This was the second marriage for both, and they each intended to leave all their assets to their respective children. The problem? Margaret and Joe owned their house as joint tenants with right of survivorship. Joe died, and to everyone's dismay (including Margaret's, who wanted to keep peace in the blended family), his share of the house went to Margaret and not to his children. They had all agreed beforehand that the survivor should be able to live in the house and that the children would sell it and split the proceeds after both Margaret and Joe were dead. But suddenly Margaret owned the whole house. If she left Joe's share to his children at her death, her estate would have to pay taxes on it so the tax would be coming out of her children's share. But Joe's children didn't think it was fair to expect them to pay the taxes either. You can see how easy it is to strain family relationships over estate issues.

Third, tell your family members *where* your will is and whether trusts have been created. Also tell them who the executor is (and be sure to ask any potential executor in advance before you put him in your will). You will prevent a lot of family anguish and hard feelings if you make it clear where your will and trust are located. You do not have to tell your relatives what the documents *say*, just make sure that they know where the documents *are* (and remember not to put your will in the safe-deposit box).

Finally, be as clear as possible about your wishes in your will (and trust, if you have one). In 1994, more than two hundred years after Benjamin Franklin died and left much of his estate to be used for education in Massachusetts, various nonprofit organizations were still battling over who would receive the $4.6 million remaining in Franklin's estate: the Franklin Institute, which provides hands-on skilled training for mostly minority students, or the general state public school budget. The Massachusetts Supreme Judicial Court had to step in, and the issue was set to be resolved by—you guessed it—the state legislative body.

Most of *The Money Diet* is focused on helping you meet your lifetime goals. But whether you like to admit it or not, there are also goals that you have at death, and they usually cannot be met unless you make the right provisions during your lifetime. Having an estate plan with a will and perhaps even a trust will help ensure that the goals you have for your family can be met if you are not around. It is truly a mark of caring for your family to take the time to do this last bit of planning right.

CHAPTER FIFTEEN

Putting It All Together

MORE THAN A FEW TIMES, people have said to me, "I could solve all my financial problems if I only had a million dollars." It would be great if life were so simple (and we could find a million dollars for everybody), but unfortunately it just is not that easy. Even when a million dollars does land in your lap, it's not that easy. A couple came to me last year because they had just inherited close to a million dollars and wanted to make sure they managed it right so they could meet all their goals. Elliott and Gloria had been living on a modest income, so the prospect of a million dollars sitting in the bank seemed like a dream come true. Of course, it was a wonderful event, but by the time we had our second meeting it was clear that "goal inflation" had taken hold. Goal inflation is, quite simply, that very human characteristic of having one's financial goals suddenly get more and more grandiose the minute we have a chance to get our hands on some money. A million dollars sounded like unbelievable wealth to Elliott and Gloria, and they decided that it was time to live like millionaires. Unfortunately, living like millionaires in the 1990s is not the same as living like millionaires in the 1960s, '70s, or '80s—even with the million dollars this couple would not have been able to meet their new goals.

By the time they met with me, they had already picked out a new house and enrolled their children in expensive private schools. Elliott and Gloria also had their eye on a cottage at the beach. Therefore, you can imagine their shock when I ran some numbers and told them they would be destitute before they reached retirement if they followed through on all these goals. They were asking too much of that million dollars, and it simply could not stretch that far. They were expecting this inheritance to pay off their $25,000 in credit card and consumer debts, pay for sixteen years of private school education for two children, provide a $150,000 down payment on a new home, purchase a $100,000 cottage outright, and generate adequate retirement income for a couple who did not have a single retirement asset to their names.

I told them they had four choices and could select one or more of them. First, they could live the way they were dreaming of living and run out of money before the kids got out of college. Second, they could give up all their new goals, maintain their old spartan existence, and at least be able to balance their budget and not keep running up credit card debts. Third, they could reduce the size of some goals (such as only private high school for the kids instead of private elementary and high school) and give up others—such as the cottage—altogether. Finally, they could cut their living expenses so they would not have to use up the interest and asset growth from their inheritance. I told them that if they did not plan now, they would have to face these possibilities at different times, whether they liked it or not. The bottom line was, they would run out of money.

This is certainly a depressing thought—that even inheriting a million dollars cannot provide financial salvation—but I use Elliott and Gloria as an example because the one thing they thought would solve their financial problems would not. In fact, it might even make their problems worse because the family could become accustomed to a higher standard of living and then have to drastically cut back. After all, it is much harder to cut yearly spending from $100,000 to $35,000 than from $45,000 to $35,000. Inheriting money was not enough to live on Easy Street; Elliott and Gloria would have to change their financial behavior as well—as you already know from reading this far in *The Money Diet*. And, because nothing in this world is certain, it makes sense for us to plan as if some miracle will not come along and bail us out even if we do expect an inheritance at some future date. We need to make ourselves as financially fit as possible, starting today.

What makes it so difficult to get our minds around our financial situations is that we focus on different financial issues at different times of the day, week, or year and at different times in our lives. For example, we think about taxes around April 15, but probably not a whole lot at other times during the year. We worry more about retirement when we get older than when we are younger. We do not think much about funding our children's education if we do not have kids yet or if they are very small. And many of us never think at all about what would happen if we die, because this thought is too depressing and we would rather focus on living.

Putting all the different pieces of the Money Diet together is the key to making it work. It is just like a food diet, where you focus on all aspects of your health—nutrition, exercise, counting calories, and so on. It is synergy at work: The value of the whole plan is greater than the value of the sum of its parts. *The Money Diet* truly is the sum of the different chapters we have already covered, but it does not do any good to come up with the best education funding strategy in the world if doing so bankrupts your retirement, or to develop a sophisticated investment strategy without a will or life insurance. Financial planning is the process of constantly balancing one need against another. What you need is a strategy to help you balance these needs. Here is where we put together everything you have learned in this book.

If you feel overwhelmed at this point, this is actually a good sign: You are already 90 percent of the way to making the Money Diet work for you. You have already determined what your financial goals are, and you have some idea of what it will take to reach those goals. Now it is time to set priorities among your goals—to determine which ones you can forgo altogether and which others you are willing to reduce in size. Remember, I am being realistic, not negative, by assuming that you will not be able to meet every one of the goals you listed in chapter 4. Life is too hard these days, and even my wealthiest clients rarely can meet all their financial goals unless they make major changes. And by wealthy, I am talking about clients with $10 million or more. So, if you are in a position where you have to make trade-offs between one goal and another and watch your pennies carefully so you can save more, you are in the company of some of the richest people around.

This chapter first will help you establish your priorities and decide which goals you can eliminate altogether and which can be achieved at lower costs. Then it is time to look at increasing your annual savings so you will have more in the future, as well as investing better to meet these long-term future goals. Again, my premise is that you cannot do everything you want. Your goals may seem perfectly reasonable now, but it is only human nature that as soon as you get any extra money your goals will suddenly inflate, as they did with Elliott and Gloria. Just as most people cannot eat everything they want and stay thin, you cannot meet all the financial goals you want because your "money metabolism" simply cannot handle it.

There are three building blocks you can use to meet your goals— the assets you currently have, your future annual savings, and how well you invest those assets and future earnings. We have talked about these building blocks in great detail already, so now is the time to move back from the "micro" to the "macro." Look at **Putting the Money Diet Together** (page 305) so you can start to make sense of all the different parts of the Money Diet.

The information for part 1 of this exercise, the Additional Assets You Need to Meet Your Goals, comes from the charts you completed in previous chapters. For each of your goals, you have already determined approximately how much you need in today's dollars. In line A of **Putting the Money Diet Together,** write down the amount of additional assets you need for retirement after taking into account Social Security, other retirement benefits, and your existing assets. This number is in **How Much More Do You Need for Retirement?** (page 146, line J). If you have more assets than you need for retirement, write the surplus (from that same retirement chart, line K) on line B of **Putting the Money Diet Together.** Now, write the amount of money in today's dollars (in other words, what it would cost today) you estimate you will need for education on line C. This can be found in **Setting Your Financial Goals** (page 42, line D). You may want to reduce the amount needed by estimating how much in financial aid

Putting the Money Diet Together

Part 1: Additional Assets You Need to Meet Your Goals

A. Retirement Shortfall _or_ (How Much (More) Do You line J	A. +
B. Retirement Surplus Need for Retirement? p. 146) line K	B. −
C. Plus: Education Funds Needed* (Setting Your Financial Goals, p. 42, line D)	C. +
D. Plus: Down Payment on Home	D. +
E. Plus: Big-Ticket Item # 1	E. +
F. Plus: Big-Ticket Item # 2	F. +
G. Plus: Big-Ticket Item # 3	G. +
H. Total Additional Assets You Need to Meet Your Goals (Add lines A–G)	H. =

Note: If line H is negative, it shows you do not need additional assets. Congratulations! You can stop here.

Part 2: Your Total Annual Savings Until Retirement

I. Annual Savings with the Money Diet (Spending and Saving, p. 28, line I; plus new savings possible, and less new expenses required (insurance premiums, etc.))	I. =
J. Plus: Times Number of Years Until Retirement	J. ×
K. Equals: Total Annual Savings Until Retirement	K. =

Part 3: Your Financial Planning Shortfall/Surplus

H. Total Additional Assets You Need to Meet Your Goals (see line H above)	H.
K. Less: Total Annual Savings Until Retirement (see line K above)	K. −
L. Your Financial Planning Shortfall (If K is less than H)	L. =
_or_	
M. Your Financial Planning Surplus (If H is less than K)	M. =

Note: All numbers in today's dollars.
* You may be able to reduce the amount you estimated for education expenses in
Setting Your Financial Goals because of the many college funding sources available
which are described in Chapter 10.

scholarships and grants you will be entitled to, and how much you expect your children to contribute by assuming responsibility for loans, etc. If you plan to make a down payment on a new house, write that amount in today's dollars on line D. And if you plan to buy a new car and/or other big-ticket item, write these amounts on lines E through G of **Putting the Money Diet Together.** The total additional assets you need to meet your goals, line H, is the sum of adding lines A through G. However, if you have written a retirement surplus amount on line B, you should subtract that number. (This is one of those times when a negative number is good.) If line H shows you do not need additional assets, congratulations! You can stop here unless you want to figure out just how solid your financial situation is.

Certain other goals will need to be taken care of if you die or become disabled, so you may have to set aside a few hundred dollars for a will and estate plan as well as whatever additional annual insurance premiums you need. We are focusing on the big picture now—those few hundred dollars here and there will not make a major impact over the long haul.

In part 2 of **Putting the Money Diet Together,** you will have a chance to figure out the total amount of annual savings you may have until you retire, not taking inflation or any increases in savings into account. Take the Total Annual Savings you came up with in **Spending and Saving** (page 28, line I), and estimate the additional savings as well as the additional expenses (such as insurance) that you will have by following the Money Diet. Write your answer on line I of **Putting the Money Diet Together.** Then multiply it by the number of years you have until retirement (line J). The result, on line K, is the amount of savings you may in fact have available to invest until you reach retirement age if your salary increases with inflation and all those increases are used for increased taxes and living expenses, or if everything stays exactly the same as it is now.

In part 3 of **Putting the Money Diet Together,** you can find out your financial planning shortfall or surplus. Subtract your Total Annual Savings Until Retirement (line K) from the Total Additional Assets You Need to Meet Your Goals (line H). If line K is less than line H, write Your Financial Planning Shortfall on line L. If K is more than H, write Your Financial Planning Surplus on line M. Do not be dismayed if you just came up with a large negative number. Before you panic, consider these four things:

- First, this rough calculation does not take your investment earnings into consideration, unless they are deposited in your checking account and you included them in your annual savings calculation in **Spending and Savings.**
- Second, we haven't counted on it, but we hope that you will be able to invest to get an overall rate of return that is several percentage points higher than inflation.
- Third, we have not taken into account any further increased savings you might be able to achieve once you master the Money Diet.
- Fourth, there are many variables involved in this calculation— from how much achieving your goals will cost, how much you can save, what your employer's retirement contributions will be, and what rate of return you earn, to the generalities of inflation, increases in Social Security benefits, tax changes, and changes in other government programs such as federal education programs. We are coming up with numbers for many years in the future, and who knows what her life will be like ten, twenty, or thirty years from now?

To start to put the whole Money Diet into action, however, it is important to follow a number of steps. Here's where **Making Trade-offs** (page 308) can help. (If you have a financial planning surplus, you do not need to complete this chart. However, you may want to do so anyway because it's smart to practice defensive planning in case your situation changes.) Start by writing Your Financial Planning Shortfall (**Putting the Money Diet Together,** line L) on line A. Now, go back and look at the goals you wrote down in **Putting the Money Diet Together;** think about which goals are more important and decide which, if any, you can eliminate. If you can eliminate any of your goals, that directly reduces your shortfall. For example, the fancy new car or vacation home should be the first to go if you don't have enough money to do everything you want. Next, look at your other goals and see if you are willing to reduce them in any way (public col-

Making Trade-offs

Note: You only have to complete this chart if **Putting the Money Diet Together** shows you have a financial planning shortfall. However, if your financial planning surplus does not appear to be enough of a cushion, you may want to do so anyway in order to protect against unforeseen changes in your financial situation.

A. Your Financial Planning Shortfall (Putting the Money Diet Together, p. 305, line L)	A.
B. Reduction in Retirement Goal	B.
C. Plus: Reduction in Education Goal	C. +
D. Plus: Reduction in Home Down Payment Goal	D. +
E. Plus: Reduction in Big-Ticket Items Goal	E. +
F. Equals: Total Reduced Needs for Goals (Add lines B+C+D+E)	F. =
G. Financial Planning Shortfall After **Reducing Goals** (line A minus line F)	G. =
H. Further Annual Savings Possible*	H.
Times Number of Years to Retirement	×
I. Equals Total Increased Savings Possible	I. =
J. Financial Planning Shortfall After Making **Trade-offs** (line G minus line I)	J. =

* This amount is in addition to the annual savings amount you listed on
Putting the Money Diet Together, p. 305, line I.

lege instead of private, $50,000 less in assets at retirement, less expensive car, etc.).

In terms of goals, you have to set priorities. One of your top two priorities should probably be a basic retirement income. That's because if push comes to shove you could probably do without the more expensive house, or paying for all of your children's college education yourself, or the new car with all the extras, but you *have* to have money to live on. I'm not talking about a jet-set lifestyle but an income that covers your essential needs. Of equal priority is insurance against catastrophes—not insuring against every small loss but those that can wipe you out in a split second. For most parents, education is the next goal. (You may now agree with the idea of putting basic retirement needs before education, but if you are like most parents, you probably had these two priorities reversed when you started. See how *The Money Diet* has changed your money thinking?) Any reductions you can come up with here will shrink that bottom-line number of your shortfall. The idea is to make the biggest reductions in the least important goals. Add all the goal reduction amounts from lines B through E in **Making Trade-offs,** and write the answer, Total Reduced Needs for Goals, on line F. Then subtract line F from line A (Your Financial Planning Shortfall) to get your new, lower shortfall on line G. Next, make a commitment to yourself to save even more than you wrote on line I of **Putting the Money Diet Together** and write your Further Annual Savings Possible on line H. Multiply that by the number of years to retirement to get your Total Increased Savings Possible (line I). Subtract your Total Increased Savings Possible (line I) from the Financial Planning Shortfall After Reducing Goals (line G). The result is your Financial Planning Shortfall After Making Trade-offs (line J). Finally, make a commitment to change your investment strategy (if need be). This may mean taking more risk if you will be investing more in the stock market, but you need to invest at a higher rate than inflation if you want to reduce your financial planning shortfall. And remember, by using asset allocation, diversification with no-load mutual funds, and dollar cost averaging, you are reducing the amount of risk you are taking.

What you have left is your first attempt at putting the Money Diet together and making it work. If you are like most people, you probably *still* show a shortfall, but you now have an overall framework within which you can make financial decisions. Remember how we talked about keeping the Money Diet method in mind whenever you are making financial decisions? It is just like visualizing yourself at your ideal weight so that you have an incentive to eat less and exercise more. The same is true with the Money Diet, and keeping in mind the method as well as your shortfall amount in **Putting the Money**

Diet Together is a great motivator to spend less, save more, and invest better. Obviously, as you go through life your priorities and your financial situation will change, but you now have the framework in which to plan for all those changes.

There are some other ways to improve your bottom line besides reducing or eliminating goals, saving more, and investing better. Probably the most important of these is to make sure that whenever you change jobs you take a close look at the benefits that come with those jobs. This is because the dollar value of those benefits to you may literally be $10,000 a year or more. For example, your employer may be matching retirement plan contributions to the tune of a hefty percentage of your salary. You may have company-paid disability, medical, and/or life insurance. All these benefits add up, and having your employer (instead of you) pay for them will decrease your bottom-line shortfall. If you are not working or are working part-time now, you may decide to change to a job with more income or take a job so you can whittle away at that bottom line. You should also expect your children to set aside some of their job earnings for education (or for other "important" expenses like the concert tickets or $100 sandals). Finally, you may decide to start a small business on the side to make a hobby profitable, or do some off-hours consulting in your field of expertise. All these things will reduce your shortfall and improve your bottom line.

At my firm, when we finish a financial plan for clients and show them exactly what they need to do in order to meet various goals, there is always the question of deciding which recommendations to follow and which to deal with later. This is because any assets you use up for one goal are then taken away from another. The $5,000 you spend on extras when you remodel the bathroom means you have $5,000 less to save for retirement. *Life is a constant financial balancing act.* You may have already tried to balance your goals with your assets and savings in the worksheet **Making Trade-offs** by reducing or eliminating some goals and committing to an increased savings program. Now let's look at a couple of specific recommendations that don't show up in **Making Trade-offs** because instead of a big chunk of money they require only small one-time or annual payments. First, you *must* cover your catastrophic insurance needs, including life insurance and disability insurance to protect you and your family if a disaster strikes. Adequate insurance also means having enough home-owners and automobile coverage in case you are sued. At the same time, you need to get a will or review the one you have to make sure that your estate planning is up-to-date. These two recommendations are based on the advice that virtually every financial planner I know gives to clients—namely, that *you should protect against loss before you take any action for potential gain.* After all, you have the possibility of losing much more (your lost income, a large lawsuit) than you can possibly gain by putting another thousand dollars into your annual savings.

Once you have covered your insurance needs and have gotten your estate-planning documents in order, it is time to think about where to invest your annual savings. First, you need to review your asset allocation and make any changes necessary so your investments are placed in the right categories—fixed income, equities, etc. (see chapter 8). Then any new savings you are able to generate should first go to fund your retirement plans. There are some major tax benefits to do so, and remember my overall recommendation that you must cover your own basic needs first. Keep in mind that it often is a good idea to put money into retirement plans even if you may have to take it out later (either through borrowing or outright distribution) so you can apply it to other goals such as a child's college tuition. In the meantime, you will have benefited from tax deductions and tax deferral of the investment earnings until the time you take it out. You may have to pay a 10 percent penalty as well as income taxes on outright withdrawal, but if you invest well (even if you keep money in the retirement plan for only a few years), you may come out ahead. Remember, my example in **Who Is Smarter?** (page 154) in chapter 9, with "Smart" putting money in a retirement plan and "Stupid" saving in a regular account? You can see that after only a few years, "Smart" is better off because he has had the chance to defer income taxes each year, so he has more money to grow each year. Even after paying a 10 percent penalty, "Smart" comes out ahead. In the meantime, you will be less tempted to spend that money, and if you are trying to qualify for college financial aid, your retirement plans usually are not taken into account.

Next, commit to saving a specific dollar amount this year through a combination of spending less, reducing your debt, and saving taxes. Use the one biggest money-saving suggestion that most appeals to you in each of these categories (spending less, reducing debts, saving taxes) rather than making changes in only one of the categories and ignoring the others. For example, Wendy can start to make her annual savings tax-deductible and tax-deferred by setting up an IRA, keeping track of her biggest spending problem area (clothes), and paying off her credit card balances faster. She will probably see more bottom-line results if she does some of each of these different things than if she concentrates on finding three ways to spend less. This is because there is a law of diminishing returns when it comes to changing your money behavior. As you were reading this book, I hope you were able to figure out the one change in your behavior that would generate the most significant long-term financial improvement in each of the areas covered. For example, you are probably better off making a commitment to reduce your restaurant expenses and getting organized so you can take more tax deductions than by choosing to follow two of my suggestions in the tax chapter and ignoring your spending problems.

Believe it or not, the worst thing you can do is take *The Money Diet* and try to implement every single recommendation I have given that makes sense for you. It becomes just like tracking every penny you spend—doing all these things is just too much trouble in our busy lives. It is better to make the few changes that will create the biggest bottom-line impact so you get more "bang for your buck."

Combining the different aspects of the Money Diet is difficult, even if you have a trained financial planner to assist you along the way. The key is to keep the four steps of the Money Diet in mind:

- **Step 1: Find out your current financial weight.** Remember to stay focused on the big picture so you don't get bogged down in details.
- **Step 2: Set your Money Diet goals.** Make these goals realistic ones that are based on your current lifestyle.
- **Step 3: Develop your Money Diet plan.** Stay focused on trying to decrease your bottom-line financial shortfall (or improving

your surplus) through a combination of goal reduction, saving more, and investing better. Then decide on your plan of action—choosing one or two Money Diet "to do's" from each chapter to implement.

- **Step 4: Review your Money Diet plan regularly.** Make a commitment to review your plan on a regular basis so you are setting up daily, weekly, monthly, and annual goals. Your chances of Money Diet success improve every time you review your progress.

Putting the Money Diet into action will not be smooth sailing all the way. Even the most self-disciplined person would not be able to immediately act on all my recommendations. But every time you make a smart money decision in a situation where before reading this book you would have done just the opposite will make the *next* positive decision that much easier. After almost two years of working with me, a client recently made the decision to dramatically change his lifestyle so that he could retire in comfort ten years from now. Even six months ago, Thomas could have never imagined giving up his boat and lavish vacations. But he started changing his money behavior a little at a time, and after about a year, suddenly he found that his perspective had changed so much that giving up the boat and vacations were easy. Do not be hard on yourself; remember that you are changing a lifetime of money behavior. The good news is that no matter how small the step, each one will change your financial future for the better.

CHAPTER SIXTEEN

Choosing Your Financial Advisers

EVERY ONCE in a while when I give a speech, someone comes up to me afterward and says, "I just came to listen—to prove to myself that I don't need a financial adviser." My response is always "You may not need a financial planner but you probably have already used more financial advisers in your life than you can imagine." Every time you have opened a bank account, bought insurance, bought or sold a house, borrowed money, applied for a credit card, or made any of a plethora of financial or legal transactions, chances are someone acted as a financial adviser to you during that process. If you own a home, think about when you applied to refinance a mortgage. The person sitting behind the desk may not have been much older than you or your own children or might have been new in the job, but chances are he or she gave you advice about how many points to pay, whether to apply for a fifteen- or thirty-year mortgage, whether to finance any improvements or use up cash you've saved. The advice *may* have been just fine; the problem is, you were relying on the advice of someone who knew only one part of your financial story. This "adviser" probably knew little about your retirement plans, your cash flow, your method of saving for education, your tax bracket, and your individual financial preferences—if, for example, you are the kind of person who psychologically needs to have as small a monthly payment as possible. You probably did not know much about the customer service rep, insurance agent, loan officer, or other person acting as the "adviser" either. But you may have relied on his or her advice about transactions worth hundreds and perhaps hundreds of thousands of dollars.

Whenever I start working with a new client, as we go through the data-gathering process I ask where they got advice to make various buying and selling decisions. It never fails to shock me how easily we take another person's financial advice as gospel if she appears to be even a tiny bit more knowledgeable or confident than we do about the subject. Some of my all-time-favorite amateur financial advisers are the brothers-in-law, the mechanics, the hairdressers, or the guys in the car pool who probably had no idea how seriously their advice would be taken. Perhaps you have noticed the warning on virtually every diet and exercise book, package of diet food, and exercise video that says "Consult your doctor before using this." Most people know by now that taking the wrong diet and exercise advice can have serious implications for their physical health. The same is true for financial advice: You really should consult an experienced financial adviser before making any major money decision. But just as we tend to get our diet advice from a wide variety of unprofessional sources (a friend, a "lose-ten-pounds-in-ten-days" magazine article, the person at the next locker in the gym), we take as gospel the financial pronouncements of anyone who seems to know what he is talking about. Unfortunately, the financial world has gotten too complex and the stakes are too high to rely on just anyone's advice.

As previously mentioned on pages 133–34, *Consumer Reports'* survey of mutual fund advice given by salespeople at banks raised serious questions about the quality of that advice. The magazine judged the salesperson's advice to be adequate and appropriate, based on the customer's situation, less than 25 percent of the time. The problem of poor financial advice is not just confined to banks, either. Always keep in mind that just because a person is sitting in a wood-paneled office, or works in an environment as "safe" as a bank, or has a title, that doesn't mean you should accept his advice at face value.

It is no wonder we are confused about where to get financial advice, especially since we are surrounded by conflicting financial advice every day in the media—and studies have shown that people who do not use financial planners rely on the media as their primary source of financial advice. Most daily newspapers have a business section with personal finance articles, and every major publication seems to have at least one item devoted to money or to the economy. You can find articles on "the best stocks for the 1990s," "how to cut taxes," "when to refinance your mortgage," "where to invest your savings for education." This advice may be perfectly fine for someone else, but it may be *totally wrong* for your particular circumstances. Another source of financial advice that is becoming more common is the "free" seminar to talk about estate planning, insurance planning, investing, and/or retirement. Just like they always say, there is no free lunch, even if the seminar is advertised and led by an "independent financial adviser," or an insurance agent, or an attorney. Many people go to these events because they are free, not realizing that the bias of the presentation is to get you to buy the presenter's products or use the presenter's services. And some of these seminars *seem* acceptable because they are being sponsored by some organization you belong to, or are held in your library, or are given in conjunction with a college near you.

There are all kinds of "financial planners" offering a broad spectrum of financial advice. These "financial planners" can include comprehensive financial planners, stockbrokers, insurance agents, bank officers, investment advisers, CPAs, tax attorneys, enrolled agents, other people who provide accounting and tax preparation services, computer program services, CLUs, ChFCs, CFPs, and so on. Some computer programs even have built-in "artificial intelligence" that helps the program analyze your financial information the way an expert would if she were dealing with your situation one-on-one with you, generate a series of financial calculations similar to those you have made in the *Money Diet* worksheets, and print out a written report containing specific recommendations. (I know because I was part of a large software project in the 1980s that did just that.) The problem is the label "financial planner"; there is no regulation of the term, so anyone can claim to be one. (I once threatened to register my dog Grizzly as a member of a particular financial planning organization to protest the lack of regulations.)

Choosing a financial planner is also confusing because with financial planners, "What you see is *not* always what you get." With most advisers, compensation arrangements are clear. In general, stockbrokers and insurance agents earn commissions. CPAs, tax attorneys, and enrolled agents earn fees. Bank employees used to be strictly on salary, although now many of them are on a commission system as well. But with "financial planners," you do not know (unless they tell you or you ask directly) how they are compensated. (The only exception is that when a planner gives you investment advice, he is required by law to give you an SEC brochure in which his method of compensation is spelled out—often buried in the middle pages and "spelled out" in legalese.) The new stockbroker trainee can call you up her first day on the job and refer to herself as a financial planner. The same is true with insurance agents who sell insurance and don't give investment or tax advice. Therefore, it is worth taking a few minutes to learn the differences between *commission-based, fee plus commission* or *fee-based,* and *fee-only* financial planners.

The fee-or-commission-or-both topic is hotly debated within the financial planning profession. Let me start out by saying that every financial planner has a bias about what makes a good practitioner. I would like to think that I have fewer prejudices than most; although I am totally fee-only now, I started out in my early twenties earning commissions (but I didn't make much money because I kept giving out advice *not* to buy the products I was supposed to sell!). In my thirties I was a partner at a firm that mostly earned fees but did get a small part of its revenues via commissions. Interestingly enough, the path I took is the same trend (toward fee-only) that the planning profession is taking in general.

Recently a client called me with a very thorny technical financial problem. I called three people—a CPA, an insurance agent, and another financial planner. Each gave me the one right answer, and each had a different perspective that was very helpful in devising a solution to this client's problem. When I thought about it, I realized I had just called someone who earned money only through fees (the CPA), someone else who earned money only through commissions (the insurance agent), and a third person who charged a combination of the two (the fee-plus-commission financial planner). Because I know these advisers well, their answers all had equal validity for me. But the problem is, you usually can't get to know an adviser that well before you have to make a decision whether or not to use her. For many people, it feels safer to use a financial planner whose income is not dependent upon what products you buy. That's why, when Americans are asked who they would prefer to deal with, the surveys overwhelmingly show a preference for someone who does not charge commissions.

Because this issue is so important, let us look at it in more detail. The first type of planner is *commission-only*. The advantage here is that you do not have to pay them separate fees, they are compensated directly by the companies they sell investments, insurance, etc., for, and they may be very knowledgeable about specific products because they work with them all the time. *Fee-plus-commission* planners usually charge you a flat fee to prepare a written financial plan and then earn commissions on any products you buy to implement the recommendations in the plan. Sometimes fee-plus-commission planners will work on a fee-offset basis; they reduce their fees by the amount of any commissions earned. For example, Mary Beth is charged $500 for a simple financial plan. But she then buys an insurance policy that pays the financial planner $300 in commissions. So, instead of writing out a check for $500, she owes only $200 ($500 less the commissions of $300). The advantage of the fee-plus-commission arrangement is that the actual financial planning fees tend to be lower than with fee-only planners. The disadvantage of using a planner who is compensated in any way by what you buy is that you may wonder whether the plan recommendations were written just so that certain products can be sold.

The third type of planner is the *fee-only* planner, charging only hourly or retainer fees for advice and selling no products. The advantage is that you can be sure that investments, insurance policies, etc. are not being recommended just to put dollars in the planner's pocket. The disadvantage, however, is that you may still have to buy products on which commissions are charged unless you buy "no-load" products that do not charge commissions. You have to decide what arrangement feels comfortable to you and what it will take to trust a financial planner enough to take his advice.

If you look through your local Yellow Pages you will no doubt see a number of display ads heralding certain financial planing firms as "fee-based." It is these I sometimes find most offensive, because "fee-based" sounds like "fee-only" but in fact it can—and often does—mean "fee-plus-commission." Or it may be that the firm itself charges only fees but the planner has set up another company that handles the product sales. If you are shopping for a planner and run into someone who says he is "fee-based" but in reality accepts commissions, run in the other direction. When I went through the Boston phone book, I found a number of firms listed as "fee-based" that I know quite well sell products. It's not the product sales that I find appalling (there are many excellent planners who earn commissions) but the deliberate deception. My personal belief is that until there is some regulation of the term *financial planner* and until planners are required to disclose fully and in simple language, in advance, *all* fees and commissions they would earn in working with a client, we are going to continue to have this confusion among consumers.

When you are considering using a financial planner, the first thing to do is figure out how much help you want or need. Here's how you know when you need help. Professional assistance is needed when you read *The Money Diet* and know:

- you do not have the time,
- you do not have the knowledge, and/or
- you do not have the motivation to do it on your own.

Of course, there are certain areas in which you should always get professional help, like in estate planning. In other financial areas, how much outside help you need depends on your individual situation. With cash flow and credit management, you can track expenses on your own or hire a bookkeeper for a few hours a month to keep track of them for you and to motivate you. (Just the shame of having someone else see the money that is flowing out may be enough for you to change your spending ways. This can be especially useful if you are single or a single parent and no one else ever looks at how you are spending your money.) You can do your taxes on your own, with or without the help of a tax preparation book or software program, or you can have someone do them for you. With investments, now you can make your own decisions and buy investments inexpensively through a "discount broker" (look for ads in the business section of the paper) or even commission-free by buying no-load mutual funds. Even in insurance, you can now purchase "low-load" insurance where there is no commission and you buy directly from the insurance company or through a fee-only financial planner or insurance adviser. The trend is definitely toward "do it yourself," but at different times of your life it may make sense to use the services of a professional financial planner. There are a number of questions to ask any person who is in a position to give you advice for a fee and/or a commission.

They are:

1. What areas of personal finance do you specialize in? Stockbrokers and FSAs (Financial Securities Analysts) specialize in investments, CPAs and enrolled agents specialize in taxes, some attorneys may specialize in estate planning and personal taxes, and insurance agents specialize in insurance. You should rely on financial recommendations *only* if they are given by a professional who gives advice in that particular area a large part of the time. A financial planner may say that she is a "generalist"; this usually means that she offers advice in all the areas of financial planning covered in *The Money Diet*. A general financial planner is fine to use, provided he tells you he's willing to get more specific help if needed (you can usually predict if an adviser's ego is so big that he is convinced he knows all the answers himself). Anyone who calls herself a financial planner should engage in overall financial planning—not just work in one or two areas such as investment management, insurance, or estate planning. *The Money Diet* focuses on the fact that you have competing needs and goals—so upping your IRA contribution may affect your plans to buy a new house next year. You need a planner who understands your whole financial situation so he can make sure the decisions you make are good for your overall financial health.

2. How long have you been in this field? Ideally, you are looking for someone who has been working at least five years (if you have a complicated situation) because you do not want anyone to make mistakes at your expense. It is fine to use someone with less experience, provided that person's recommendations are overseen by someone with five years of experience or more and you meet that supervisor in person. Especially in insurance, investments, and financial planning, it takes a number of years to be sure the person has survived the "weeding-out" period and is good enough to make a living at it.

3. What are your credentials? What you are looking for here is letters after the person's name. It used to be that some investment advisers and financial planners would put "RIA" after their names, meaning "Registered Investment Adviser." To become a Registered Investment Adviser, all you have to do is send $150 to the Securities and Exchange Commission, have your application approved, and follow certain SEC regulations. But the SEC did not like the fact that people were passing "RIA" off as an educational degree. The SEC made using the initials "RIA" a no-no. But there *are* professional designations that are meaningful. Most have minimum experience requirements and require written exams. They include the following:

> **CFP** (Certified Financial Planner)—general financial planning
> **ChFC** (Chartered Financial Consultant)—primarily insurance or general financial planning
> **EA** (Enrolled Agent)—usually tax advice
> **CPA** (Certified Public Accountant)—emphasizing taxation, but more and more CPAs are specializing in personal financial planning, and the American Institute of Certified Public Accountants has an additional designation **APFS** (Accredited Personal Finance Specialist) that CPAs can earn
> **CLU** (Chartered Life Underwriter)—specializing in insurance
> **FSA** (Financial Securities Analyst)—investments
> **LLB, JD,** and **LLM**—legal degrees

4. How do you get paid? We talked about fee-only, fee-plus-commission, and commission-only. Because there are fewer potential conflicts of interest, I recommend that you use a fee-only planner unless you already have had good experience with a particular fee-plus-commission or commission-only planner or you have a very strong referral to one. But regardless of who you use, find out how—and how much—they will be paid. Pressure anyone who is earning commissions to disclose to you *in writing* approximately what those commissions would be, not just for this year but for future years as well, including commissions you would have to pay if you decided to sell the product. If the person earns fees, make sure you understand the basis—flat retainer, hourly fees, percentage of assets (yours) under management—upon which you will be charged and what the upper limit of those fees will be. Also find out if the fee-only planner will help you purchase "no-load" or "low-load" products (without commissions). Brokerage firm "wrap" accounts can have notoriously high fees (a "wrap" account is a brokerage account where a percentage of assets under management is charged instead of commissions), and I personally believe the fees some planners charge to manage a portfolio of no-load mutual funds are too high. In this last case, you are already paying the fees of each particular mutual fund; to pay the adviser another 1½ to 2 percent on top of that is too high unless your account is under $100,000. Money management fees should also decline as a percentage as your account gets larger. Whenever you are looking at cost, look at *total* cost including commissions, not just what you are paying the planner directly. Some planners even use another professional money management firm as adviser, so you end up paying two different fees.

5. Where will investments be held? Whenever someone is managing your money for you, make sure that an accredited financial institution is physically holding the investments, *not* the planner himself. *Never give anyone the ability to hold money in their name for you, and never make out a check for an investment directly to the planner.* Reputable planners and investment managers always have a "third-party custodian" such as a brokerage firm or a bank. For example, we manage money using no-load mutual funds, and all checks for investments must be made out directly to the discount brokerage firm we use as custodian. There are too many instances of financial advisers or their employees absconding with client funds to give anyone else access to your money.

6. Can I see your ADV-1? ADV-1 is SEC shorthand for "Advisory Form #1," a brochure that all investment advisers *must* give potential clients before they buy anything. It provides answers to most of the questions here, and then some. Actually, if you even have to ask this question after meeting with any adviser about investment advice, think twice before proceeding. Why? Any firm or individual giving you advice about investments and/or selling investment products must be registered with the Securities and Exchange Commission and agree to distribute their ADV-1 brochures to prospective customers. Read the ADV-1 carefully.

7. May I have the names of references? Preferably, you want two client references and one from a professional in a related field, such as an estate planning attorney or CPA, if you are considering working with a Certified Financial Planner. Your client references should be people who face similar financial concerns.

8. Could I ask you to get an answer to my tax or investment question [or whatever]? In other words, do the responsiveness test. Remember that the advice you are getting is critical to your financial future, and you want this particular financial adviser to be around to pay attention to you when you need help (another reason to work with an established planner!). Ask him to get back to you with some small piece of information before you make a decision whether or not to use him. If a potential adviser does not call back (and you would be surprised how many do not follow through), you obviously do not want that person as your adviser.

In addition to these questions, there are certain potential financial advisers you want to avoid. First, *avoid anyone who pressures you. Period.* When you are under pressure or feeling manipulated, that is when you can end up making bad decisions. The only time to possibly be concerned about waiting is with insurance, where a delay may cost you coverage if you become uninsurable while you wait to make up your mind. Also, in some instances, there may be a tax decision that needs to be made before the end of the year. Otherwise, there will always be other investments, other loans, and other chances to make decisions.

I believe that when someone pressures you, she is in effect admitting that her product or service cannot stand on its own merits or that she has not explained it well enough so you can clearly see its merits. And if you are buying products, you do not want a financial planner who is not selling the best products or who cannot explain those products to you in a comprehensible way. Women in particular seem to have trouble saying no because for the most part we have been treated like second-class citizens in the financial decision-making process. If someone is pressuring you, use this book as your excuse: Tell them I said you need time to think about it and that if they continue to pressure you, you will no longer work with them.

The second type of adviser to avoid is anyone with a "party line." By "party line" I mean the adviser who says "I am a *better* adviser because . . .": such as "I am male" (or "female"), or "I practice a particular religion," or "I don't sell products," etc. Believe me, greed and the resulting impulse to empty a client's pockets know no gender, no religion, and no single way of getting paid. However, it's fine to use a planner who states he is fee-only because he feels more comfortable that way or does so to avoid conflicts of interest.

The third type of adviser to avoid is *anyone* you have never met or anyone who sells solely by phone. You learn a lot just by seeing how a person looks and behaves. Phone scams have become very sophisticated, and a cultured accent and fancy company name can mask a host of deceptive sales practices. And it goes without saying that you should never buy an investment over the phone with a credit card.

Here, in alphabetical order, are some organizations that can give you information about planners in your area (most have extensive experience requirements and all have stringent continuing education requirements so that members must stay abreast of current tax laws, etc.):

AICPA
American Institute of Certified Public Accountants
201-938-3100
This organization is for CPAs; you can also get referrals to CPAs who have earned the APFS (Accredited Personal Finance Specialist) designation.

ASCLU/ChFC
American Society of Chartered Life Underwriters and Chartered Financial Consultants
800-392-6900
This organization is for those who have passed ten exams for the CLU (focuses on insurance) and/or ChFC (focuses on all financial planning topics).

ICFP
Institute of Certified Financial Planners
800-322-4237
This is an organization of individuals who have earned the Certified Financial Planner designation (either six individual exams or one comprehensive exam on all areas of financial planning).

NAEA
National Association of Enrolled Agents
800-424-4339
This association is for individuals who are Enrolled Agents authorized to represent you before the IRS. The requirements are an IRS examination or five years of audit-level experience with the IRS.

NAPFA
National Association of Personal Financial Advisers
800-366-2732
This is an organization for fee-only financial planners.

RFPP
Registry of Financial Planning Practitioners/International Association for Financial Planning
800-945-IAFP
This is an organization for individuals who have passed an examination and had a financial plan scrutinized by the RFPP.

If this chapter scared you, I wanted it to do precisely that. Each year, hundreds of millions of dollars are lost through financial scams. And each year, legitimate and ethical financial advisers have to untangle the nasty messes their shady brethren have caused. The only way to become self-sufficient on the Money Diet is to know *what* is going on and know *who* is giving you advice at all times. *The Money Diet* will not make you an expert in all areas of your financial life, but I hope it will give you all the tools you need so that you can judge for yourself the validity of a piece of advice. That way, the next time you get a hot stock tip from your hairdresser, you will know exactly what to do with it—nothing!

CHAPTER SEVENTEEN

Scheduling Regular Financial Checkups

THIS MORNING, before I sat down to write this chapter, I had a semiannual review meeting with two of my very favorite clients. We have been working together for years, and although there is always work to be done, for much of the time it feels as if their financial planning is on "autopilot." I relish our meetings, though, because they refocus and re-energize all of us and remind us all how far we have come together. There have been many challenges since they first walked through my door—a major job change, an unexpected addition to the family, financing of a new home, even a medical scare—but because the groundwork was done and they always stayed on top of their financial progress, each new challenge stopped short of becoming a crisis. Financial planning has become such an ingrained part of their life and their daily behavior that they do not consciously think about it anymore, except at review time.

Telling you that it is important to review your financial progress regularly is like saying "Brush your teeth" or "Eat your vegetables." But this piece of financial advice may be a bit harder than admonitions to take care of your health. Changing the way you spend and save money involves changing major habits, and if you get off track, it is tempting to give up altogether. In this way, conducting regular financial checkups is like getting on the scales periodically after you have lost all that weight. It ensures that all of the hard work you have done so far is not forgotten, reinforces all the progress you have made, and helps to head off backsliding before you are tempted to fall back into old habits. But in many ways the Money Diet is much more important than a food diet. A few extra pounds should not affect your happiness and future goals, but poor money management can mean long-term unhappiness. And the negative results can affect more than one generation.

Changing habits is tough, and changing money habits is the toughest of all. Money is bound up in just about everything we do, and it is integrally connected to our emotions. Having or not having money can make us euphoric or nervous wrecks, and we also use it as a mood-enhancer to make ourselves and others happy. With the Money Diet, you are changing the way you conceptualize money, spend money, save money, invest money, and visualize the future.

If sticking to the Money Diet is so important, how often should you review your financial situation to make sure that you are staying on track? I generally recommend that at least once a year you review and update the key worksheets and tables in *The Money Diet*. "Key" are those that *you* found most helpful and useful in addressing your particular money issues as you proceeded through this book. If you are like most people, your annual review should be done around January 1 to see how close you came last year to your spending and saving goals and to set goals for the upcoming year. In the area of expenses, I recommend that you keep track of your spending for three months running when you first start trying to cut expenses on the Money Diet (this is in addition to the two months of spending the same way you always do but keeping track of your expenses). Then pick two months of every year plus December in years thereafter to keep track. Most people find it easier to break big tasks down into small ones, so I have come up with **Your Money Diet Calendar** (page 332) that has suggested tasks for each of the months of the year. This worksheet provides a place where you can create your own personalized Money Diet calendar to use and update each year.

In the left-hand column of **Your Money Diet Calendar**, I have listed my suggested timetable. The Your Tasks column is for you to write down your own money tasks. You can use my order or create your own. This is my suggested timetable, but it may not be exactly right for you. After all, every household has its own money rhythm. For example, the "doing taxes" timetable is all over the map for different people: Some people have their taxes done by the middle of January, others do them all in one day in April, and still others spread the task over a three-month period. Similarly, some people balance their checkbooks every month (which is a good time to look at monthly expenses). Other people balance their checkbooks once every quarter, or every six months, and some never balance their checkbooks at all. I don't want to chastise you and pressure you to make changes in your money behavior that are doomed to failure because you will never do them. However, if you fall into the last category of never balancing your checkbook, try to do so at least twice a year; that way you can create an accurate **Spending and Saving** worksheet. Looking over your deposits, checks, and ATM withdrawals is a great way to gain perspective on the money decisions you are making every day. You may track your investment portfolios with a computer, or you may never look at your investments at all. Some people might find it easier to do everything at once so that they think about the Money Diet only two or three times a year. Others like to break tasks down into smaller activities, which is why you may want to use the Money Diet calendar I put together.

The important thing is to experiment and figure out the schedule that makes sense for you. Do not set up a schedule that you know you will not be able to keep! If all of the things I have listed are too much for you to handle, pick out the two or three that seem most important for your particular situation and focus just on them for this year. You can graduate to a more detailed schedule after you have mastered these tasks.

When constructing **Your Money Diet Calendar**, think carefully about your spending "danger months." For most people these are the months when they take vacations, and of course December (thanks to holiday shopping). Major birthdays and anniversaries can also present problems in certain months. Think carefully about when you will be out of your everyday routine, because this is when you are most likely to overspend.

Once a year, you should set aside a day for an overall financial review. Here are some tricks to make sure this actually happens:

Your Money Diet Calendar

Month	Suggested Tasks	Your Tasks	Check When Done
Jan.	• Review totals from last year • Set expense budget for year • Set savings and debt-reduction goals for year		
Feb.	• Organize tax information • Set vacation budget for year • Review your investments		
March	• Do your taxes		
April	• Track all of your expenses for the month • Finish your taxes, if necessary		
May	• Review your savings goals for year • Review investments and investment allocations		
June	• Review your debt position and look for ways to pay off faster		

Your Money Diet Calendar (cont.)

Month	Suggested Tasks	Your Tasks	Check When Done
July	• Review expenses year-to-date; then modify expense projections • Review yearly savings goal; is it on track?		
Aug.	• Review your investments • Track all of your expenses for the month		
Sept.	• Review your will and trust for any changes		
Oct.	• Set realistic holiday budget • Review your insurance coverages		
Nov.	• Review investments and investment allocations (to make sales before the end of the year)		
Dec.	• Track all of your expenses for the month		

From *The Money Diet*, by Ginger Applegarth.

- First, decide in advance that you will accomplish this goal on a specified date in the future so that you can get your papers together beforehand. It is very demoralizing to set aside a day to review your finances and to spend most of it looking for various documents.

- Second, if you are married, make sure that your spouse is involved so that both of you can work on your financial past and future together. This will improve your chances of success and reduce the friction which will inevitably occur as you try to change your money habits and actions.

- Third, set aside a specific place and time. You may find this hard to believe, but some of my clients take their checkbooks and review their expenses when they are on vacation, because it is the only time they have a free moment to do so. Others actually take a day off from work, when they will be alone in the house, in order to do their annual financial review.

The key in making the Money Diet work for you is to design a to-do calendar that will motivate you to review your financial progress regularly so that the Money Diet becomes an automatic part of your life. Every review you do consolidates all of what you have learned to date and re-energizes you to stick to your plan. The goal is to make managing your money such an integral part of your life that it happens as part of your daily living and does not become just another task that you put off doing, making yourself miserable in the process. If you follow the Money Diet, a few years from now you will look back and be amazed at your financial state of mind before you started. You will look forward to your financial checkups because you will actually be able to measure your progress. Just think how pleasurable it is to get on the scales when you have been on a diet and know that a substantial amount of weight has been lost. Your Money Diet began when you started this book; make it your companion and you will reap the rewards of financial fitness for life.

Conclusion

ALMOST EVERY OTHER CHAPTER of this book has started out with a story about someone else trying to improve his or her financial situation. Here, it is time to put the emphasis on you and the fact that you have just made a very powerful investment in your financial future by finishing this book. If you have read the preface and the previous seventeen chapters, you now know all of the basics of financial planning. I have no doubt, however, that you may have found the going rough at times. First, few people find every financial topic riveting, and as hard as I have tried to make things entertaining and easy, I suspect that your eyes glazed over more than once. Second, if you are like most people, you probably discovered that your finances are not in perfect shape, and you may have been tempted to put this book down forever. But you did not, so it is time to congratulate yourself.

I have worked with clients since the 1970s, so I have been around long enough to know where people usually have the most trouble managing their money. Frankly, I see it almost every time I start to work with a new client. Getting your information together and developing your financial plan is the hardest part. From here on out—putting the Money Diet into action, regularly reviewing your progress, and making any needed changes—you should find it much smoother sailing. I am not saying that your financial problems are over, but at this point you understand the big picture, which puts you ahead of millions of other Americans.

You may be amazed at how this knowledge starts to permeate your everyday thinking. When you open up the menu at a restaurant, *The Money Diet* squeezed dollar may pop into your head and you may find yourself ordering a less expensive meal. When you think about your goals—retirement, education, a new house—you may find that the those particular *Money Diet* worksheets come to mind and you are mentally filling in the blanks. As the author of this book, I would find that particularly exciting because it would mean that I have been able to positively change the way that you think about an important part of your everyday life.

You may have just skimmed this book and not filled in a single worksheet. If so, that is okay too. Even if you did not study the book in detail, you probably picked up the most important concepts—and you may be motivated at some point to go back and complete some or all of the charts. After all, the reason I call them Willpower Worksheets is that completing them will increase your willpower to stick to your Money Diet. But there are certainly plenty of ideas, tips, and advice in the text to use for making your financial future better, even if you never wrote down a single number.

Whatever reaction *The Money Diet* prompts, keep in mind that my goal has been to make you feel better about yourself and your money management skills by being knowledgeable and more in control. Professionally, as a financial adviser, and personally, as a single parent with two long-term medical crises under my belt thus far in life, I know the anxiety and emotional pain that money problems can cause. But our personal and family relationships are far too important to allow money to affect them any more than necessary. With the Money Diet, you cannot control every financial event but you can have more control over how you react to events and how you take advantage of opportunities to improve your financial future.

My final word of advice is: Be easy on yourself. Let your accomplishment of having completed this book absolve you of any past, present, or future guilt about how you manage your money and the fact that you cannot guarantee everyone in your life—including yourself—everything they want. Look for the satisfaction in whatever positive money moves you take so that following the Money Diet will prove to be as satisfying as for you as it has been for me and others.

You may remember that I mentioned in the preface that I want to hear from you. Any author wants to know if his or her book has made an impact on readers. In this case, I have the larger interest of passing some readers' Money Diet success stories on to others so that they can be motivated by and benefit from them. You can write to me at the following address:

Ginger Applegarth, CFP, CLU, ChFC
President
Applegarth Henderson Advisors, Inc.
6 Mt. Vernon St., Suite 225
Winchester, MA 01890

I cannot imagine a more satisfying role than being the conduit for Americans helping other Americans to have better financial lives. If that is the case, *The Money Diet* will have been successful beyond my wildest dreams.

Index